Civil Society and Social Change

Series Editors: **Ian Rees Jones** and
Paul Chaney, Cardiff University,
Mike Woods, Aberystwyth University

This series provides interdisciplinary and comparative
perspectives on the rapidly changing nature of civil society
at local, regional, national and global scales.

Also in the series:

Analysing the Trust–Transparency Nexus
By **Ian Stafford, Alistair Cole** and **Dominic Heinz**

Local Civil Society
By **Robin Mann, David Dallimore, Howard Davis,
Graham Day** and **Marta Eichsteller**

City Regions and Devolution in the UK
By **David Beel, Martin Jones** and **Ian Rees Jones**

Civil Society and the Family
By **Esther Muddiman, Sally Power** and **Chris Taylor**

Civil Society through the Lifecourse
Edited by **Sally Power**

The Foundational Economy and Citizenship
Edited by **Filippo Barbera** and **Ian Rees Jones**

Putting Civil Society in Its Place
By **Bob Jessop**

Find out more at
**policy.bristoluniversitypress.co.uk/
civil-society-and-social-change**

Forthcoming:

Youth Unemployment and Precarity
By **Sioned Pearce**

Single Mothers and the Welfare Trap
By **Helen Blakely**

Editorial Advisory Board

Published with the Wales Institute of Social and
Economic Research and Data

Find out more at
**policy.bristoluniversitypress.co.uk/
civil-society-and-social-change**

CIVIL SOCIETY IN AN AGE OF UNCERTAINTY

Institutions, Governance and Existential Challenges

Edited by
Paul Chaney and Ian Rees Jones

First published in Great Britain in 2022 by

Policy Press, an imprint of
Bristol University Press
University of Bristol
1–9 Old Park Hill
Bristol
BS2 8BB
UK
t: +44 (0)117 374 6645
e: bup-info@bristol.ac.uk

Details of international sales and distribution partners are available at
policy.bristoluniversitypress.co.uk

British Library Cataloguing in Publication Data
A catalogue record for this book is available from the British Library

ISBN 978-1-4473-5341-6 hardcover
ISBN 978-1-4473-5345-4 ePub
ISBN 978-1-4473-5344-7 ePdf

Cover design: Hayes Design and Advertising
Front cover image: freepik
Bristol University Press and Policy Press use environmentally responsible
print partners.
Printed in Great Britain by CPI Group (UK) Ltd, Croydon, CR0 4YY

Contents

List of tables and figures

Notes on contributors

David Beel is Senior Lecturer in Political Economy at Manchester Metropolitan University based within the Future Economies team. He has authored a broad range of international journal articles and reports and is co-author of D. Beel, M. Jones, I. Rees Jones (2021) *City Regions and Devolution in the UK: The Politics of Representation*, Policy Press. He is currently leading and conducting research on the *Civil Society and Place Based Strategies for Sustainable Development* project which is part of the Wales Institute of Social and Economic Research Data and Methods (WISERD) Civil Society Research Centre.

Paul Chaney is a co-director of WISERD and Professor of Policy and Politics at Cardiff School of Social Sciences. He has authored a number of books and peer-reviewed journal articles.

Alistair Cole is Professor and Head of Department, Government and International Studies at Hong Kong Baptist University. His research interests include comparative research in governance: territorial and multi-level governance (especially comparative devolution), public administration and the State, public policy (education, training, research, the knowledge economy), Europeanisation and European integration (mainly through the specific lens of the Franco-German relationship and of Franco–British relations). He is author and contributor to an extensive range of leading publications and is an affiliate professor with WISERD.

Stephen Drinkwater is Professor of Economics at the Business School at the University of Roehampton, London. He is also a research fellow at the Institute for the Study of Labor (IZA) in Bonn, the Centre on Dynamics of Ethnicity (CoDE) at the University of Manchester and the Centre for Research and Analysis of Migration (CReAM), University College London. His main research interests lie in applied microeconomics, particularly within the labour market, as well as regional issues – including labour market discrimination, self-employment, industrial relations, international and interregional migration, the effect of language on economic activity and voting behaviour.

Taulant Guma is Lecturer in Human Geography at Edinburgh Napier University and was previously a Post-Doctoral Research Associate with WISERD at Aberystwyth University. He is currently the Principal Investigator on the ESRC-funded project: Investigating the use of temporary accommodation to house asylum seekers and refugees during the COVID-19 outbreak. He has published extensively in leading international journals. His research interests lie in the field of migration studies, covering a wide range of topics and issues, including civil society and participation; place and belonging; 'race' and ethnicity; social security and risks; transnationalism and healthcare; online networks and digital communities; Brexit and EU migration.

Dominic Heinz is Lecturer for the German Academic Exchange Service (DAAD) at the Türk-Alman Üniversitesi/Türkisch Deutsche Universität. Previously he was based at Geschwister-Scholl-Institute for Political Science, Munich School of Politics, and WISERD, Cardiff University. His research interests include comparative politics; German politics; joint-decision making; joint-decision trap; and federalism.

Ian Rees Jones is Professor of Sociological Research at Cardiff University and Civil Society Centre Director of WISERD. He is a Fellow of the Learned Society of Wales, Fellow of the UK Academy of Social Sciences and Trustee of the Foundation for the Sociology of Health & Illness. His research interests include social change and processes of social change. Specific areas of research focus include civil society and social change; inequalities in health; ageing and later life; lifestyles and social relations; class, community and social change; and transparency and trust in health and welfare. He is the Principal Investigator on a series of major research grants and author of multiple books and leading international journal articles.

Martin Jones is Professor of Human Geography and Vice-Chancellor at Staffordshire University as well as a Fellow of the Royal Society of Arts and Academician, Academy of the Social Sciences. He is an interdisciplinary researcher, working in the broad area of society and space and specifically on the interface between economic and political geography. He is the author or editor of 13 books and has given evidence to UK Government Select Committees on skills, business support and regional development and worked alongside the European Commission through its Week of Regions and Cities.

Rhys Jones is Professor of Human Geography in the Department of Geography and Earth Sciences at Aberystwyth University. His research interests focus on a range of interrelated themes linked to political geography, including: the geography of group identities, the geography of the state and behavioural insights in public policy. He has published widely on these themes, including 11 books and over 80 articles and book chapters. His work has been supported by research grants from the ESRC, the AHRC, the Leverhulme Trust, Horizon 2020, INTERREG and the Welsh government.

Rhys Dafydd Jones is Lecturer in Human Geography at Aberystwyth University. His research interests centre around migration, religion and belonging. Specifically, these include lifestyle migration and regional inequalities, transnational belonging and non-belonging in minority nations, international migration and religious diversity in rural regions, and civic participation as place-making activities.

Fiona O'Hanlon is Senior Lecturer in Language Education at Moray House School of Education and Sport, IETL, University of Edinburgh. Between 2014 and 2017 she was a board member of Bòrd na Gàidhlig, the executive non-departmental public body which works to promote the use and understanding of Gaelic language, education and culture. Her research interests include bilingual education, languages education, attitudes to language, language policy, language planning and mixed methods research. She is author of leading articles in international journals including *Language, Culture and Curriculum* and *Language Policy*.

Lindsay Paterson is Professor of Education Policy at Edinburgh University. He currently holds a Leverhulme Major Research Fellowship: Education and Society in Scotland. He has served on the Research Resources Board of the UK Economic and Social Research Council and has been an adviser to the Scottish Parliament's Education Committee, and to several government departments since the early 1990s. He was elected a Fellow of the Royal Society of Edinburgh in 2004 and a Fellow of the British Academy in 2013. His research interests include the sociology of education, Scottish politics, quantitative methods in social research, and education policy. He is the Principal Investigator on a series of major research grants and author of multiple books and leading international journal articles.

Elin Royles is Senior Lecturer at the Department of International Politics, at Aberystwyth University. Her research interests include territorial politics and post-devolution UK politics; sub-state diplomacy and nation-building; sub-state climate change and sustainable development policy; civil society; and language planning and policy. She is currently the Chair of the Aberystwyth University Branch of the Coleg Cymraeg Cenedlaethol and leader on the 'Language, Culture and Identities' theme of the Centre for Welsh Politics and Society. She has published widely in leading books and international journals including, *Environment and Planning C: Politics and Space*, *Geoforum* and the *British Journal of Politics and International Relations*.

Christala Sophocleous is Research Associate at WISERD, Cardiff University. Her research interests lie in the dynamic relationship between the state and civil society in the development and delivery of public policy, particularly as it relates to communities and social care. She is interested in issues of governance, citizenship and third sector policy and the shifting institutional formations that shape them. She has published in leading international journals such as *Regional and Federal Studies* and the *Journal of Social Policy*.

Ian Stafford is Senior Lecturer in Politics in the Department of Politics and International Relations, School of Law and Politics, Cardiff University. His research interests include devolution and territorial politics, British politics and public policy, theories of public policy analysis, and comparative politics. He has been investigator on a series of major projects including 'Building Trust? Institutions and interactions of multi-level governance in the UK, Germany and France' (with Professor Alistair Cole) and research on transport policy within Wales (with Professor Jonathan Bradbury, Swansea University). He has published extensively on a wide range of topics, including 'States of convergence in territorial governance' in *Publius: The Journal of Federalism* (with Alistair Cole, Jean-Baptiste Harguindeguy, Romain Pasquier and Christian de Visscher) and the books *Devolution and Governance: Wales between capacity and constraint* (with Alistair Cole; Palgrave) and *Analysing the Trust-Transparency Nexus: Multi-level governance in the UK, France and Germany*, (with Alistair Cole and Dominic Heinz; Policy Press).

Michael Woods is Professor in the Department of Geography and Earth Sciences, Aberystwyth University. His research interests focus on rural geography and political geography. He is Co-Director of WISERD and Co-Director of the Centre for Welsh Politics and Society. He has led a series of major projects including European Research Council Advanced Grant GLOBAL-RURAL, on globalisation and rural localities, and Horizon 2020 project IMAJINE, on spatial justice and territorial inequalities. He is a former editor of the *Journal of Rural Studies* and author or co-author of books including *An Introduction to Political Geography* (Routledge, 2016) and *Rural* (Routledge, 2010).

Sophie Yarker is Research Associate in the Manchester Institute for Collaborative Research on Ageing (MICRA) at Manchester University, currently working on the Leverhulme Ageing in Place in Cities project. She was previously a Post-Doctoral Research Associate with WISERD at Aberystwyth University. Her research interests include inclusive urban neighbourhoods, urban regeneration and population change. In particular, collaborative and inclusive forms of urban development, social innovation within the community and voluntary sector, and conceptualising local neighbourhoods and feelings of belonging and attachment to local communities. She has published in leading international journals such as *Quality in Ageing and Older Adults*.

*Cydnabyddiaethau/*Acknowledgements

This book would not have been possible without the contribution of those that generously agreed to give their time and participate in the data gathering for the different projects covered in this volume. *Diolch o galon am rhanu eich sylwadau a gwybodaeth* – heartfelt thanks for sharing your views and knowledge.

Thanks also to the Economic and Social Research Council for funding the research presented here under two Centre grants L009099/1 and ES/S012435/1 – Principal Investigator Ian Rees Jones.

The editors would also like to thank all contributing authors – your good natured and friendly support for this volume is much appreciated. Thanks also to Laura Vickers-Rendall (Commissioning Editor) and her team at Policy Press, for the excellent support for this and all the other titles in the *Society and Social Change* book series. The helpful and constructive comments of three anonymous reviewers of the original proposal and typescript of this volume are also gratefully acknowledged.

Sincere thanks to the wider WISERD community – your enthusiastic and insightful input to civil society-related research and events was invaluable in informing the research outlined in the following pages.

Last, many thanks to the WISERD hub Professional Services Staff, past and present, for their excellent oversight and administration of WISERD – with notable thanks to Tina Woods and Alex Williams.

Unwaith eto, diolch i chi gyd – once again, thanks to you all.

Paul Chaney and Ian Rees Jones

Introduction: Locating civil society

Paul Chaney and Ian Rees Jones

This volume explores a range of contemporary challenges facing civil society organisations in the early twenty-first century. As the following chapters reveal, each may arrest or subvert the beneficial effects of associative life and negatively impact upon governance, culture and welfare. The overall argument of this volume is the importance of civil society to individual and collective well-being, as well as the health of democracy. On the one hand, the following chapters note the resilience of civil society and its adaptability to meet uncertainties, yet on the other, we argue that civil society's ability to prevail in the face of the existential challenges is far from assured. Rather, it is contingent in nature and requires ongoing vigilance, social self-organisation and criticality. A further strand of our argument underlines the point that while the contemporary 'project' to reconfigure the state might be normatively sound, its execution can be subverted by dogma, and the failure of political elites to listen and engage exogenous interests, as well as civil society organisations' mistrust and lack of capacity to participate. Accordingly, this is the first of two short introductory chapters to this volume. Here we summarise core aspects of the history and theory associated with the concept of civil society. This is followed by a discussion of the key features of civil society in the nations of the UK. In the next chapter we summarise contemporary political and social changes and how these contribute to the existential challenges facing civil society today.

The concept of civil society has been variously advanced as: a corrective to the negative effects of neo-liberal, market-driven policies; an answer to the challenges of state down-sizing and declining welfare capacity; and a bedrock of democracy and good governance through which citizens can hold political elites to account. Moreover, it has been styled as a space where culture, identity and norms can be transmitted and valued. However, the reality is that, far from being a panacea, civil society is itself intimately wrapped up in the uncertainties of the age. These are wide-ranging and include austerity, inequality, the climate emergency, Brexit and the COVID-19 pandemic, as well as the crisis of traditional forms of social welfare. As if this was not enough, as the following pages reveal, further threats emerge from increasing governance complexity and fragmentation, declining trust in government, political alienation, xenophobia and a loss of community cohesion.

This volume explores such globally resonant challenges principally with reference to developments in the different nations of the UK. This is apposite for, as Naidoo (2003: 32) observes, 'democracy, freedom and nation-building by free citizens: these appear to be under threat by the actions of some of our oldest democracies. Civil society's space is being squeezed and must be restored.' We explore the contemporary challenges by drawing on a series of studies undertaken as part of the pioneering, ESRC-funded Civil Society research programme at Wales Institute of Social and Economic Research and Data (WISERD) 2015–2021.[1] WISERD was founded in 2008 and is a partnership between five Welsh universities (Cardiff, Aberystwyth, Bangor, Swansea and South Wales). In addition to the present volume, our multi-disciplinary research also features in the other titles in the Policy Press *Civil Society and Social Change* book series.

Conceptualising civil society

A broad literature attests to the contested nature of 'civil society' (Cohen and Arato 1992; Kumar 1993; Ehrenberg 1999; Edwards 2004; Powell 2007). This volume reveals how existential threats stemming from prevailing uncertainties reinforce this sense of contestation as new forms of governance and associative practices continue to redefine the civil sphere; subjecting it constantly to change from powerful internal and external forces. These blur boundaries and produce ever more complexity and fragmentation. Thus, the concept of civil society (Gramsci 1971; Cohen and Arato 1992) needs to be framed in relation to the family, civic and political associations, and state political institutions, while at the same time noting that 'these elements are intertwined such that their boundaries are effectively seamless' (Eto 2012: 78). So conceived, civil society comprises a diverse range of associational activities extending beyond the family, to encompass non-governmental organisations (NGOs), pressure groups, charities, community groups, social movements and campaigning organisations (Keane 1988; Salamon and Anheier 1992; Casey 2004). The third sector – or 'non-profit sector' in North America (Dekker and Van den Broek 1998) – intersects with civil society and, according to Salamon and Anheiers' classic typology (1992, 1996), is a collection of entities that share five crucial characteristics; they are: (1) organised, (that is, institutionalised to some extent), (2) non-governmental (in the sense of being structurally separate from the instrumentalities of government), (3) non-profit-distributing, (that is, not returning profits generated to their owners or directors), (4) self-governing, (that is, in a position to control their own activities through internal governance procedures and enjoy a meaningful degree of autonomy); and (5) voluntary, (that is, involving some meaningful degree of voluntary participation). In addition, there are three further types of third sector organisation that are properly part of the wider non-profit sector, although, reflecting its contested nature, they are not always included in social analyses: trades unions, religious/sacramental organisations and political parties.

To understand contemporary thinking on civil society we need to briefly reflect on its antecedents. Early Aristotelian ideas emphasised the collective identity of the state *and* society, whereby civil society is conceived of as a work of nature (Barker 1946). Here, it is indistinguishable from the state. In the *polis* (or city state), both spheres are merged, constituting an 'association of associations' (Pérez-Díaz 2014: 819). This constellation enabled citizens to share in the virtuous task of ruling and being ruled. As Edwards (2004: 6) notes, according to this conception, 'the state described the "civil" form of society – and "civility" described the requirements of good citizenship'.

In contrast, the modern classical era began to view the state and civil society as two independent entities. Thus, for example, in the seventeenth century, Hobbes (1651) and Locke (1689) asserted that societies are the product of a social contract between individuals. According to this view, civil society is an arena for people to act in a civil manner, cooperating rather than acting in self-interest. A key motive for people to associate in this way is the fear of coercive common power exercised by the state. It is a standpoint emphasised both by Hegel (1991 [1820]) and De Tocqueville (1956 [1835]). The former characterised the defining features of civil society as a system of human needs wherein individuals seek to reconcile individual interests (including private property) with social demands and expectations that are mediated by the state. Whereas, De Tocqueville (1956 [1835]) distinguishes between 'political' society and civil society, asserting that civilian and political associations act as a counterbalance to liberal individualism and the state. According to this view, the effectiveness of civil society depends upon its organisational form.

Later twentieth-century thinkers such as Gramsci (1948) and Habermas (1962) advance a more nuanced perspective; highlighting the fluidity of relations between the state and civil society and, notably, claiming that civil society both resists and reinforces hegemonic ideas about economic and social life. Three core strands can be identified in this body of work. First, rather than a passive transmitter of established norms and practices, civil society constitutes a site of social contestation wherein collective identities, moral values and associative norms interact. Second, civil society is at once generative and dynamic, for it is responsible for the creation of informal networks and social movements. Third, it can be seen as constitutive of the public sphere, an arena that facilitates discussion and reciprocal learning in a manner that is free from state coercion and over-intrusion by the market. It is characterised by claims-making and criticality directed at the state, and advances democracy by holding ruling elites to account.

Notably, in the latter half of the twentieth century, the earlier Tocquevillean view, which placed citizens' associations at the core of civil society and democracy, was reasserted by Bourdieu (1986), Coleman (1988) and Putnam (Putnam et al 1993, Putnam 1995). They stressed the production and accumulation of social capital as integral to the effective functioning of society and democracy. Social capital here refers to the 'features of social organization, such as trust, norms, and networks, that can improve the efficiency of society by facilitating coordinated actions' (Putnam et al 1993: 167). The formation of social networks founded upon trust and sociability between individuals serves to enhance their capacity to perform the key tasks that comprise the political process; the pursuit of common ends and resolution of collective problems (compare Coleman 1988; Tonkiss 2000). For authors like Bourdieu (1986), Coleman (1988) and Putnam et al (1993), civic virtue is most powerful when embedded in norms and networks of trust and reciprocity. According to these views, as Laine (2014: 59) observes, civil society can be conceived of as 'an arena, a public space with blurred borders, where diverse societal values and interests interact'.

In their different ways, the foregoing conceptions of civil society engage with the work of Foucault-influenced scholars of governance (see Foucault 1991, 2007; Enroth 2014). Among these, Rod Rhodes and John Keane provide a useful underpinning for the following chapters in this volume. This is because they seek to locate prevailing challenges in the context of the institutions and structures of contemporary governance and global processes. As Hindess (2004: 40) explains, governance and governmentality

> should be understood more widely than the supreme authority in states, [but instead] as action aimed at influencing the way individuals regulate their own behaviour ... the aim of modern government of the state is to conduct the affairs of the population in the interests of the whole. This is not restricted to the government but is performed also by agencies in civil society.

It is a view that is promulgated in the classic literature on new governance (Rhodes 1997). According to this paradigm, social and political organisation is best viewed as 'a new process of governing; or a changed condition of ordered rule; or the new method by which society is governed' (Rhodes 1997: 1245). This resonates with Keane's (2009) work on monitory democracy that is defined by the rapid growth of many different kinds of extra-parliamentary, power-scrutinising mechanisms. In short, it is an historical form of democracy that presents a 'post-electoral' view of politics and government. As Feenstra and Keane (2014: 1265) note, 'in the name of "the public", "public accountability", "the people", "stakeholders" or "citizens" – the terms are normally used interchangeably in the age of monitory democracy – power-scrutinising institutions spring up all over the place, both within the fields of government and beyond [crucially, including civil society], often stretching across borders'. Thus, monitory institutions extend representative democracy to enfranchise many more citizens' voices in the political process, thereby changing the political and geographic dynamics of existing representative democracies (Chaney 2002, 2016).

Together, these conceptions resonate with the ensuing chapters, for the uncertainties and existential challenges of the age are leading to new forms of governance, and, civil society is at the heart of this process of change. For this reason, it is worth reflecting on Rhodes' original characterisation (1997: 53) of governance. He posits that it should be conceived of as a system characterised by the following:

1. Interdependence between organizations. Governance is broader than government, covering non-state actors. Changing the boundaries of the state mean the boundaries between public, private and voluntary sectors become shifting and opaque.
2. Continuing interactions between network members caused by the need to exchange resources and negotiate shared purposes.
3. Game-like interactions, rooted in trust and regulated by rules of the game negotiated and agreed by network participants.
4. A significant degree of autonomy from the state. Networks are not accountable to the state; they are self-organising. Although the state does not occupy a privileged, sovereign position, it can indirectly and imperfectly steer networks.

All of these defining characteristics remain important in understanding contemporary change. Based on analysis of the shifting form of the British state, they underpin what Rhodes dubbed 'the differentiated polity' (Rhodes and Weller 2005). As he (Rhodes 2007: 1258) proceeds to explain, it

> opens new avenues of exploration on key issues confronting policymaking and policy implementation ... including: the sectoral character of policymaking; the mix of governing structures; the 'philosopher's stone' of central coordination; devolution to the constituent territories of the UK ... [in short, we can] use it to develop a new way of seeing state authority in its relationship to civil society.

It is a point more recently articulated by Jessop (2015: 20), who argues that 'state powers ... are activated through changing sets of politicians and state officials located in specific parts of the state apparatus, *in specific conjunctures* ... the state's structural powers and capacities cannot be fully grasped by focusing on the state alone' (see Jessop, 2020). As Rhodes' (2017: 23) later revisiting of his earlier work also underlines, 'governance poses questions about the shifting boundaries between state and civil society. Governance has no essential characteristics; *it is a contingent mix*' (emphasis added).

In conceptual terms, over recent decades the academic use of contingency theory in social and political science has ebbed and flowed. In part, the use of contingency theory is the result of critiques of positivism and inductive generalisations about universalist norms (Bonacker 2006). As Walzer (1990) notes, norms around meaning and understanding of the social world can only be validated when there is cognisance of local, contextual phenomena. This volume adopts a similar position in relation to the present age of uncertainty and the challenges facing civil society. Ergo, the mere existence of particularistic factors (for example, civic activism, institutional capacity, norms promoting social well-being and so on) do not, in and of themselves mean that existential challenges facing civil society will be overcome. There is no inductive certainty involved. The straightforward co-presence of a core set of factors or preconditions applied across polities will not deliver universal results. Instead, contingency adds to civil society studies by underlining the complex interplay of contextual influences shaping social and political processes in a given civil society setting.

In conceptual terms, contingency is expressed in the literature of critical realism (Sayer 2000; Jessop 2005; Bhaskar 2008 [1975]). As Gerrits and Verweij (2013: 172) explain: 'reality is contingent. This means that any explanation [of social processes] is temporal in time and local in place. In this way, critical realists allude to the existence of innate causal powers (or what is dubbed "natural necessity") in society' (see Sayer 1992, 2000). Thus, in a given social situation there may be sufficient conditions for a particular event or process to occur, but it only happens when the 'natural necessity' is triggered. To put it another way, the actualising mechanism is contingent upon the alignment or co-presence of social objects with causal powers. Crucially, as the following chapters reveal, this has both temporal and spatial components. Again, this is relevant to civil society studies for the following reason: it underlines that any attempt to understand social processes in a given civil society setting needs to be cognisant of how the social space for action is at once shaped by the historical development of the polity and also the areal qualities specific to different geographical localities (*inter alia*, patterns and processes of social capital, social stratification, the existence of inequalities in class and/ or wealth – and so on). All of this resonates with the need to locate civil society challenges in a wider governance frame. In turn, this resonates with the 'spatial turn' in complexity theory and emergent properties at different spatial levels, the importance of 'locality' and spatial levels as nested systems in the social world (Byrne 1998). As

Jessop (2015: 246–7) observes: 'Rather than trying to define the core of the state in *a priori* terms, we need to explore how its boundaries are established through specific practices within and outside the state. ... The boundaries of the state and its relative unity as an ensemble or agency would instead be contingent.'

It is outwith current purposes to outline all aspects of the literature on citizenship (see Turner 1993). However, the present volume links with civic republican conceptions of citizenship that view the individual in terms of civic self-rule, embodied in institutions and practices (White and Ypi 2010). The work of classical thinkers (Rousseau, Hobbes, Locke) tells us that it is the co-authoring of laws via the general will that makes citizens free and laws legitimate. Active participation in collective processes, including deliberation and decision-making, ensures that individuals are citizens, not subjects (Elster 1998; Gutmann 2004). In essence, the republican model emphasises political agency. It is in this context that David Lockwood's (1996) work on civic stratification offers a useful framework to analyse contemporary developments. It posits that 'the institutional unity of citizenship, market and bureaucratic relations is central to social cohesion' (p 531) as played out in civil society. As Morris (2016: 697) explains, 'civic stratification constitutes a system of inequality by virtue of the granting or denial of rights by the state, which cuts across the treatment of both citizens and migrants, potentially providing a unifying framework of analysis for a whole regime of rights'. In turn, as Lockwood argues, this allows us to explore 'questions of how inequalities of class and status affect the institutionalization of citizenship and thereby its integrative function' (1996: 531).

Lockwood continues, 'citizenship can be seen to exert a force-field of its own. Four main types of "civic stratification" are distinguished by citizens' differential enjoyment of, and abilities to exercise, rights, their social categorization by the rights themselves and by their motivation to extend and enlarge them' (p 532). By addressing these factors in empirical research, we can explore change in civil society in terms of civic exclusion, civic gain and deficit, and civic expansion and increased and pronounced patterns and processes of civic stratification. In this way, Lockwood's concept of civic stratification and civil loss and gain at once 'talk to' the contemporary uncertainties and challenges facing civil society – and resonate with De Tocqueville's (1956: 202) classic statement that:

amongst the laws which rule human societies, there is one which seems to be more precise and clear than all others. If men [*sic*] are to remain civilised, or to become so, the art of associating together must grow and improve in the same ration in which equality of conditions is measured.

Figure 1.1: Civic stratification

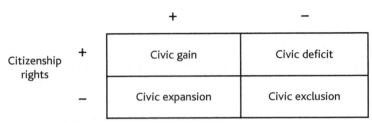

Source: Lockwood 1996

Echoing Enlightenment-era thinking typified by the work of Hobbes and Locke, Lockwood (1996: 536) explains (see Figure 1.1):

> Citizenship rights (+) denotes 'full citizenship', namely that the same existing rights are shared by all citizens. Citizenship rights (−) denotes either new rights that are aspired to but not yet achieved (civic expansion) or a lack of existing rights (civic exclusion). In definitional terms, 'moral resources' refers to advantages conferred by social standing and social networks, command of information, and general know-how, including the ability to attain one's ends through the activation of shared moral sentiments, whether or not the actor's orientation to such standards is sincere or disingenuous.

The appropriateness of linking this volume's analysis to governance theory and Lockwood's framework is implicit in Morris's work on the UK. Here she alludes to the ways that different governance contexts and styles of governing impact on social rights and diversity in civil society, observing that 'civic stratification is being pressed into use to limit the social rights of citizens ... citizens are increasingly subject to disciplinary techniques comparable to those imposed on migrants – by virtue of the appropriation of a conditional system of rights as a vehicle for monitoring and control' (Morris 2016: 697). By also drawing upon contingency theory and emphasising temporality (changing governance contexts and challenges facing civil society organisations over time) and spatiality (notably, the UK's move to a 'differentiated polity' with national devolution to Wales, Scotland and Northern Ireland), the chapters in this volume allow us to better understand how the existential challenges facing civil society in the UK and beyond reflect and reinforce ongoing processes of change.

Civil society in the nations of the UK

At the turn of the twenty-first century, the third sector in the UK grew at a significant rate. In part, this was aided by the expansion of state support, which increased from £8.4 billion in 2000/01 to £16 billion in 2009/10 (Clark et al 2009: 14). Yet, in the wake of the Great Recession (c. 2008) there has been a significant retrenchment 'suggest[ing] a fundamental shift in the relationship between the sector and the state' (Macmillan 2011: 115–124). Third sector organisations have been increasingly subject to conflicting pressures from different stakeholders. Service users and beneficiaries pay greater attention to the nature and quality of services provided, while funders and donors place more scrutiny on the value for money for the type of causes to which they contribute (Chew and Osbourne 2017: 92).

The latest data reveal there are 166,592 civil society organisations across the UK. These have a combined income of £53.5 billion (of which £15.7 billion is derived from government) and they employ 909,088 people (NCVO 2020: 9).[2] The sector continues to grapple with major income fluctuations. Post-2008 austerity has had a significant impact. For example, in the social services sector there was a 52 percentage point reduction in government income (decreasing from £294m in 2009/10 to £141m in 2015/16) and a 57 percentage point reduction for umbrella bodies (decreasing from £345m in 2009/10 to £148m in 2015/16) (NCVO 2018). The COVID-19 pandemic has subsequently caused further major funding losses. In 2021, 52.3 per cent of civil society organisations surveyed said they had been subject to a 25 per cent reduction in funding compared to the pre-pandemic situation, and almost a third more than 50 per cent (DCMS 2021: 7).

Alongside the economic uncertainties, there are also questions about prevailing patterns and processes of voluntarism and whether we are seeing the decline of civic engagement (Putnam 2000; Stolle and Hooghe 2005). Notwithstanding successive government programmes aimed at boosting voluntary action (such as the Blair government's Millennium Volunteers Programme (c.1999),[3] GwirVol in Wales,[4] Volunteer Development Scotland,[5] 'Volunteer Now' in Northern Ireland,[6] and 'The Big Society' from the Cameron–Clegg government in England, (c.2010, see Scott 2011)), the rate of volunteering in society has largely remained static over the last 20 years (Nichols and Ralston 2011: 2977). As Alcock (2018: 6) observes, 'the bad news is that despite generally rising prosperity, and increased levels of participation in higher education, neither have they [that is, rates of volunteering] risen'. The latest data present a mixed picture. They show that the majority of adults do not volunteer on a regular, ongoing basis. According to the National Council for Voluntary Organisations (NCVO 2020: 9), just over a third (36 per cent) of people volunteered at least once during the year in 2018/19, equating to 19.4 million people (NCVO 2020: 9). More recent data indicate 26 per cent of people in Wales volunteered between April 2019 and March 2020 (Welsh Government 2020a). The foregoing raises wider questions about the health of associative life in the UK. Other recent data also point to decline. For example, in communities across the UK, 'positive engagement with our neighbours, such as exchanging favours or stopping to talk, fell by three and four percentage points, respectively, between 2011/12 and 2017/18' (ONS 2020: 4).

Loneliness indicates shortcomings in associative life. It compromises people's health, affecting mortality, depression and suicide. At the turn of the century, data showed feelings of loneliness had increased over the previous decade (Victor et al (2006: 32). In 2016 to 2017, there were 5 per cent of adults in England who reported feeling lonely 'often' or 'always' (ONS 2018: 3). The pandemic exacerbated the situation. From October 2020 to February 2021, the proportion of the adult population (in Great Britain) feeling lonely increased to 7.2 per cent (about 3.7 million adults) (ONS 2021). A further key challenge lies in the fact that another component of social capital, trust, appears to be in decline (see Chapter 7). In England, for example, there was an overall drop in the proportion of adults reporting that 'many people in the neighbourhood can be trusted'; down from 48 per cent in 2013/14 to 42 per cent in 2016/17 (DCMS, 2017: 11), while trust in the UK government fell by 11 percentage points in the year to autumn 2019 (ONS 2020: 3).

Prior to the pandemic, trust in civil society organisations also appeared to be waning. According to the index used by one study, 'in 2016, the overall level of trust and confidence in charities has fallen to 5.7 out of 10. This is a significant decrease from a headline figure of 6.7 in 2012 and 2014.'[7] This research also found that one-third of the public said that their trust and confidence in charities had decreased over the preceding two years (Charity Commission 2016: 7). Moreover, a major inquiry on civil society in England concluded that 'relationships within civil society have corroded as everyone competes for funding. Big changes are needed to allow smaller groups and more informal networks to flourish – but the large institutions need to change fastest and most profoundly, learning from the best of what's new' (Civil Society Futures 2018: 17).

Reflecting the 'governance frame' of this volume, it should be noted that the formal administration of civil society in the UK has operated on a 'devolved' basis since the first half of the twentieth century, with separate national representative bodies linking the third sector with government in Wales, Scotland, England and Northern Ireland (Chaney et al 2020). Data derived from these bodies show that across territories there is significant variation in the profile of the third sector (Table 1.1).

Devolution and the (re)establishment of national legislatures in Wales, Scotland and Northern Ireland in 1998/99 has led to increasing divergence in the legal and policy context shaping civil society in the constituent countries

Table 1.1: Key statistics: voluntary sector profiles in each country

	Wales	Scotland[1]	N. Ireland	England
No. of third sector organisations (TSOs)	49,044[2]	40,000+	6,122	133,505[3]
No. of registered charities	8,100[4]	19,884	6,000[5]	161,000
Third sector workforce	99,750[6]	107,432	53,620	592,000[7]
Third sector income	£1,258 million[8]	£6.92 billion	£729 million	£44.59 billion[9]

Sources: SCVO 2020; WCVA 2021; NCVO 2021; Charity Commission Northern Ireland 2021.

[1]Data from https://scvo.scot/policy/sector-stats (last updated February 2020).

[2]Circa July 2021, no. of organisations in WCVA third sector support database. Available at: https://wcva.cymru/the-voluntary-sector-in-wales/

[3]NCVO Almanac figure for 2017/18 latest available.

[4]6,100 according to the Charity Commission, July 2019, via https://wcva.cymru/the-voluntary-sector-in-wales/; 8,100 according to https://wcva.cymru/wp-content/uploads/2020/04/2020-data-hub-update-E.pdf (circa 2020).

[5]Circa July 2021, https://www.charitycommissionni.org.uk/start-up-a-charity/register-of-charities/

[6]In 2017, according to https://wcva.cymru/wp-content/uploads/2020/04/2020-data-hub-update-E.pdf (circa 2020).

[7]Calculated: UK workforce figure given by https://www.ncvo.org.uk/policy-and-research/vol-sec tor-workforce (circa July 2021) minus Welsh, Scottish and N. Irish totals.

[8]According to https://wcva.cymru/wp-content/uploads/2020/04/2020-data-hub-update-E.pdf (circa 2020).

[9]Calculated: UK figure given by NCVO Almanac 2020 minus Welsh, Scottish and N. Irish totals.

of the UK (Law and Mooney 2012; Chaney 2015; Gormley-Heenan and Birrell 2015). This has been driven by territorial electoral politics following the move away from sole reliance on single, state-wide elections in 1998/9 (Bradbury and Mitchell 2005; Keating and Laforest 2018). Existing work on this governance shift shows that electoral discourse is a driver of policy divergence in multi-level systems. The result is differing policy prescriptions for the third sector that (re-)define governance practices and underpin the rise and territorialisation of welfare pluralism (Chaney 2014, 2020, 2021).

The process of divergence in the legal and policy contexts shaping civil society is further underpinned by 'post-devolution' party politics, with key contrasts across territories in party mix/dynamics, dominance/period in government, and ideological stance (Chaney and Drakeford 2004; Birrel and Gray 2012; Chaney 2015), as well as the distinctive legal and institutional structures linking the third sector with government (Chaney and Fevre 2001; Fyfe 2005; Ford 2011). Overall, the UK's move to quasi-federalism over the past 20 years has seen increasing policy divergence that is shaping and redefining relations between civil society and the state

(Birrell and Gray 2016; Chaney 2017; Kaehne et al 2018). This is related to ongoing debates about post devolution 'policy styles' (that is, the way that governments make and implement policy; see Richardson 1982: 2). While some make the case for key aspects of continuity between 'devolved' and British/Westminster styles (Cairney 2008, 2011), others underline elements of discontinuity (Birrell and Heenan 2013). This volume aligns with more recent arguments that, with the passing of time, there is increasing divergence in policy styles between Cardiff and Edinburgh compared to Westminster; not least regarding the rise of territorial rights and the need for government to engage with territorial (that is, meso-level) policy communities. A key factor in this is the rise of overarching, distinctive and prescriptive legal duties on devolved policy makers *requiring ongoing, future adherence in all areas of devolved policy making* to specified policy aims, implementation and outcomes. Examples of such duties stem from progressive enactments covering areas such as the well-being of future generations and the incorporation of UN human rights treaties into Welsh and Scottish law (for a discussion, see Chaney 2022).

Having outlined the development of civil society and related social theory, as well as a profile of civil society in the different nations of the UK, in the next chapter attention turns to recent political and social changes and how these form part of the existential challenge facing civil society today. This is followed by a summary of the remaining chapters.

Notes

1 ESRC awards nos. ES/L009099/1 and ES/S012435/1.
2 Due to the pandemic, the latest NCVO Almanac (circa 2020) reports 2017/18 data for key, headline indicators. At the time of writing these were the latest available.
3 See for example, 'Millennium volunteers wanted', BBC News, 01.09.1999. Available at: http://news.bbc.co.uk/1/hi/uk/435247.stm and http://webarchive.nationalarchives.gov.uk/20060715202434/http://www.millenniumvolunteers.gov.uk/
4 See http://www.gwirvol.org/
5 See http://www.vds.org.uk/
6 See http://youngcitizens.volunteernow.co.uk/millennium-volunteers
7 Respondents were asked to score their feelings of trust on a Likert scale where 0 = no trust and 10 = complete trust.

References

Alcock, P. (2018) 'Foreword', in R. Lindsey, J. Mohan, E. Metcalfe and S. Bulloch, *Continuity and Change in Voluntary Action: Patterns, trends and understandings*, Bristol: Policy Press.

Barker, E. (1946) *The Politics of Aristotle*, Oxford: Clarendon Press.

Bhaskar, R. (2008 [1975]) *A Realist Theory of Science*, London: Routledge.

Birrell, D. and Gray, A. (2012) 'Coalition government in Northern Ireland: Social policy and the lowest common denominator thesis', *Social Policy and Society*, 11(1): 15–25.

Birrell, D. and Gray, A. (2016) *Delivering Social Welfare: Governance and service provision in the UK*, Bristol: Policy Press.

Birrell, D. and Heenan, D. (2013) 'Policy style and governing without consensus: Devolution and education policy in Northern Ireland', *Social Policy & Administration*, 47(7): 765–782.

Bonacker, T. (2006) 'Disclosing critique: The contingency of understanding in Adorno's Interpretive Social Theory', *European Journal of Social Theory*, 9(1): 369–392.

Bourdieu, P. (1986) 'The forms of capital', in John G. Richardson (ed.), *Handbook of Theory and Research in the Sociology of Education*, New York: Greenwald Press, pp 241–258.

Bradbury, J. and Mitchell, J. (2005) 'Devolution: Between governance and territorial politics', *Parliamentary Affairs*, 58(2): 287–302.

Byrne, D. (1998) *Complexity Theory and the Social Sciences: An introduction*, London and New York: Routledge.

Cairney, P. (2008) 'Has devolution changed the "British policy style"?', *British Politics*, 3(3): 350–372.

Cairney, P. (2011) 'The new British policy style: From a British to a Scottish political tradition?', *Political Studies Review*, 9(2): 208–220.

Casey, J. (2004) 'Third sector participation in the policy process: A framework for comparative analysis', *Policy & Politics*, 32(2): 241–257.

Chaney, P. (2002) 'Social capital and the participation of marginalized groups in government', *Public Policy and Administration*, 17(4): 20–38.

Chaney, P. (2014) 'Multi-level systems and the electoral politics of welfare pluralism: Exploring third-sector policy in UK Westminster and regional elections 1945–2011', *Voluntas: International Journal of Voluntary and Nonprofit Organizations*, 25(3): 585–611.

Chaney, P. (2015) 'Exploring the pathologies of one-party-dominance on third sector public policy engagement in liberal democracies: Evidence from meso-government in the UK', *Voluntas: International Journal of Voluntary and Nonprofit Organizations*, 26(4): 1460–1484.

Chaney, P. (2016) 'Gendered political space: Civil society, contingency theory, and the substantive representation of women', *Journal of Civil Society*, 12(2): 198–223.

Chaney, P. (2017) '"Governance transitions" and minority nationalist parties' pressure for welfare state change: Evidence from Welsh and Scottish elections – and the UK's "Brexit" referendum', *Global Social Policy*, 17(3): 43–57.

Chaney, P. (2020) 'Examining political parties' record on refugees and asylum seekers in UK party manifestos 1964–2019: The rise of territorial approaches to welfare?', *Journal of Immigrant & Refugee Studies* (online first). Available at: https://www.tandfonline.com/eprint/J6W5JTQV4FGNZ W7GMJZQ/full?target=10.1080/15562948.2020.1839620

Chaney, P. (2021) 'Exploring the politicisation and territorialisation of adult social care in the UK: Electoral discourse analysis of state-wide and meso elections 1998–2019', *Global Social Policy* (online first). Available at: https:// journals.sagepub.com/eprint/AXFIYEECRKWXTYSSNBAA/full

Chaney, P. (2022 forthcoming) 'Social policy in Wales', Chapter 25 in Pete Alcock, Tina Haux, Vikki McCall and Margaret May (eds), *The Student's Companion to Social Policy*, London: Wiley.

Chaney, P. and Drakeford, M. (2004) 'The primacy of ideology: Social policy and the first term of the National Assembly for Wales', *Social Policy Review*, 16: 211–243.

Chaney, P. and Fevre, R. (2001) 'Inclusive governance and "minority" groups: The role of the third sector in Wales', *Voluntas: International Journal of Third Sector Research*, 12(2): 131–156.

Chaney, P., Sophocleous, C. and Wincott, D. (2022) Exploring the meso-territorialization of third sector administration and welfare delivery in federal and union states: Evidence and theory-building from the UK, Regional & Federal Studies, 32:2, 231–254. DOI: 10.1080/13597566.2020.1822341

Charity Commission (2016) 'Public trust and confidence in charities', London: Charity Commission. Available at: https://assets.publishing.serv ice.gov.uk/government/uploads/system/uploads/attachment_data/file/ 532104/Public_trust_and_confidence_in_charities_2016.pdf

Charity Commission for Northern Ireland (2021) 'Register of charities', Belfast: CCNI. Available at: https://www.charitycommissionni.org.uk/ start-up-a-charity/register-of-charities/

Chew, C. and Osbourne, S. (2017) 'Exploring strategic positioning in the UK charitable sector: Emerging evidence from charitable organizations that provide public services', *British Journal of Management*, 20: 90–105.

Civil Society Futures (2018) *Civil Society in England: Its current state and future opportunities*, London: Civil Society Futures https://civilsocietyfutures.org/ wp-content/uploads/sites/6/2018/11/Civil-Society-Futures__Civil-Soci ety-in-England__small-1.pdf

Clark, J., Dobbs, J., Kane, D. and Wilding, K. (2009) *The State and the Voluntary Sector: Recent trends in government funding and public service delivery*, London: NCVO.

Cohen, A. and Arato, A. (1992) *Civil Society and Political Theory*, Cambridge, MA: MIT Press.

Coleman, J. (1988) 'Social capital in the creation of human capital', *American Journal of Sociology*, 94: 95–120.

Dekker, P. and Van den Broek, A. (1998) 'Civil society in comparative perspective: Involvement in voluntary associations in North America and Western Europe', *Voluntas: International Journal of Third Sector Research*, 9(1): 11–38.

De Tocqueville, A. (1956 [1835]) *Democracy in America*, R. D. Heffner (ed.), New York: Mentor.

DCMS (Department for Digital, Culture, Media & Sport) (2017) *Community Life Survey 2016–2017*, London: DCMS.

DCMS (2021) *DCMS Coronavirus Impacts Third Sector Survey: Results*, London: DCMS.

Edwards, M. (2004) *Civil Society*, Cambridge: Polity Press.

Ehrenberg, J. (1999) *Civil Society: The critical history of an idea*, New York: New York University Press.

Elster, J. (1998) *Deliberative Democracy*, Cambridge; New York: Cambridge University Press.

Enroth, H. (2014) 'Governance: The art of governing after governmentality', *European Journal of Social Theory*, 17(1): 60–76.

Eto, M. (2012) 'Reframing civil society from gender perspectives: A model of a multi-layered seamless world', *Journal of Civil Society*, 8(2): 101–121.

Feenstra, R. and Keane, J. (2014) 'Politics in Spain: A case of monitory democracy', *Voluntas: International Journal of Voluntary and Nonprofit Organizations*, 25(5): 1262–1280.

Ford, P. (2011) 'Third sector regulation in post-devolution Scotland: Kilting the cuckoo', in Susan Phillips and Steven Rathgeb Smith (eds), *Governance and Regulation in the Third Sector: International perspectives*, London: Routledge, pp 37–48.

Foucault, M. (1991) 'Governmentality', in G. Burchell, C. Gordon and P. Miller (eds), *The Foucault Effect: Studies in governmentality*, Chicago, IL: University of Chicago Press.

Foucault, M. (2007) *Security, Territory, Population: Lectures at the Collège de France, 1977–1978*. New York: Palgrave Macmillan.

Fyfe, N. (2005) 'Making space for "neo-communitarianism"? The third sector, state and civil society in the UK', *Antipode*, 37(3): 536–557.

Gerrits, L. and Verweij, S. (2013) 'Critical realism as a meta-framework for understanding the relationships between complexity and qualitative comparative analysis', *Journal of Critical Realism*, 12(2): 166–182.

Gormley-Heenan, C. and Birrell, D. (2015) *Multi-Level Governance and Northern Ireland*, Basingstoke: Palgrave Macmillan.

Gramsci, A. (1948) *Selections from Prison Notebooks*, New York: International Publishers.

Gutmann, A. (2004) *Why Deliberative Democracy?* Princeton, NJ: Princeton University Press.

Habermas, J. (1962) *The Structural Transformation of the Public Sphere: An inquiry into a category of bourgeois society*, Cambridge, MA: MIT Press.

Habermas, J. (1996) *Between Facts and Norms: Contributions to a discourse theory of law and democracy*, trans. William Rehg, Cambridge, MA: MIT Press.

Hegel, G. W. F. (1991 [1820]) *Elements of the Philosophy of Right*, Cambridge: Cambridge University Press.

Hindess, B. (2004) 'Power, government, politics', in Kate Nash and Alan Scott (eds), *The Blackwell Companion to Political Sociology*, Malden, MA: Blackwell, pp 40–49.

Hobbes, T. (1909 [1651]) *Leviathan*, Oxford: Clarendon Press.

Jessop, B. (2005) 'Critical realism and the strategic-relational approach', *New Formations: A Journal of Culture / Theory / Politics*, 56: 40–53.

Jessop, B. (2015) *The State: Past, present, future*, Cambridge: Polity Press.

Jessop, B. (2020) *Putting Civil Society in Its Place: Governance, metagovernance and subjectivity*, Bristol: Policy Press.

Kaehne, A., Birrell, D., Miller, R. and Petch, A. (2018) 'Bringing integration home: Policy on health and social care integration in the four nations of the UK', *Journal of Integrated Care*, 25(2): 84–98.

Keane, J. (ed.) (1988) *Civil Society and the State: New European perspectives*, London: University of Westminster Press.

Keane, J. (2009) 'Monitory democracy', in *Democracy and Media Decadence*, Cambridge: Cambridge University Press, pp 77–108. doi:10.1017/CBO9781107300767.002

Keating, M. and Laforest, G. (eds) (2018) *Constitutional Politics and the Territorial Question in Canada and the United Kingdom*, Basingstoke: Palgrave Macmillan.

Kumar, K. (1993) 'Civil society: An inquiry into the usefulness of an historical term', *The British Journal of Sociology*, 44(3): 375–395. https://doi.org/10.2307/591808

Laine, J. (2014) 'Debating civil society: Contested conceptualizations and development trajectories', *International Journal of Not-for-Profit Law*, 16(1): 59–77.

Law, A. and Mooney, G. (2012) 'Devolution in a "stateless nation": Nation-building and social policy in Scotland', *Social Policy and Administration*, 46(2): 161–177.

Locke, J. (1965 [1689]) *Two Treatises of Government*, New York: Mentor Books.

Lockwood, D. (1996) 'Civic integration and class formation', *The British Journal of Sociology* 47(3): 531–550.

Macmillan, R. (2011) '"Supporting" the voluntary sector in an age of austerity: The UK coalition government's consultation on improving support for frontline civil society organisations in England', *Voluntary Sector Review*, 2(1): 115–124.

Morris, L. (2016) 'Squaring the circle: Domestic welfare, migrants rights, and human rights', *Citizenship Studies*, 20(6–7): 693–709.

Naidoo, K. (2003) 'Civil society at a time of global uncertainty, Organisation for Economic Cooperation and Development', *The OECD Observer*, May 2003, no. 237.

NCVO (National Council for Voluntary Organisations) (2018) *Civil society almanac 2018*, London: NCVO. Available at: https://data.ncvo.org.uk/category/almanac/voluntary-sector/introduction/

NCVO (2020) *Civil society almanac 2020*, London: NCVO. Available at: https://data.ncvo.org.uk/category/almanac/voluntary-sector/introduction/

NCVO (2021) *Civil society almanac 2021*, London: NCVO. Available at: https://data.ncvo.org.uk/category/almanac/voluntary-sector/introduction/

Nichols, G. and Ralston, R. (2011) 'Social inclusion through volunteering: The legacy potential of the 2012 Olympic Games', *Sociology*, 45(5): 900–914. Doi:10.1177/0038038511413413

ONS (Office for National Statistics) (2018) *Loneliness: What characteristics and circumstances are associated with feeling lonely?* Newport, Wales: ONS. Available at: https://www.ons.gov.uk/peoplepopulationandcommunity/wellbeing/articles/lonelinesswhatcharacteristicsandcircumstancesareassociatedwithfeelinglonely/2018-04-10

ONS (2020) *Statistical Bulletin: Social capital in the UK*, Newport, Wales: ONS. Available at: https://www.ons.gov.uk/peoplepopulationandcommunity/wellbeing/bulletins/socialcapitalintheuk/2020#glossary

ONS (2021) *Mapping loneliness during the coronavirus pandemic*, Newport, Wales: ONS. Available at: https://www.ons.gov.uk/peoplepopulationandcommunity/wellbeing/articles/mappinglonelinessduringthecoronaviruspandemic/2021-04-07

Pérez-Díaz, V. (2014) 'Civil society: A multi-layered concept', *Sociology Review*, 62(6): 812–830.

Powell, F. (2007) *The Politics of Civil Society*, Bristol: Policy Press.

Putnam, R. (1995) 'Bowling alone: America's declining social capital', *Journal of Democracy*, 6: 65–78.

Putnam, R. D. (2000) *Bowling alone: The collapse and revival of American community*, New York: Simon & Schuster.

Putnam, R., Leonardi, R. and Nanetti, R. (1993) *Making Democracy Work: Civic traditions in modern Italy*, Princeton, NJ: Princeton University Press.

Rhodes, R. A. W. (1997) *Understanding Governance*, Buckingham and Philadelphia: Open University Press.

Rhodes, R. A. W. (2007) 'Understanding governance: Ten years on', *Organization Studies*, 28(8): 1243–264. DOI:10.1177/0170840607076586

Rhodes, R. A. W. (2017) 'Understanding governance: 20 years on'. Available at: http://www.raw-rhodes.co.uk/wp-content/uploads/2017/07/National-Governance-Review.pdf

Rhodes, R. A. W. and Weller, P. (2005) 'Westminster transplanted and Westminster implanted: Explanations for political change', in H. Patapan, J. Wanna and P. Weller (eds), *Westminster Legacies: Democracy and responsible government in Asia, Australasia and the Pacific*, Sydney: University of New South Wales Press, pp 1–12.

Richardson, J. J. (1982) 'Convergent policy styles in Europe?', in J. J. Richardson (ed.), *Policy Styles in Western Europe*, London: Allen & Unwin, pp 32–43.

Salamon, L. and Anheier, H. (1992) 'In search of the nonprofit sector I: The question of definitions', *Voluntas: International Journal of Third Sector Research*, 3(2): 125–151.

Salamon, L. M. and Anheier, H. K. (eds) (1996) *Defining the Nonprofit Sector: A cross-national analysis*, Manchester: Manchester University Press.

Sayer, A. (1992) *Method in Social Science: A realist approach* (2nd edition), London: Routledge.

Sayer, A. (2000) *Realism and Social Science*, London: SAGE.

Scott, M. (2011) 'Reflections on The Big Society', *Community Development Journal*, 46(1): 132–137.

SCVO (Scottish Council for Voluntary Organisations) (2020) 'The state of the sector 2020', Edinburgh: SCVO. Available at: https://scvo.scot/policy/sector-stats

Stolle, D. and Hooghe, M. (2005) 'Inaccurate, exceptional, one-sided or irrelevant? The debate about the alleged decline of social capital and civic engagement in Western Societies', *British Journal of Political Science*, 35(1): 149–167.

Tonkiss, F. (2000) 'Trust, social capital and economy', in F. Tonkiss and A. Passey (eds), *Trust and Civil Society*, London: Macmillan, pp 72–89.

Turner, B. (1993) 'Outline of a theory of citizenship', in B. Turner and P. Hamilton (eds), *Citizenship: Critical Concepts*, London: Routledge, pp 56–72.

Victor, C., Scambler, S., Marston, L., Bond, J. and Bowling, A. (2006) 'Older people's experiences of loneliness in the UK: Does gender matter?' *Social Policy and Society*, 5(1): 27–38.

WCVA (Wales Council for Voluntary Action) (2021) *The Third Sector Data Hub*, Cardiff: WCVA. Available at: https://wcva.cymru/the-voluntary-sector-in-wales/

Walzer, M. (1990) *Kritik und Gemeinsinn*, Berlin: Fischer.

Welsh Government (2020a) *Volunteering (National Survey for Wales): April 2019 to March 2020*, Cardiff: Welsh Government. Available at: https://gov.wales/volunteering-national-survey-wales-april-2019-march-2020-html

White, J. and Ypi, L. (2010) 'Rethinking the modern prince: Partisanship and the democratic ethos', *Political Studies*, 58(4): 809–828.

2

Existential challenges

Paul Chaney and Ian Rees Jones

This volume explores a range of existential challenges facing civil society organisations in the early twenty-first century, a period that has been dubbed 'the age of uncertainty' (Bauman 2007; Gagnon 2018; Obeng-Odoom 2021). Such a focus is grounded in existential humanist studies of social welfare. As originally propounded by Mohan (1979, 1985a, b), these highlight how a concern for the well-being of others underpins associative life and impacts on people in diverse ways, including the way they think about themselves, behave and interact. It links to deeper questions about meaning and the values that shape associative life, welfare, culture and democracy. As Dixon (2010: 180) explains,

> The cognitive and behavioural changes induced by public social welfare provision are the causal link between that provision and the observed levels of poverty, deprivation, income inequality, social exclusion, and quality of life. To an existential humanist, social welfare provision must seek to enhance the human condition (dominated, as it is, by feelings of aloneness, absurdity, pointlessness, anxiety, guilt and alienation).

In contrast to the North American tradition where 'welfare' is often defined narrowly 'to mean income transfers or direct services which support the poor and give a minimum standard of living' (Gamble 2016: 3), this volume follows the European approach, defining it as associative action and services designed to improve the general well-being of citizens. In other words, service provision and interventions to promote well-being involving voluntarism and collective action 'to pool collective risks and to provide investment in the human capital of all citizens' (Gamble 2016: 3; see also Beveridge 1943; Titmuss 1958; Greve 2013). Beresford (2016: 2) puts it simply: '[I]t is essentially concerned with how we take care of each other as human beings.'

To better understand the notion of existential threats facing civil society we need to briefly remind ourselves of the underpinnings of existentialist thought. As Dixon (2010: 178) explains, 'first-person subjective experiences are dominated by the self's awareness of individuality, temporality and nothingness, which means people are left only to contemplate the absurdity of living a life without reason or purpose, where self is just a contingent fact engulfed by the infinite'. In response, associative life and collective action may realise both individual and collective freedoms through acting for the greater good (Stone 1987). In this regard it is germane to focus on civil society, because acting for collective well-being is an altruistic act (Carpenter and Knowles Myers 2010; Lindsey et al 2018: 7). As a burgeoning literature attests, altruism lies at the heart of voluntary action (for example, Horton Smith 1981; Bussell and Forbes 2002; Burns et al 2006; Vakoch 2013; Kahana et al 2013; Veludo-de-Oliveira et al 2015; Bennett and Einolf 2017). This literature, itself, reinforces the idea of an age of uncertainty by providing conflicting evidence on prevailing trends in voluntarism. While some authors point to a decline in social capital (Putnam 2000; Hustinx and Meijs 2011: 5), others report 'a counter-trend towards tighter modes of organising volunteering, aimed at countering and/or better accommodating the individualising forces that are current in present-day Western European societies' (see also Stolle and Hooghe 2004).

As noted in Chapter 1, civil society is a key arena where many efforts to improve the human condition play out. Not only is it the bedrock of associative life, but it also captures the contemporary blurring of boundaries as new forms and practices of governance increasingly draw civil society organisations into the delivery of public services and the advancement of well-being. In the twenty-first century, existential challenges not only stem from the quest for meaning and how this shapes motivations for voluntary action; they are also a function of modernity. As Barberis (2001: 115) explains: 'Among the more salient characteristics of modernity are disorganization, decomposition, disaggregation, flexibility, variegation and even incongruence – whether of structures, systems, processes or values. … Structures have become more fragmented, organisations more difficult to classify, procedures more convoluted.'

A survey of the recent international academic literature supports the foregoing view and underlines the breadth of existential challenges facing civil society organisations. They encompass promoting societal well-being in the context of governance shifts (such as devolution and Brexit), new and contested forms of identity (for example, Mycielski 2016; Sanchez Salgado 2017; Beel et al 2018), austerity (for example, Giugni and Grasso 2016; Simiti 2017; Tzifakis et al 2017; Beel et al 2018), and upholding citizen well-being and social cohesion in the context of new and pronounced flows of migration and asylum seeking (for example, Semino 2015; Simsa 2017). Technology is a further driver of uncertainty, not least because of unequal access and growing digital divides (see, Jones 2015; Papachristopoulos and Zafiropoulou 2016; Theocharis et al 2017). Other challenges stem from the negative effects of neo-liberalism (for example, Pianta 2013; Keane 2005; Knutsen 2017), declining state capacity (see, Zafiropoulou 2014; Murphy

2015); as well as curbs on democratic freedoms and the undermining of civil society independence from the state (for example, Cepić and Kovačić 2015; Drakaki and Panagiotis 2017; Chaney 2018). The rise of populism, individualism and economic nationalism (Wright 2017; Kazin 2016; Alvares and Dahlgren 2016; Fevre 2016; Gusterson 2017) also presents key challenges, as does the decline of local practices and traditions in the face of dominant corporate and globalised practices (for example, Taylor 2016), and the need to address widespread human rights violations (see, Luengo 2018; Chaney 2018). Two major existential challenges have emerged during the writing of this book: Brexit and the COVID-19 pandemic.

Brexit stems from the inter-play of populist politics, revised governance structures, economic nationalism and migration (see Chapter 8). Over recent years, relations between the EU and the UK state, as well as Wales, Scotland and Northern Ireland, have been shaped by instrumentalist calculations of the benefits of collective European governance versus (albeit contrasting notions of) independence (Chaney 2014). Several authors have underlined how UK civil society organisations were slow to realise the threat of Brexit and engage in the referendum debates (Ishkanian 2019; Parks 2019). As Kaldor (2019: 15) observes, over the years civil society has been a progressive force in the EU. Recent accounts offer a range of insights on the emerging implications of Brexit for civil society. First, it disrupts established governance structures and practices that link organised civil society and EU institutions. Second, it ends direct civil society engagement in delivering EU directives, such as tackling discrimination and inequality (Minto 2020). Third, it is a significant financial threat. Hitherto, and most notably in the devolved nations, the EU extended considerable support to civil society organisations through structural funds, enabling them to pursue programmes on employability, equality and sustainability (Birrell and Gray 2017). Fourth, it also threatens the position of large numbers of EU citizens who work for charities in the UK (Morris 2018).

In the case of the pandemic, a burgeoning international literature reveals how civil society organisations made diverse interventions during the COVID-19 emergency, with increased levels of volunteering, donations and service delivery (Cai et al 2021; Nicolaides and Lim 2020; Saha 2020; Mikecz and Oross 2020; Dayson et al 2021). Thus, 'thousands of people came together in more than 700 mutual aid groups across the country while the NHS Volunteer Responder Scheme[1] received around 750,000 volunteer applications' (NCVO 2020: 8). The literature also shows how different countries' responses were shaped by contrasting governance arrangements, institutions and party politics (Schwartz 2014; Dayson and Damm 2020; Tandon and Aravind 2021; Doğan and Genç 2021). A core emerging strand of this literature highlights how civil society organisations have suffered during the pandemic. As Thiery et al (2021) note, 'the funding landscape for voluntary organisations is uncertain, demand for services is overwhelming, and staff and volunteers are suffering from fatigue' (see also Hyndman 2020; Kim and Mason 2020). Again, data from the UK affirm this and show that 72 per cent of civil society organisations surveyed said they were not wholly able to meet demand for their services because of the pandemic, and 49.3 per cent had closed their service delivery operations entirely. The main causes were social distancing regulations, insufficient income and a shortage of volunteers (DCMS 2021: 11).

At this juncture it is germane to reflect on the limitations of this volume. As the foregoing outline of the literature associated with civil society theory and prevailing existential challenges suggests, space constraints do not allow for an exhaustive exploration of all challenges facing civil society. Rather, as the following section describes, we present salient examples emerging from WISERD's Economic and Social Research Council-funded civil society research programme.

The structure of this book

In Chapter 3, 'Civil society and the governance of city region economic development', David Beel, Martin Jones and Ian Rees Jones analyse how new spatial political units of governance for economic development are (re-)positioning civil society. The challenges posed to civil society by agglomerative, city regional economic development models are an internationally salient issue. Citing parallel analysis of North America's 'metro' areas (for example, Glaeser 2012), this chapter uses semi-structured interviews with key actors operating across case study city regions in Wales and England to reveal how they are creating several significant tensions as well as presenting opportunities for civil society actors. To highlight how the ongoing process of restructuring the sub-national economic space has significant impacts upon the ways in which civil society actors think and mobilise, the analysis draws out thematic tensions that straddle the development of each city region. This is important because, to date, much of the city region agenda has been primarily focused upon economic development. In contrast, Chapter 3 addresses a key lacuna by exploring the implications for civil society positioning, autonomy and criticality.

A burgeoning international literature (Pierson 2001; Barberis 2001; Clark 2011; Taylor-Gooby et al 2017) charts the decline and reconfiguration of traditional forms of state welfare provision. The UK is no exception to the wider trend, for over recent decades there have been significant cuts to welfare services hitherto provided by the state (Edmiston 2017). Amid contemporary concerns over a crisis in state welfare provision (Castles 2004; Rueda 2014), in Chapter 4, 'Civil society, pandemic, and the crisis of welfare: exploring mixed economy models of welfare in domiciliary adult social care in a devolved UK', Paul Chaney and Christala Sophocleous draw on the literature of welfare pluralism (Johnson 1987; Nirmala 1996; Wigell 2017) and present new empirical evidence. They discuss whether civil society is the answer to meeting modern welfare needs and explore the challenges that this presents.

The chapter focuses on the example of social care. An ageing population coupled with austerity presents considerable challenges in meeting rising demand (Higgs and Gilleard 2010; Meier and Werding 2010; Hastings et al 2015; Mazzola et al 2016). As noted, this has often been framed in terms of a 'crisis in social care' (Ehrenstein 2012; Oliver 2015; Kaehne 2017; Ogden 2017). To address this, governments are presented with limited choices. With tax rises to pay for expanded state provision often viewed as electorally unpalatable by ruling elites (Wilensky 2002), they have instead tended to turn to the private sector, or seek solutions based on partnership working with civil society (Taylor-Gooby 2012). In the wake of devolution in 1998–9, the devolved administrations have tended to embrace the latter option. This is a product of the territorialisation of electoral politics which has seen Left-of-Centre, civic nationalist-leaning parties govern in Wales and Scotland. In contrast, successive Westminster governments have followed a neo-liberal agenda (Danson et al 2012).

Devolution has created a natural experiment in welfare mixes. This chapter presents comparative analysis of stakeholders' views of the efficacy of the different mixes in the four nations of the UK and the challenges facing civil society organisations. It also examines whether mixed economy approaches are the answer to meeting modern welfare needs with reference to the pre-COVID policy frameworks in Wales, Scotland, England and Northern Ireland. Underlining the present age of uncertainty, the analysis then considers the subsequent pandemic response, revealing key contrasts and commonalities between polities.

Chapter 5, 'The contemporary threat to minority languages and cultures: civil society, young people and Celtic language use in Scotland and Wales' by Rhys Jones, Elin Royles, Fiona O'Hanlon and Lindsay Paterson, explores civil society's past and present role in addressing the existential threat facing two 'minority' languages: Welsh and Scottish Gaelic. This is an internationally salient issue with many minority languages under threat (Mooko 2006; Sherris and Penfield 2019). In part driven by globalisation, experts predict that a half of the estimated 6,800 languages spoken today will have disappeared by the end of the twenty-first century.

In addition to summarising past civil society activism from the 1960s onwards to defend the languages, the analysis presents a series of new findings on the contemporary role of national festivals in seeking to promote minority language use in social contexts. This matters because while both languages have seen an increase in the number of speakers, much of the gain has been associated with formal state education. The wider literature warns us that a language which is confined to the educational sector is not a living language. Therefore, much depends on civil society organisations co-working with state agencies to promote language use in social settings. The case studies are the *Eisteddfod Cenedlaethol* (National Eisteddfod) in Wales and *Am Mòd Nàiseanta Rìoghail* in Scotland. Both are national festivals of language, culture, history and heritage. Interview data with young people reveal their experiences and views of the efficacy of the cultural festivals in promoting minority language use in social settings. Based on the timely empirical analysis, contrasts, commonalities and transferable lessons are identified.

In Chapter 6, 'Digital threat or opportunity? Local civil society in an age of global inter-connectivity', Michael Woods, Taulant Guma and Sophie Yarker examine the challenges and opportunities for local civil society arising from digital technologies, especially social media. Drawing upon case studies of local civil society groups in three localities in Wales, they explore the dynamics of reconfiguration of local civil society. Specifically, they consider how digital technologies shape the articulation of issues within local civil society; how digital technologies have impacted on the ways in which local civil society groups operate and organise within their localities; and how digital technologies impact upon local civil society groups' ability to forge connections beyond their locale.

As the chapter details, such issues matter because new digital technologies have created a new universal space of social consciousness, identity, belonging and collective action. Against the backdrop of studies suggesting the erosion of bonding social capital in American communities and beyond (Putnam 2000, MacMillan 1995; Lane et al 2000; Sarracino and Mikucka 2017), a key issue is the extent to which this poses an existential threat to local civil society, with the global and the local pitted against each other. Accordingly, this chapter provides new insights about the impact of digital technologies on local civil society groups and discusses their implications.

In Chapter 7, 'Democratic decline? Civil society and trust in government', Alistair Cole, Ian Stafford and Dominic Heinz examine the contemporary decline of political trust and the potential existential threat that this poses to democracy. Drawing on comparative analysis from the UK, France and Germany, they examine governance-trust configurations and their likely propensity to foster co-production and co-creation between state and civil society. The chapter explores how the development of trust varies within and between different states and civil society. In addition, the analysis considers the role of civil society in potential solutions for restoring political trust and reversing the perceived decline of democracy. Consideration is also given to the impact of history and identity on attempts to adopt co-creation or co-production to build trust with civil society actors, as well as the extent to which the restructuring of governance arrangements within a territory impacts on cooperation between the state and civil sphere. The analysis also examines the territorial dimension to the impact of COVID-19 on political trust and how this affects developments at the sub-state level.

In Chapter 8, 'Xenophobia, hostility and austerity: European migrants and civil society in Wales', Stephen Drinkwater, Taulant Guma and Rhys Dafydd Jones focus on the internationally salient issue of turbulence and uncertainty in relation to contemporary patterns and processes of migration. As they discuss, this has been driven by a variety of causes including the international rise of populism and Brexit, with its inflammatory discourse surrounding immigration, and accompanying sharp increase in reported hate crimes. Many EU citizens have been targeted in xenoracist incidents. Further drivers of uncertainty include substantial cuts to public services, including those for immigrants, refugees and asylum seekers – as well as Brexit's implications for migration. This chapter's timely analysis examines migrants' roles and experiences of civil society in the context of ongoing hostile and austere environments. It asks whether contemporary empirical analysis supports the dominant integrationist view of migrants' participation in the UK evident in the academic and policy literature. This presents them as passive and requiring support, rather than as being resourceful agents and civil society makers. The analysis also examines migrants' views and experiences of the Brexit referendum result. Furthermore, it provides rich new insights into migrants' experiences of setting up and running new civil society initiatives to tackle dominant negative discourses of migrants in the UK. In addition, the chapter examines the evidence on a participation gap in civil society between migrants and non-migrants. It also reflects on the post-Brexit environment for xenophobia and xenoracism, the reporting of hate crimes, and the adequacy of the wider policy environment for upholding migrants' rights and sustaining civil society.

In Chapter 9, 'Meeting the challenge? Prospects and perils for civil society in the twenty-first century', Paul Chaney and Ian Rees Jones reflect upon the implications of the earlier empirical analyses of developments in the UK and elsewhere and summarise the core challenges and lessons emerging from this multi-disciplinary set of studies. Drawing upon David Lockwood's (1996) conceptualisation, we also consider how the existential challenges and the uncertainties facing civil society impact on civic stratification; specifically, civic gain and expansion as well as civic deficit and exclusion. Last, we consider the prospects and perils for civil society organisations in the context of ongoing existential challenges in an age of uncertainty.

Note

[1] An initiative of the English National Health Service whereby volunteers undertake tasks such as greeting and guiding people at vaccination centres; collecting their shopping,

medicines; helping people to get to medical appointments by giving lifts. https://nhsvolu nteerresponders.org.uk/

References

Alvares, C. and Dahlgren, P. (2016) 'Populism, extremism and media: Mapping an uncertain terrain', *European Journal of Communication*, 31(1): 46–57.

Barberis, P. (2001) 'Civil society, virtue, trust: Implications for the public service ethos in the age of modernity', *Public Policy and Administration*, 16(3): 111–126.

Bauman, Z. (2007) *Liquid Times: Living in an age of uncertainty*, Cambridge: Polity Press.

Beel, D., Jones, M. and Jones, I. R. (2018) 'Regionalisation and civil society in a time of austerity: The cases of Manchester and Sheffield', in C. Berry and A. Giovannini (eds), *Developing England's North: The political economy of the northern powerhouse*, Basingstoke: Springer/Palgrave MacMillan, pp 241–260.

Bennett, M. R. and Einolf, C. J. (2017) 'Religion, altruism, and helping strangers: A multilevel analysis of 126 countries', *Journal for the Scientific Study of Religion*, 56(2): 323–341. https://doi.org/10.1111/jssr.12328

Beresford, P. (2016) *All Our Welfare: Towards participatory social policy*, Bristol: Policy Press.

Beveridge, W. (1943) *The Pillars of Security*, London: Allen and Unwin.

Birrell, D. and Gray, A. (2017) 'Devolution: The social, political and policy implications of Brexit for Scotland, Wales and Northern Ireland', *Journal of Social Policy*, 46(4): 765–782.

Burns, D. J., Reid, J. S. and Toncar, M. (2006) 'Motivations to volunteer: The role of altruism', *International Review on Public and Non-Profit Marketing*, 3: 79–91. https://doi.org/10.1007/BF02893621

Bussell, H. and Forbes, D. (2002) 'Understanding the volunteer market: The what, where, who and why of volunteering', *International Journal of Voluntary Sector Marketing*, 7(3): 244–257.

Cai, Q., Okada, A., Jeong, B. and Kim, S. (2021) 'Civil society responses to the COVID-19 pandemic: A comparative study of China, Japan, and South Korea', *China Review*, 21(1): 107–138.

Carpenter, J. and Knowles Myers, C. (2010) 'Why volunteer? Evidence on the role of altruism, image, and incentives', *Journal of Public Economics*, 94: 911–920.

Castles, F. (2004) *The Future of the Welfare State: Crisis myths and crisis realities*, Oxford: Oxford University Press.

Cepić, D. and Kovačić, M. (2015) 'Civil society going political: The crisis of democracy and the rise of participatory political parties in Croatia', *Contemporary Southeastern Europe*, 2(1): 24–44.

Chaney, P. (2014) 'Instrumental Europeans? Minority nationalist parties' discourse on the European Union: the case of UK meso-elections 1998–2011', *Perspectives on European Politics and Society*, 15(4): 464–482.

Chaney, P. (2018) 'Civil society, "traditional values" and LGBT resistance to heteronormative rights hegemony: Analysis of the UN Universal Periodic Review in the Russian Federation', *Europe-Asia Studies*, 70(4): 638–665.

Clark, J. (2011) 'Civil society in the age of crisis', *Journal of Civil Society*, 7(3): 241–263.

Danson, M., MacLeod, G. and Mooney, G. (2012) 'Devolution and the shifting political economic geographies of the United Kingdom', *Environment and Planning C: Government and Policy*, 30(1): 1–9.

Dayson, C. and Damm, C. (2020) 'Re-making state–civil society relationships during the COVID 19 pandemic? An English perspective', *People, Place and Policy Online*, 14(3): 282–289.

Dayson, C., Bimpson, E., Ellis-Paine, A., Gilbertson, J. and Kara, H. (2021) 'The "resilience" of community organisations during the COVID-19 pandemic: Absorptive, adaptive and transformational capacity during a crisis response', *Voluntary Sector Review* (online first), doi: 10.1332/204080521X16190270778389

DCMS (Department for Digital, Culture, Media & Sport) (2021) *DCMS Coronavirus Impacts Third Sector Survey: Results*, London: DCMS.

Dixon, J. (2010) 'Comparative social welfare: The existential humanist perspective and challenge', *Journal of Comparative Social Welfare*, 26(2–3): 177–187.

Doğan, E. and Genç, H. D. (2021) 'Early-responding civil society and a late coming state: Findings from Turkey during the pandemic', *Nonprofit Policy Forum*, 12(1): 127–146.

Drakaki, M. and Tzionas, P. (2017) 'Community-based social partnerships in crisis resilience: a case example in Greece', *Disaster Prevention and Management*, 26(2): 203–216. https://doi.org/10.1108/DPM-09-2016-0190

Edmiston, D. (2017) 'Welfare, austerity and social citizenship in the UK', *Social Policy and Society*, 16(2): 261–270.

Ehrenstein, A. (2012) *Precarity and the crisis of social care: Everyday politics and experiences of work in women's voluntary organisations.* Unpublished PhD thesis, Cardiff University.

Fevre, R. (2016) *Individualism and Inequality: The future of work and politics*, Cheltenham & Northampton, MA: Edward Elgar Publishing Limited.

Gagnon, A. (2018) *Minority Nations in the Age of Uncertainty: New paths to national emancipation and empowerment*, Toronto: University of Toronto Press.

Gamble, A. (2016) *Can the Welfare State Survive?* Malden, MA: Polity Press.

Giugni, M. and Grasso, M. T. (ed.) (2015) *Austerity and Protest: Popular Contention in Times of Crisis*, London: Routledge.

Glaeser, E. (2012) *Triumph of the City*, London: Macmillan.

Greve, B. (2013) *The Routledge Handbook of the Welfare State*, London: Routledge.

Gusterson, H. (2017) 'From Brexit to Trump: Anthropology and the rise of nationalist populism', *American Ethnologist*, 44: 209–214.

Hastings, A., Bailey, N., Gannon, M., Besemer, K. and Bramley, G. (2015) 'Coping with the cuts? The management of the worst financial settlement in living memory', *Local Government Studies*, 41: 601–621.

Higgs, P. and Gilleard, C. (2010) 'Generational conflict, consumption and the ageing welfare state in the United Kingdom', *Ageing & Society*, 30(8): 1439–1451.

Horton Smith, D. (1981) 'Altruism, volunteers and volunteerism', *Journal of Voluntary Action Research*, 10(1): 21–36.

Hustinx, L. and Meijs, L. (2011) 'Re-embedding volunteering: In search of a new collective ground', *Voluntary Sector Review*, 2(1): 5–21.

Hyndman, N. (2020) 'UK charities and the pandemic: Navigating the perfect storm', *Journal of Accounting & Organizational Change*, 16(4): 587–592.

Ishkanian, A. (2019) 'Social movements, Brexit and social policy', *Social Policy and Society*, 18(1): 147–159.

Johnson, N. (1987) *The Welfare State in Transition: The theory and practice of welfare pluralism*, Brighton: Wheatsheaf.

Jones, I. R. (2015) 'Connectivity, digital technologies and later life', in J. Twigg and W. Martin (eds), *Routledge Handbook of Cultural Gerontology*, London: Routledge, pp 438–446.

Kaehne, A. (2017) 'Last word: Crisis in social care', *Political Insight*, 8(1): 40–40.

Kahana, E., Bhatta, T., Lovegreen, L., Kahana, B. and Midlarsky, E. (2013) 'Altruism, helping, and volunteering', *Journal of Aging and Health*, 25(1): 159–187.

Kaldor, M. (2019) 'Democracy and Brexit', *Soundings*, 72, Summer 2019, 17–30.

Kazin, M. (2016) 'Trump and American populism', *Foreign Affairs*, 95(6): 17–24.

Keane, J. (2005) 'Eleven theses on markets and civil society', *Journal of Civil Society*, 1(1): 25–34.

Kim, M. and Mason, D. (2020) 'Are you ready? Financial management, operating reserves, and the immediate impact of COVID-19 on nonprofits', *Nonprofit and Voluntary Sector Quarterly*, 49(6): 1191–1209.

Knutsen, W. (2017) 'Retaining the benefits of government-nonprofit contracting relationship: Opposites attract or clash'? *Voluntas: International Journal of Voluntary and Nonprofit Organizations*, 28(4): 1373–1398.

Lane A. P., Wong, C. H., Močnik, Š., Song, S. and Yuen B. (2020) 'Association of neighborhood social capital with quality of life among older people in Singapore', *Journal of Aging and Health*, 32(7–8): 841–850. Doi:10.1177/0898264319857990

Lindsey, R., Mohan, J., Metcalfe, E. and Bulloch, S. (2018) *Continuity and Change in Voluntary Action: Patterns, trends and understandings*, Bristol: Policy Press.

Lockwood, D. (1996) 'Civic integration and class formation', *The British Journal of Sociology*, 47(3): 531–550.

Luengo, M. (2018) 'Gender violence: The media, civil society, and the struggle for human rights in Argentina', *Media, Culture & Society*, 40(3): 397–414.

Macmillan, R. (1995) 'Changes in the structure of life courses and the decline of social capital in Canadian society: A time series analysis of property crime rates', *The Canadian Journal of Sociology / Cahiers Canadiens de Sociologie*, 20(1): 51–79. https://doi.org/10.2307/3340986

Mazzola, P., Rimoldi, S., Rossi, P., Noale, M., Rea, F., Facchini, C., Maggi, S., Corrao, G. and Annoni, G. (2016) 'Aging in Italy: The need for new welfare strategies in an old country', *The Gerontologist*, 56(3): 383–390.

Meier, V. and Werding, M. (2010) 'Ageing and the welfare state: Securing sustainability', *Oxford Review of Economic Policy*, 26(4): 655–673.

Mikecz, D. and Oross, D. (2020) 'Political participation and volunteering during the COVID-19 pandemic in Hungary', *Corvinus Journal of Sociology and Social Policy*, 11(2): 175–177.

Minto, R. (2020) 'Sticky networks in times of change: The case of the European women's lobby and Brexit', *Journal of Common Market Studies*, 58(6): 1587–1604.

Mohan, B. (1979) 'Conceptualization of existential intervention', *Psychology – A Journal of Human Behavior*, 16(3): 39–46.

Mohan, B. (1985a) 'Comparative social welfare: Beyond ideology, Utopia, and despair', in B. Mohan (ed.), *Toward Comparative Social Welfare*, Cambridge, MA: Schenkman, pp 1–23.

Mohan, B. (1985b) 'Social policy: Beyond illusion and reality', in B. Mohan (ed.), *New Horizons in Social Welfare and Policy*, Cambridge, MA: Schenkman, pp 1–25.

Mooko, T. (2006) Counteracting the threat of language death: The case of minority languages in Botswana, Journal of Multilingual and Multicultural Development, 27(2): 109–125.

Morris, M. (2018) *The Charity Workforce in Post-Brexit Britain: Immigration and skills policy for the third sector*, London: IPPR, the Institute for Public Policy Research. Available at: https://www.cfg.org.uk/userfiles/docume nts/Policy%20documents/Brexit_and_the_charity_workforce_April18_ PROOF_V3.pdf

Murphy, M. (2015) 'Irish civil society: Rearranging the deckchairs on the Titanic? A case study of fighting Irish social security retrenchment', *Journal of Civil Society*, 23(1): 1–16.

Mycielski, M. (2016) 'The crisis of European identity and awakening of civil society', *European View*, 15(2): 223–232.

NCVO National Council of Voluntary Organisations (2020) *Voluntary Sector Almanac*, London: NCVO.

Nicolaides, A. and Lim, A. (2020) 'Undergoing the experiences of the COVID-19 pandemic as ruptures in American civil society create conditions for right action', *Reflective Practice*, 21(6): 844–860.

Nirmala, R. (1996) *Towards Welfare Pluralism: Public services in a time of change*, Aldershot: Dartmouth.

Obeng-Odoom, F. (2021) *The Commons in an Age of Uncertainty: Decolonizing nature, economy, and society*, Toronto; Buffalo; London: University of Toronto Press.

Ogden, J. (2017) 'Rising cost of dementia care risks social care funding crisis', *Progress in Neurology and Psychiatry*, 21(1): 5–5.

Oliver, D. (2015) 'We cannot keep ignoring the crisis in social care', *BMJ: British Medical Journal*, 21: 350.

Papachristopoulos, K. and Zafiropoulou, M. (2016) 'Greek civil society's online alternative networks as emergent resilience strategies in time of crisis', *Social Communication*, 2: 6–19.

Parks, L. (2019) 'All quiet on the Brexit front? UK civil society before and after the UK's referendum on membership of the EU', in L. Antoniolli, L. Bonatti and C. Ruzza (eds), *Highs and Lows of European Integration*, Cham: Springer, https://doi.org/10.1007/978-3-319-93626-0_7

Pianta, M. (2013) 'Democracy lost: The financial crisis in Europe and the role of civil society', *Journal of Civil Society*, 9(2): 148–161.

Pierson, P. (2001) 'Coping with permanent austerity: Welfare state restructuring in affluent democracies', in P. Pierson (ed.), *The New Politics of the Welfare State*, Oxford: Oxford University Press, pp 127–135.

Putnam, R. (2000) *Bowling Alone: The Collapse and Revival of American Community*, New York: Simon & Schuster.

Rueda, D. (2014) 'Dualization, crisis and the welfare state', *Socio-Economic Review*, 12(2): 381–407.

Saha, G. (2020) 'Civil society and volunteerism in the COVID-19 pandemic', *Indian Journal of Social Psychiatry*, 36(2): 34–42.

Sanchez Salgado, R. (2017) 'Europeanization of civil society organizations in times of crisis? Exploring the evolution grant-seeking strategies in the EU multi-level system', *European Politics and Society*, 18(4): 511–528.

Sarracino, F. and Mikucka, M. (2017) 'Social capital in Europe from 1990 to 2012: Trends and convergence', *Soc Indic Res*, 131: 407–432. https://doi.org/10.1007/s11205-016-1255-z

Schwartz, J. (2014) 'Achieving effective pandemic response in Taiwan through state–civil society cooperation: The role of the Li Zhang', *Asian Survey*, 54(6): 1136–1157.

Semino, S. (2015) 'Governmental promotion of social cohesion and its effect on local civil society organisations: How these institutions respond to the inclusion of vulnerable groups as active citizens', *Social Policy and Society*, 14(2): 189–201.

Simsa, R. (2017) 'Leaving emergency management in the refugee crisis to civil society? The case of Austria', *Journal of Applied Security Research*, 12(1): 78–95.

Stolle, D. and Hooghe, M. (2004) 'Inaccurate, exceptional, one-sided or irrelevant? The debate about the alleged decline of social capital and civic engagement in Western societies', *British Journal of Political Science*, 35: 149–167.

Stone, B. (1987) 'Simone de Beauvoir and the existential basis of socialism', *Social Text*, No. 17 (Autumn, 1987), pp 123–133.

Tandon, R. and Aravind, R. (2021) 'Source of life or kiss of death: Revisiting state-civil society dynamics in India during COVID-19 pandemic', *Nonprofit Policy Forum*, 12(1): 147–163.

Taylor, J. (2016) 'Crises in civil society organisations: Opportunities for transformation', *Development in Practice*, 26(5): 663–669.

Taylor-Gooby, P. (2012) 'Root and branch restructuring to achieve major cuts: The policy programme of the 2010 UK coalition government', *Social Policy and Administration*, 46: 61–82.

Taylor-Gooby, P., Leruth, B. and Chung, H. (eds) (2017) *After Austerity: Welfare state transformation in Europe after the Great Recession*, Oxford: Oxford University Press.

Thiery, H., Cook, J., Burchell, J., Ballantyne, E., Walkley, F. and McNeill, J. (2021) '"Never more needed" yet never more stretched: Reflections on the role of the voluntary sector during the COVID-19 pandemic', *Voluntary Sector Review* (online first), doi: 10.1332/204080521X16131303365691

Theocharis, Y., Vitoratou, S. and Sajuria, J. (2017) 'Civil society in times of crisis: Understanding collective action dynamics in digitally-enabled volunteer networks', *Journal of Computer-Mediated Communication*, 22(5): 248–265.

Titmuss, R. (1958) *Essays on the Welfare State*, London: Allen and Unwin.

Vakoch, D. (ed.) (2013) *Altruism in Cross-Cultural Perspective*, New York: Springer.

Veludo-de-Oliveira, T., Pallister, J. and Foxall, G. (2015) 'Unselfish? Understanding the role of altruism, empathy, and beliefs in volunteering commitment', *Journal of Nonprofit & Public Sector Marketing*, 27(4): 373–396.

Wigell, M. (2017) 'Political effects of welfare pluralism: Comparative evidence from Argentina and Chile', *World Development*, 95: 27–42.

Wilensky, H. (2002) 'Tax-welfare backlash: How to tax, spend, and yet keep cool', in *Rich Democracies: Political economy, public policy, and performance*, Berkeley: University of California Press, pp 363–397.

Wright, T. (2017) 'The road to somewhere: The populist revolt and the future of politics', *Political Quarterly*, 88(4): 726–727.

Zafiropoulou, M. (2014) 'Exclusion from healthcare services and the emergence of new stakeholders and vulnerable groups in times of economic crisis: A civil society's perspective in Greece', *Social Change Review*, 12(2): 141–160.

Civil society and the governance of city region economic development

David Beel, Martin Jones and Ian Rees Jones

Within the UK, and further afield, the spatial delineations of the 'city region' have seen a renaissance as the de facto spatial political units of governance for economic development (Clarke and Cochrane 2013, Sykes et al 2021). In the UK, successive governments have sought to reshape the ways in which economic development takes place, and although this shift in governmental delivery began under New Labour, it has been much vaunted by the UK coalition government (Deas 2013), and subsequently by the continuing Conservative administrations (Conservative Party 2015) and the Welsh Labour Party (Bristow and Healy 2015). This chapter, therefore, addresses the (re-)positioning of civil society within these new structures of city region governance. Based on stakeholder mapping and semi-structured interviews with key actors operating across each city region, the chapter illustrates how this has created several significant tensions as well as opportunities for civil society actors.

The chapter draws from four UK case study city regions (two in Wales and two in England from 2015 to 2019) and specifically looks at the ways city and devolution deals have impacted upon the positioning of civil society actors. It was funded by the Economic and Social Research Council under grant No: ES/L009099/1; part of WISERD's ongoing civil society research programme. This methodology takes the form of thematically grouping stakeholder responses to look across the four differing city regions for points of convergence and divergence. This allows the chapter to consider the ways in which civil society organisations and individuals have sought to interpret, rationalise and respond to the challenges of the city region agenda. In doing this, we draw out three thematic tensions that straddle the development of each city region; the purpose being to highlight how the ongoing processes of restructuring sub-national economic space has significant impacts upon the ways in which civil society actors think and mobilise. This is important when much of the city region agenda has been primarily focused upon economic development, often to the detriment of more social concerns. In turn, this has significant implications for civil society autonomy and criticality. It is important to note that the delivery of city regions in Wales and England is layered onto differing political and geographical contexts. This is especially pertinent in relation to Welsh devolution and the role the Welsh government has played alongside the UK government in the delivery of city regions (see Beel et al 2018; Waite and Bristow 2019; Waite and Morgan 2019). Despite these substantial differences, as we will highlight, the overarching rationale for city region delivery, creates a number of comparable tensions for civil society actors whether based in Wales or England.

The chapter will develop as follows: the first section looks at the underpinning rationale for developing city regions and presents a brief narrative detailing who was given agency to do this. Following this, the chapter moves to consider three themes in regard to the tensions that have arisen from the delivery of city regions in terms of civil society (re)positioning. The first will focus on the changes this creates in terms of central/local relations in the way in which city regions create new scalar relations. The second will consider questions of accountability. The third will consider what this implies with regard to economic and social relations. The chapter concludes by reflecting back on these thematic concerns.

City region 'growth machine'?

City regions in their current guise in the UK are still very much nascent spatial or territorial entities, that are actively assembling in terms of their creation and delivery (see Beel et al 2021). Some have progressed through to their second terms as Mayoral Combined Authorities (Greater Manchester, West Midlands), whereas others have been slower in the process (such as the Sheffield City Region and developments in Wales). City regions in England have developed out of the demise of regional development agencies (Pike et al 2016), whereas in Wales city regions followed the demise of the Wales Spatial Plan (Jones et al 2016), with both being spatial fixes for a number of economic deficiencies in the UK's growth model. In part this relates to the enduring impact of the global financial crisis (Omstedt 2016) but also in relation to longer-term issues such as regional imbalances and disparities (Martin et al 2016). This also dovetails with academic and policy literatures that vaunt the city region and city first economic growth through agglomeration (Nathan and Overman 2013) as the key strategy in terms of unlocking growth potential in a global economy (Storper 2013). The following section will now consider, at least in its initial format, what was envisioned for city regions and why in the context of civil society actors this makes for potential turbulence.

The development of regional disparity in the UK is based upon historical precedent; it is also one which is further perpetuated into the present by specific UK governmental policies (McCann 2016). At all scales, but especially those based upon the consolidation of London as a world city

(Smith 2003), it has meant that this disparity has perpetuated over time and is continuing. This, as SPERI (2015a, 2015b) has shown, is very much backed by UK government policy whereby London, despite being celebrated as a capital of world economy and the free market, is also subsidised heavily in comparison with the rest of the UK. Therefore, there is a paradox in play with regard to current economic development and policy being implemented within the UK. Despite there being an awareness that London is way ahead in terms of economic development and that the north of England, but more broadly the rest of the UK, is in some way 'lagging', there is still not the change in policy direction to create a greater sense of balance (see figures in ONS (2016) for further evidence). This has been developed further, in recent debates, with regard to the notion of 'levelling up' that again attempts to address issues of economic imbalance in the UK economy (BEIS Committee 2021). This is due to a variety of reasons, but it predominately is ideological and relates to application of those theories of agglomeration that have become dominant in developing neo-liberal city region building whereby the 'golden goose' needs to be protected and allowed to grow at all costs (Pike et al 2012). It is, therefore, the model that is laid down by London's 'success' that should then be developed elsewhere in the UK. This has led to the metropolitan city region becoming the dominant scale upon which urban policy and development is being enacted (Neuman and Hull 2013).

Work by Scott (2001, 2019) is a prime example in delineating the eminent positions world cities find themselves in as indicators of the success city regions can have. The focus upon scale is important because a key feature of their success has been their urban centres' ability to dominate the region surrounding them. Agglomeration in urban theory refers to processes whereby an urban centre enlarges by engulfing more land, labour and infrastructure into its region (Rigby and Brown 2013). This allows for a suitable supply of labour, as well as the space to spread, as city agglomeration grows (Storper 2013). Agglomeration at the city region scale, then, is the current ideological discourse that is dominant within the neo-liberal growth model of urban development thinking (Haughton et al 2013). Its proponents (such as Fujita and Krugman 1995; Scott and Storper 2003; Harding 2007; Nathan and Overman 2013; and Florida 2014) set out a model that celebrates the development of the urban while ignoring the structural inequality it creates. There has also been a strong influence on UK policy-makers from North American accounts of urban development, where a focus upon the 'metro' areas approach (Glaeser 2012; Barber 2014; Katz and Bradley 2014) has had a strong influence upon structuring UK urban policy (RSA 2014). This is done by focusing solely on 'successful' metro/regional case studies (Harrison 2007) which are highly spatially selective, highlighting only a narrow narrative of economic success through agglomeration (Lovering 2007). The proponents of this approach conceptualise the city region as

Figure 3.1: The geography of jobs across the Northern Powerhouse

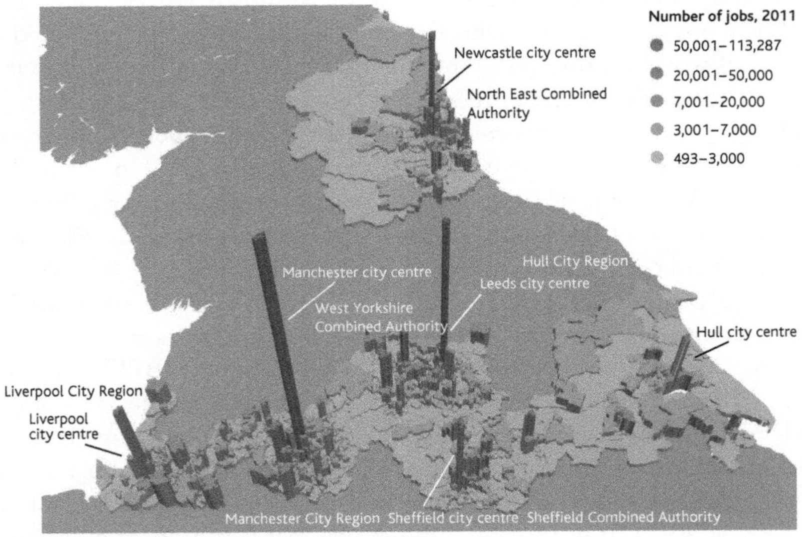

Source: Centre for Cities Northern Powerhouse Factsheet

the focus for generating growth (Harding 2007) in which the city should be mobilised to pull in capital as best it can. The city region is constructed as a 'growth machine' (Logan and Molotch 1987), which aims to develop a critical mass of investment so that such expansion can then lead to a trickledown effect for the city region as a whole (Overman et al 2010). Figure 3.1 vividly represents this agglomeration thinking by attempting to show how urban centres and their peripheries within the 'Northern Powerhouse' can create and centralise employment. The 'spikiness' focuses attention on how such urban cores are key in generating growth for cities. Manchester, for instance, is seen as the central 'power', as the UK government attempts to deliver a Northern Powerhouse by agglomerating selected cities together. At the centre of this is the belief that, despite issues caused by uneven development, in overall economic performance terms it is better to ignore economic and historical imbalances and concentrate on continuing growth.

In the words of one interesting commentator on this perspective:

Investing in more successful cities to either enhance the economy or reduce cost of living clearly exacerbates uneven spatial development. But I have tried to argue that this may make for good economic policy in a world where who you are matters more than where you are and the government can't do much to offset the market forces that make some places perform worse than others. Of course, adopting such a course, and prioritising growth over rebalancing makes for very difficult politics for constituency based politicians. (Overman 2012: 1)

Success creates success, and the city region is thus seen as a tool for economic growth, which focuses upon building an economic mass, the skills base and the transport links of the region (City Regions Task and Finish Group 2012). It has a very specific spatiality in play whereby the city region's projected territorially looks to harness surrounding areas in order to serve the economic growth of the centre. The political project of city regionalism is, therefore, to rescale the central city into a much larger territory and to bring surrounding territories under its purview. It pushes the dominant centre's identity and politics out into its hinterland (Vainikka 2015) through an economic rationalism for growth. Due to this, all other concerns become secondary (Peck and Tickell 1994, 2012).

Critiques of this position have been varied and there have been a variety of heated debates in the academic literature which have opened up discussions about city region development. This will be developed further below, but, with regard to city regions and agglomeration, Haughton et al (2014) neatly point out the failure of agglomeration to develop even growth due to its boosterish potential. In discussion with Overman (2014), Haughton et al (2014) detail how a desire to relax planning constraints in urban areas for 'growth' suffers from 'short-term' thinking that focuses upon the centres of successful agglomeration while ignoring the uneven growth this creates within the city and its surroundings (Etherington and Jones, 2009; Massey 2015). Such approaches fail to counter this evidence with empirical work from other less successful locations, therefore not taking into account the way in which such processes, although potentially good for one city region, could be highly constraining for another (Lovering 1999; Henderson and Ho 2014).

Harrison (2007) argues that this represents a shift in terms of the spatial scale upon which economic competition takes place, as 'New Regionalist' thinking (Keating et al 2003; Brenner 2004) is then rescaled to the city region. As mentioned previously in the UK context, by moving from the region to the city region, the system of city regional development only serves to increase the competition between urban areas rather than breaking it down; or alternatively it attempts to create uneasy growth coalitions such as the Northern Powerhouse which is as fractious as it is cooperative. The need to compete in a relentless globalised economy and with the city region being seen as the appropriate scale on which to do this (Scott 2001, 2019), as Harrison (2007) suggests, forces city regions to compete for growth and territory (in some cases) in an attempt to secure their position of dominance. Lovering's (1999) critique of 'New Regionalism' as the policy and theoretical forerunner to city regionalism is exceedingly valid at this point as it offers perhaps the most stinging critique whereby he distils such approaches down to 'a set of stories about how "parts" of a regional economy might work, placed next to a set of policy ideals which "might" just be useful in "some cases"' (Lovering 1999: 384). What is perhaps most important in the context of the initial phase of city region building is that the focus is almost completely on economic issues (Schneider and Cottineau 2019).

To date, then, there have been both theoretical and empirical literatures, operating at a variety of scales, arguing both for and against the practices of city regional development. What becomes apparent, though, is that there is a pressing need to contextualise, comprehend and place the current economic developments and growth-orientated agendas of city regions (in the UK) within the broader processes of state spatial restructuring (Hoole and Hincks 2020). This point has been made on several occasions by MacLeod (2001) and Jones (2001), who, contra Lovering (1999), remain sympathetic to the new regionalist project, but note a conceptual void around the geographical political economy of city region-making (see Axinte et al (2019) for a more progressive reading of city regional futures). It is in this void which we now move to consider the positioning of civil society actors.

Civil society (re)positioning

It is in the wake of the above policy developments that civil society organisations have been seeking to respond to this overtly economic focus around the development of city regions that, to a certain extent, leaves such actors on the outside looking in. This is because the emphasis upon economic development (at least initially) focuses agency on those strategically significant actors – local authorities and the business sector able to mobilise and foster the growth coalitions mentioned above in the context of large-scale urban spatial agglomeration.

This chapter uses research material from four UK city regions (Swansea Bay City Region, Sheffield City Region, Cardiff City and Greater Manchester City Region). The research took place from 2015 to 2019 and involved semi-structured interviews with key civil society actors based within each city region.[1] As noted, there are significant differences in the delivery of city regions in Wales and England due to devolution yet, at the same time, a number of similar issues are raised by actors in each location from a conceptual perspective. This relates primarily to the city region agenda, as discussed above, being orientated towards a city and economy first approach to development. The following section moves to consider the conceptual concerns of civil society actors as they responded to this restricting of sub-national governance.

New scalar relations

The city region is the latest in a long line of territorial fixes for delivering economic and social development and instilling competitiveness (Deas 2013), and within this, a series of inbuilt tensions develop between the differing spatial scales and levels of regulation and governance. Without wanting to place any form of hierarchy between scales, we would simply like to point out that the city region discourse persistently ignores the tensions it creates when redefining political boundaries by purposefully creating multi-authority territories (Jones and Macleod 2002). In a very simple sense, the conflating of the city with the region, or the local with the regional, to produce the city region creates a series of spatial mismatches between policy intentions and scalar possibilities (Harrison and Growe 2014). This is highlighted below by a civil society actor discussing their positioning in relation to such changes:

'All of a sudden, we become completely insignificant so whereas at the moment locally we can lobby quite hard and push the direction on certain things, all of that power would go away. … So that for us would cause quite a significant problem. If we start working more collaboratively with other similar organisations then great, we can form a nice little consortium and then we can retain the same level of perceived power and all will be well with the world. But it doesn't fit well with how any of us work really; we work with quite defined communities, we do quite tailored things for them.' (Interview 2, Civil Society Member CCR, 2015)

Further to this and more applicable to the English case studies, but important to the broader framing of city regions as a whole in the UK, is the supposed implication at the centre of the Localism Act (HM Government 2011; Teo 2021), which was a return to local politics which would place citizens in control of their neighbourhoods and communities. In reality, much of this focus has been with regard to giving greater 'autonomy' to LAs through multi-authority agreements and devolution, which in many ways centralises power away from the local level and places it more firmly in the local authority dimension of the local state (HM Government 2015). The civil society responder below, picked up on this contradiction and brings to light the difficulties of being trapped in and between this jump in scale:

'At one point they talk about localism but if you look at regionalisation, it's huge, it's huge and actually the local voluntary community sector can't even hope to engage with, let alone deliver against that agenda. Therefore, civil society is finding itself squeezed behind/between a rhetoric that emphasises its importance but a reality which mitigates

against its ability to capture the resources to deliver against that agenda.'
(Interview 12, Bolsover 2016)

There are, therefore, rhetorical gaps between what policy on one level proposes to do with regard to localism and what it actually does with regard to city regionalism. It is also built upon a series of previous policy interventions to construct multi-scalar agreements as well as traversing onto the policy intentions of other governance institutions (Etherington and Jones 2016). This, to a large extent, reflects the neo-liberal intentions that lie at the centre of these policies in terms of talking the language of participation and autonomy, but in reality, finding ways in which to place power and participation within less democratic institutions. The development of LEPs (Local Economic Partnerships, in England) or business boards (in Wales) are prime examples of this, as those invited to participate are primarily either from business or are already elected officials. This, therefore, reflects, in the short term at least, how new scalar relations presented by city regions can place civil society actors and their interests on the outside looking in:

'My view is very much that it's about creating economic drivers within the region to regenerate and to challenge some of the key matters around things like employment which in turn should impact on poverty, etc. And I think one of the reasons that we're not at the table is we don't talk about the city regional.

Certainly, I've never picked up there being a sense of the city region having a similar if not identical ... responsibility towards things outside of the economic agenda, things like – environmental responsibilities or even more fundamental, social responsibilities. In terms of that definition of it, we're probably seen as not having much of a voice. More likely to speak to businesses and get their views on what is good and what is right about city region as opposed to the third sector.' (Interview 9, Civil Society Member CCR, 2016).

The consequence of this for development of city regions, but also for the interests of civil society organisations, is that it narrows the interests of the local state towards more market-led and consensual interests. This means issues that are more social or in itself, the social reproduction of the city region (Jones 2019), is largely ignored in its development. This, as has been highlighted above, has serious implications for civil society organisations when they are more than likely to be aligned to interests that are more social:

'So, one of the challenges we've got at the minute, and that's part of the discussion that has just happened in the meeting today, is this dilemma – or not a dilemma, this disconnect rather, between the VCSE [voluntary, community and social enterprise sector] and the work that goes in, in the whole economy plain around LEPs [Local Economic Partnerships] and everything else that's going on. And there's – social care and the VCS[Es] are quite well connected, usually, usually through contract and commissioning but then you've got this whole world around economy, employment and skills that spins close to it but never – rarely collides or isn't connected.' (Interview 6, Greater Manchester, 2016)

The quote above really highlights this tension between social and economic concerns. For the civil society actor commenting on this, from a conceptual perspective, they are aligned, but from a policy development perspective, they are separate concerns.

Added to this, when we begin to think about city regions and their constituent places, there is also a need to think critically about the ways in which such an agglomerative approach impacts upon areas outside of, or disconnected from, a metropolitan centre (Beel et al 2018). Due to the piecemeal process by which city regions are being delivered, whereby only certain cities are given a city deal, this raises a series of questions with regard to those places outside the deal-making process. This includes a number of cities and provincial towns as well as rural areas, whether they fall within the hinterland of a city region or not (Pemberton and Shaw 2012). The 'city-first' approach to sub-regional economic governance, whereby growth is delivered via agglomeration, has the potential not only to exacerbate uneven development in cities but also to further entrench it in places external to the city region:

'Now Pembrokeshire was not keen on the City Region approach I think because of our experience of City Regions. When we're sitting on the periphery of it the region looks very different sitting in west Wales than it does sitting in Swansea. So, if you're sitting in Swansea the City Region Deal looks like a pretty good thing but we're a long way from Swansea.' (Interview 14 – Civil Society Leader, 2018)

The above quote in the context of the Swansea Bay City Region reflects upon what Harrison and Heley (2015) suggest, namely, that this is particularly problematic for rural areas due to the geopolitical and spatial imaginaries being created, whereby the city region is constructed as an urban-led and controlled 'growth machine'. This, as the civil society leader suggests, as a strategy for growth, is perhaps deeply misaligned for more rural and peripheral areas. Therefore, rather than helping solve urban/rural divides it again has the potential to exacerbate them (see also Welsh and Heley 2021). This reflects Ward's (2006) warning that, if not addressed, the city region agenda will only serve to perpetuate an existing rural development problem via the reproduction of place hierarchies that marginalises non-urban centres.

Accountability

In detailing the development of new scalar relations in the building of city regions, a consistent concern that was raised by civil society actors was around the issue of accountability, defined in terms of who did or did not have agency to act. The above sections in part highlight this, but the following section will now base such concerns within the literature on this theme.

With the development of new 'spatial imaginaries' (Jessop 2016) at the city region scale, but with a whole mixture of different LAs and institutional setups in the UK, there opens up the possibility for an accountability gap to develop between the local state and civil society (Purcell 2007). In England, this is partly addressed by the creation of city region mayors, giving some form of electoral accountability and oversight. In Wales, as the development of city regions is not part of a devolution settlement, there has been no implementation of city region mayors. Swyngedouw (2009, 2010a, 2010b, 2011) has suggested that contemporary city governances have moved towards a 'post-political' condition, particularly with regard to the ability to challenge conventional democratic forms of decision-making. In moving from a conflict-based decision-making system, this is replaced, first, with a more pluralist form of political engagement and, second, with the enrolment of corporate forces supportive of neo-liberal approaches to economic and social development that seeks to build a 'consensus'. This post-political practice can be viewed across UK city regions with Combined Authorities being created out of LA leaders' boards, coalesced into new institutional partnering arrangements with LEPs and business boards (Beel et al 2021). Therefore, making such systems of governance, and the institutions that are created, directly accountable for their actions (in an elective sense) becomes very difficult as they become removed from and protected from this process (NAO 2017).

Haughton et al (2013: 217) refer to this as producing soft spaces that are 'in between' spaces of governance existing outside, alongside or betwixt the formal statutory scales of government, from area master plans to multiregional growth strategies. For Haughton et al, this further represents a shift towards more advanced forms of neo-liberal governance whereby decisions are made by individuals who hold key positions that are then deployed to serve their particular strategic interests and objectives. McCann (2007) highlights how similar processes in Austin (Texas) have taken place, where discourse focused upon 'liveability and competitiveness' serves to 'transform' Austin's inner city by extending the city's political reach beyond its territory. Its smart growth initiative engaged territories that were simultaneously more extensive (the city region) and more localised (individual neighbourhoods) than the municipality itself, in order to legitimate and facilitate new modes of policy-making and accumulation. This suggests that city regionalism frequently turns on the development of selective, strategically directional, and politically and historically contingent geographical imaginations, rather than on a singular, stable and unitary understanding of what a city region is.

> 'What opportunity will there be to genuinely involve civil society in the process? Because I think the LEP has been and I know it is an economic driver, fine and it's about inward investment, economic growth and the private sector is at the heart of that but there is very little in terms of any wider involvement. And maybe that's ok but when it comes to the combined authority, there needs to be more direct lines of accountability into localities and into local areas.' (Interview 3, Sheffield, 2015)

Here, the city's growth discourse and ability to mobilise a variety of actors allowed it to push through the policies it sought as most appropriate for growth, regardless of the social reproductive issues that this has created. For commentators, this represents a managerial and entrepreneurial turn in urban governance (Harvey 1996), though in post-political terms, a shift towards consensus politics at the same time (Rancière 2004). For Rancière, this represents the negation of democratic practice in order for elite groups to develop with respect to their specific interests. Indeed, in the case of city regions, from a civil society perspective a number have struggled with emphasis upon economic development and the presumed growth model:

> 'Well at the moment we seem to be looking at measures for economic development, transport and a market-based model. What I would – I think it's that terrible phrase, in terms of the wealth that we generate trickling down into other communities which again historically is not really showing there's much to be said for that.' (Interview 9, Civil Society Member CCR, 2016)

Within this context, the defining and reproduction of the democratic framework becomes the very process then by which the 'political' is pushed out. The ability or lack of ability to have voice within such a framework allows a consensus to be developed by those who have the right to access such spaces. Therefore, policy development and the implementation of state governance becomes a closed system which suggests that alternatives developed externally are unviable or 'undemocratic' even. In a Foucauldian sense of governmentality, consensus politics pushes a 'conduct of conduct' whereby 'the mode of assigning location, relations and distributions'

(Swyngedouw 2009: 606; see also Blakey 2021) is dominated by actors who are based within the state apparatus (Jessop 2020).

For Jones (2011), a key point to deal with is the depoliticisation of the state, and to counter this he suggests the need to purposefully engage with those tasked with implementing such strategies. This is done by following the tensions and contradictions actors face, as such activities do not exist without actors executing them on the ground. This begins to highlight who is putting such activities into operation and what agency they have within the state to do this, and it allows for the unpicking of strategies of governmentality that are in play. The city region discourse, though, deploys a series of governmental strategies in order to ensure a specific policy agenda is implemented (as Purcell (2007), McCann (2007) and Haughton et al (2013) have highlighted). Hence, these need to be fully integrated into an understanding of how city regionalism(s) are being constructed and brought into providing opportunities for a stronger representational regime (Hodson et al 2020; Beel et al 2021).

Opportunities?

The previous section perhaps presents a bleak picture concerning the positioning of civil society organisations within the context of city region building. In the following section, we consider how, despite the above, some actors are also finding ways to penetrate the city region agenda and reposition themselves within the nascent governance structures. Some would suggest (Rainnie 2021) that this sits in opposition to the above arguments on the post-political, whereby the agency of civil society actors finds new ways to interact with new forms of governance, in effect re-politicising (perhaps in a limited sense) a number of issues. Rainnie, with a regional focus, draws on the work of Osborne (2006) to suggest that, in the context of a 'New Public Governance' model, there are always opportunities for civil actors to find new partnership through which agency can be developed. The quote below highlights this with regard to opportunities arising for civil society despite the difficulties presented by changing governance arrangements:

'I think it's probably changed enormously actually. I think – well there's a number of pros and cons, I think with the current government policy and the austerity measures everything that's going on in terms of shrinking the states, promoting using third sector organisations and growing civil society has brought some opportunities for the third sector. There's definitely, for example, funding streams that the third sector can access that statutory organisations can't access, so having said that, they are highly competitive.' (Interview 6, Sheffield, Civil Society Leader, 2015)

The quote highlights how this is problematic too in terms of competition between civil society groups which has the potential for negative consequences to develop over time. Despite this, there is a sense that there is an opportunity here for such groups, but it is one that has to be very much grasped. This further echoes our work on Greater Manchester (see Beel et al 2017), whereby following the development of devolution there and a progression to the mayoral model, civil society groups have managed to embed themselves within devolved processes. The quote below highlights this:

> 'But it also means that we as an organisation are quite attractive to our colleagues in devolution as well, particularly health and social care devolution times because we've got a fair amount of evidence that we generated including some cost-benefit analysis, looking at the savings that can be generated from some of the services that we provide, and I can let you have access to that information if it would be of interest.' (Interview 11, Greater Manchester, Civil Society Leader, 2016)

It is important to note, that here the emphasis is upon health and social care devolution and not economic development, but the progress made does perhaps point to a slightly more inclusive approach to city region building.

The (re)positioning of civil society, then, in the context of city region building is perhaps best described as one of constrained agency that is built within the 'shadow of hierarchy' (Jessop 2020). The below quote neatly describes this perhaps difficult position for civil society groups negotiating new forms of governance:

> 'Strategically, you've got to be in there. Really, it's run by a bunch of old men who are predominantly private sector and statutory sector ... they really know their bag, and I don't know whether they trust the third sector or others. ... So, they're championing their own projects ... but what we ... we're aligning strategically – we all want to reduce poverty. We all want to regenerate our city centres. We all want to develop opportunities for employability and we all want to get the [electrified railway] line to Swansea, you know.' (Interview 15, Swansea Civil Society Leader, 2019)

The quote neatly highlights the opportunities available but only if such groups are prepared to 'align strategically' to the city region agenda. This is despite, as the research participant suggests, that agenda being developed by private and statutory interests. This reflects some of the points raised in previous sections and a tension around civil society involvement, especially in the creation of city regions.

Conclusions

The chapter has explored the development and delivery of city regions in England and Wales and why this has been problematic for civil society groups on a number of levels. As highlighted, the emphasis on city regions as engines for economic growth creates real tensions for civil society groups who wish to interact with this new form of sub-national governance. The agenda around the development of city regions has, in itself, been somewhat exclusionary in terms of who is given agency in the various new structures of governance. Examples the chapter has highlighted include civil society actors being squeezed between scales, a lack of voice, tensions between social and economic concerns, negative consequences for periphery regions and forms of democratic deficit and avoidance of accountability. Despite this there are opportunities, and perhaps in a constrained sense, civil society groups across all four city regions have shown an ability to push past such exclusionary factors to become involved. The important thing to note is that this would not just happen automatically; such groups have had to pressure for this and work their way into such processes:

'So, the reference group was set up when we realised that all this was going on around us and nobody was going to come banging down our door. So, the idea came from – okay, how do we make a start on this? Let's write to Tony Lloyd, he's been appointed interim mayor, several of us know him, let's just write him a letter saying, "Hi, we are here, here's five things that are fairly random and fairly bold and probably quite unrealistic, but we'd like to talk about them".' (Interview 4, Greater Manchester, Civil Society Leader, 2016)

The above quote highlights this need for civil society groups to actively seek involvement in such processes. As city regions continue to develop over the next five years, this clearly requires an ongoing process of contestation (and collaboration) in order to ensure that a city region's citizenship regime is expanded beyond the usual selection of economic actors. Such concerns are particularly important as the UK moves towards a post-European model of economic development funding centred on notions of 'levelling up' and 'shared prosperity'. The forerunner to this is the Westminster government's Community Renewal Fund, which is being locally coordinated by local government acting in tandem with local MPs in an interesting sub-regional new localist spatial fix, at the same time premised on 'super-charged' city regions (see HM Treasury et al 2021). Early indications are that local authority territorial growth interests – acting in the context of a decade of deep austerity, jaw-dropping patterns of social inequality, and focused on the immediate business and employment needs of post-COVID recovery – are dominating the projects recommended to government for funding. The agendas of civil society actors are struggling to get to the debating table and the patterns of limited social mobilisation discussed in this chapter look set to continue.

Note

1   The project consisted of 91 semi-structured interviews that were undertaken between 2015 and 2019 with a wide variety of actors working in, and connected to, the field of economic development, ranging from director and chief executive levels to civil society engaged in policy formulation and delivery on the ground. This sample size and actor cross-section was deemed appropriate for rigorous qualitative insight into city region building processes within the four case study sites. The interviews were mostly city region *in situ* office-based, digitally recorded, and draw from the governance structures and various sub-groups of economic development. Stratified actor sampling was undertaken, complemented by snowballing sampling techniques to assess more vulnerable and impenetrable groups (see Atkinson and Flint, 2001; Hitchings and Latham, 2020). For reasons of confidentiality, the individuals are not named.

References

Atkinson, R. and Flint, J. (2001) 'Accessing hidden and hard-to-reach populations: Snowball research strategies', *Social Science Update*, 33, Department of Sociology, University of Surrey.

Axinte, L. F., Mehmood, A., Marsden, T. and Roep, D. (2019) 'Regenerative city-regions: A new conceptual framework', *Regional Studies, Regional Science*, 6(1): 117–129.

Barber, B. R. (2014) *If Mayors Ruled the World: Dysfunctional nations, rising cities*. New Haven, CT: Yale University Press.

Beel, D., Jones, M. and Plows, A. (2020) 'Urban growth strategies in rural regions: Building The North Wales Growth Deal', *Regional Studies*, 54(5): 719–731.

Beel, D., Jones, M. and Jones, I. R. (2021) *City Regions and Devolution in the UK*, Bristol: Policy Press.

Beel, D., Jones, M., Jones, I. R. and Escadale, W. (2017) 'Connected growth: Developing a framework to drive inclusive growth across a city region', *Local Economy*, 32(6): 565–575.

BEIS (Business, Enterprise and Industrial Strategy) Committee (2021) *Post-pandemic economic growth: Levelling up*, House of Commons: London. Available at: https://committees.parliament.uk/work/473/postpande mic-economic-growth-levelling-up-local-and-regional-structures-and-the-delivery-of-economic-growth/

Blakey, J. (2021) 'The politics of scale through Rancière', *Progress in Human Geography*, 45(4): 623–640.

Brenner, N. (2004) *New State Spaces*, Oxford: Oxford University Press.

Bristow, G. and Healy, A. (2015) 'Written Submission to the National Assembly for Wales' Enterprise and Business Committee: City Regions and the Metro' (May), 1–8.

City Regions Task and Finish Group (2012) *City Regions: Definitions and criteria*, Cardiff: Welsh Government.

Clarke, N. and Cochrane, A. (2013) 'Geographies and politics of localism: The localism of the United Kingdom's coalition government', *Political Geography*, 34, 10–23.

Conservative Party (2015) *The Conservative Party Manifesto 2015*, London: Conservative Party.

Deas, I. (2013) 'The search for territorial fixes in subnational governance: City-regions and the disputed emergence of post-political consensus in Manchester, England', *Urban Studies*, 51(11): 2285–2314.

Etherington, D. and Jones, M. (2009) 'City-regions: New geographies of uneven development and inequality', *Regional Studies*, 43(2): 247–265.

Etherington, D. and Jones, M. (2016) 'Devolution and disadvantage in the Sheffield City Region: An assessment of employment, skills, and welfare policies', Sheffield Available at: https://www.sheffield.ac.uk/polopoly_fs/1.645005!/file/SSDevolutionPolicy.pdf

Florida, R. (2014) *The Rise of The Creative Class*, New York: Basic Books.

Fujita, M. and Krugman, P. (1995) 'When is the economy monocentric? Von Thünen and Chamberlin unified', *Regional Science and Urban Economics*, 25(4): 505–528.

Glaeser, E. (2012) *Triumph of the City*, London: Macmillan.

Harding, A. (2007) 'Taking city regions seriously? Response to debate on "City-Regions: New Geographies of Governance, Democracy and Social Reproduction"', *International Journal of Urban and Regional Research*, 31(2): 443–458.

Harrison, J. (2007) 'From competitive regions to competitive city-regions: A new orthodoxy, but some old mistakes', *Journal of Economic Geography*, 7(3): 311–332.

Harrison, J. and Growe, A. (2014) 'When regions collide: In what sense a new and regional problem?' *Environment and Planning A*, 46(10): 2332–2352.

Harrison, J. and Heley, J. (2015) 'Governing beyond the metropolis: Placing the rural in city-region development', *Urban Studies*, 52(6): 1113–1133.

Harvey, D. (1996) 'Cities or urbanization?', *City*, 1:1–2, 38–61. DOI: 10.1080/13604819608900022

Haughton, G., Allmendinger, P. and Oosterlynck, S. (2013) 'Spaces of neoliberal experimentation: Soft spaces, postpolitics, and neoliberal governmentality', *Environment and Planning A*, 45(1): 217–234.

Haughton, G., Deas, I. and Hincks, S. (2014) 'Making an impact: When agglomeration boosterism meets anti-planning rhetoric', *Environment and Planning A*, 46(2): 265–270.

Henderson, J. and Ho, S. Y. (2014) 'Re-forming the state', *Renewal: A Journal of Social Democracy*, 22(3/4): 22–41.

Hitchings, R. and Latham, A. (2020) 'Qualitative methods I: On the current conventions in interview research', *Progress in Human Geography*, 44: 389–398.

HM Government (2011) Localism Bill. Available at: http://www.legislation.gov.uk/ukpga/2011/20/contents/enacted

HM Government (2015) Cities and Local Government Devolution Bill. Available at: http://services.parliament.uk/bills/2015-16/citiesandlocalgovernmentdevolution.html

HM Treasury, MHCLG and DfT (2021) *Levelling Up Fund: Prospectus*, London: HM Treasury.

Hodson, M., McMeekin, A., Froud, J. and Moran, M. (2020) 'State-rescaling and re-designing the material city-region: Tensions of disruption and continuity in articulating the future of Greater Manchester', *Urban Studies*, 57(1): 198–217.

Hoole, C. and Hincks, S. (2020) 'Performing the city-region: Imagineering, devolution and the search for legitimacy', *Environment and Planning A*, 52(8): 1583–1601.

Jessop, B. (2016) *The State: Past, present, future*, Cambridge: Polity Press.

Jessop, B. (2020) *Putting Civil Society in Its Place: Governance, metagovernance and subjectivity*, Bristol: Policy Press.

Jones, M. (2001) 'The rise of the regional state in economic governance: "Partnerships for prosperity" or new scales of state power?' *Environment and Planning A*, 33(7): 1185–1211.

Jones, M. (2019) *Cities and Regions in Crisis: The political economy of sub-national economic development*, Edward Elgar: Cheltenham.

Jones, M., Orford, S. and Macfarlane, V. (2016) *People, Places and Policy: Knowing contemporary Wales through new localities*, London: Routledge. https://doi.org/10.4324/9781315683904

Jones, M. and Macleod, G. (2002) 'Regional tensions: Constructing institutional cohesion?', in J. Peck and K. Ward (eds), *City of Revolution: Restructuring Manchester*, Manchester: Manchester University Press, pp 176–189.

Jones, R. (2011) *People – states – territories: The political geographies of British state transformation*, Oxford: Wiley-Blackwell.

Katz, B. and Bradley, J. (2014) *The Metropolitan Revolution: How cities and metros are fixing our broken politics and fragile economy*, Washington, DC: Brookings Institution.

Keating, M., Loughlin, J. P. and Deschouwer, K. (2003) *Culture, Institutions and Economic Development: A study of eight European regions*, Cheltenham: Edward Elgar.

Logan, J. R. and Molotch, H. L. (1987) *Urban Fortunes: The political economy of place*, Berkeley, CA: University of California Press.

Lovering, J. (1999) 'Theory led by policy: The inadequacies of the "new regionalism" (illustrated from the case of Wales)', *International Journal of Urban and Regional Research*, 23: 379–395.

Lovering, J. (2007) 'The relationship between urban regeneration and neoliberalism: Two presumptuous theories and a research agenda', *International Planning Studies*, 12(4): 343–366.

MacLeod, G. (2001) 'Beyond soft institutionalism: Accumulation, regulation, and their geographical fixes', *Environment and Planning A: Economy and Space*, 33(7): 1145–1167. DOI:10.1068/a32194

Martin, R., Pike, A., Tyler, P. and Gardiner, B. (2016) 'Spatially rebalancing the UK economy: Towards a new policy model?' *Regional Studies*, 50(2): 342–357.

Massey, D. (2015) 'Vocabularies of the economy', in S. Hall, D. Massey and M. Rustin (eds), *After Neoliberalism? The Kilburn manifesto*, London: Lawrence and Wishart, pp 3–18.

McCann, E. (2007) 'Review of "Resilience in the post-welfare inner city: Voluntary sector geographies in London, Los Angeles and Sydney by Geoffery DeVerteuil, Bristol, Policy Press, 2016, 300 pp."', *Urban Geography*, 38(4): 626–628.

McCann, P. (2016) *The UK Regional-National Problem*, London: Routledge.

NAO (National Audit Office) (2017) *Progress in setting up combined authorities*, London: NAO. Available at: https://www.nao.org.uk/report/progress-in-setting-up-combined-authorities/

Nathan, M. and Overman, H. (2013) 'Agglomeration, clusters, and industrial policy', *Oxford Review of Economic Policy*, 29(2): 383–404.

Neuman, M. and Hull, A. (eds) (2013) *The Futures of the City Region (Regions and Cities)*, London: Routledge.

Omstedt, M. (2016) 'Reinforcing unevenness: Post-crisis geography and the spatial selectivity of the state', *Regional Studies*, 3(1): 99–113.

ONS (Office of National Statistics) (2016) 'UK GDP, second estimate: Apr to Jun 2016'. Available at: https://www.ons.gov.uk/releases/ukgdpseconde stimateaprtojun2016

Osborne, S. P. (2006) 'The new public governance?' *Public Management Review*, 8(3): 377–387.

Overman, H. G. (2012) 'Investing in the UK's most successful cities is the surest recipe for national growth', pp 1–2, http://blogs.lse.ac.uk/politi csandpolicy/

Overman, H. G. (2014) 'Making an impact: Misreading, misunderstanding, and misrepresenting research does nothing to improve the quality of public debate and policy making', *Environment and Planning A*, 46(10): 2276–2282.

Peck, J. and Tickell, A. (1994) 'Too many partners ... the future for regeneration partnerships', *Local Economy*, 9(3): 251–265.

Peck, J. and Tickell, A. (2012) 'Apparitions of neoliberalism: Revisiting "Jungle law breaks out"', *Area*, 44(2): 245–249.

Pemberton, S. and Shaw, D. (2012) 'New forms of sub-regional governance and implications for rural areas: Evidence from England', *Planning Practice and Research*, 27(4): 441–458.

Pike, A., Coombes, M., O'Brien, P. and Tomaney, J. (2016) 'Austerity states, institutional dismantling and the governance of sub-national economic development: The demise of the regional development agencies in England', *Territory, Politics, Governance*, 6(1): 1–27.

Pike, A., Rodríguez-Pose, A., Tomaney, J., Torrisi, G. and Tselios, V. (2012) 'In search of the "economic dividend" of devolution: Spatial disparities, spatial economic policy, and decentralisation in the UK', *Environment and Planning C: Government and Policy*, 30: 10–28.

Purcell, M. (2007) 'City-regions, neoliberal globalization and democracy: A research agenda', *International Journal of Urban and Regional Research*, 31(1): 197–206.

Rainnie, A. (2021) 'Regional development and agency: Unfinished business', *Local Economy*, 36(1): 42–55 (online first), https://doi.org/10.1177/026909 42211023877

Rancière, J. (2004) *Disagreement: Politics and philosophy*, Minneapolis, MN: University of Minnesota Press.

Rigby, D. L. and Brown, W. M. (2013) 'Who benefits from agglomeration?' *Regional Studies*, 49(1): 28–43.

RSA (Royal Society of Arts) (2014) *Unleashing Metro Growth: Final recommendations of the city-growth commission*, London: RSA. Available at: https://www.thersa.org/globalassets/pdfs/reports/final-city-growth-commission-report-unleashing-growth.pdf

Schneider, C. and Cottineau, C. (2019) 'Decentralisation versus territorial inequality: A comparative review of English city region policy discourse', *Urban Science*, 3(90): 1–22.

Scott, A. J. (2001) 'Globalization and the rise of city-regions', *European Planning Studies*, 9(7): 813–826.

Scott, A. J. (2019) 'City-regions reconsidered', *Environment and Planning A*, 51(3): 554–580.

Scott, A. J. and Storper, M. (2003) 'Regions, globalization, development', *Regional Studies*, 37(6–7): 549–578.

Smith, R. G. (2003) 'World city topologies', *Progress in Human Geography*, 27(5): 561–582.

SPERI (Sheffield Political Economy Research Institute) (2015a) 'Comparing the post crisis performance of the Sheffield, Brighton and Oxford city region economies', SPERI British Political Economy Brief 17, Sheffield: Sheffield Political Economy Research Institute, University of Sheffield. Available at: http://speri.dept.shef.ac.uk/wp-content/uploads/2018/11/SPERI-Brief-17-Comparing-the-post-crisis-performance-of-the-Sheffield-Brighton-and-Oxford-city-region-economies.pdf

SPERI (2015b) 'Public and private sector employment across the UK since the financial crisis', British Political Economy Brief 10. Available at: http://speri.dept.shef.ac.uk/wp-content/uploads/2018/11/Brief10-public-sector-employment-across-UK-since-financial-crisis.pdf

Storper, M. (2013) *Keys to the City: How economics, institutions, social interactions, and politics shape development*, Princeton, NJ: Princeton University Press.

Swyngedouw, E. (2009) 'The antinomies of the postpolitical city: In search of a democratic politics of environmental production', *International Journal of Urban and Regional Research*, 33(3): 601–620.

Swyngedouw, E. (2010a) 'Apocalypse forever? Post-political populism and the spectre of climate change', *Theory, Culture and Society*, 27(2–3): 213–232.

Swyngedouw, E. (2010b) 'Post-democratic cities for whom and for what'. Paper presented in concluding session, Regional Studies Association Annual Conference, Pecs, Budapest, 26 May 2010. Available at: http://www.variant.org.uk/events/pubdiscus/Swyngedouw.pdf

Swyngedouw, E. (2011) 'Interrogating post-democratization: Reclaiming egalitarian political spaces', *Political Geography*, 30(7): 370–380.

Sykes, O., Nurse, A. and Sykes, O. (2021) 'The scale of the century? The new city regionalism in England and some experiences from Liverpool', *European Planning Studies* (online first), https://doi.org/10.1080/09654313.2021.1931044

Teo, S. S. (2021) 'Localism partnerships as informal associations: The work of the Rural Urban Synthesis Society and Lewisham Council within austerity', *Transactions of the Institute of British Geographers*, 46(1): 163–178.

Vainikka, J. (2015) 'Identities and regions: Exploring spatial narratives, legacies and practices with civic organizations in England and Finland', *Nordia Geographical Publications*, 44(3): 1–172.

Waite, D. and Bristow, G. (2019) 'Spaces of city-regionalism: Conceptualising pluralism in policymaking', *Environment and Planning C: Politics and Space*, 37(4): 689–706.

Waite, D. and Morgan, K. (2019) 'City deals in the polycentric state: The spaces and politics of Metrophilia in the UK', *European Urban and Regional Studies*, 26(4): 382–399.

Ward, N. (2006) 'Rural development and the economies of rural areas', in J. Midgley (ed.), *A New Rural Agenda*, London: IPPR, pp 46–67.

Welsh, M. and Heley, J. (2021) 'Rural regionalism in the 21st century: A tale of no cities', *Territory, Politics, Governance* (online first), https://doi.org/10.1080/21622671.2021.1916579

Civil society, pandemic and the crisis of welfare: exploring mixed economy models of welfare in domiciliary adult social care in a devolved UK

Paul Chaney and Christala Sophocleous

A burgeoning international literature charts the decline of traditional forms of state welfare provision, leading some to question whether the welfare state can survive (Gamble 2016). The UK is no exception to the wider trend. Over recent decades there have been significant cuts to welfare services (Edmiston 2017) and extensive outsourcing to the private sector. In part, this stems from the 1980s and 90s and the New Right attack on Keynesian welfare provision (McKevitt and Lawton 1994). Amid contemporary concerns over a crisis in state welfare provision (Rueda 2014), this chapter explores emerging evidence as to whether, in contrast to statist and market-based 'for profit' service delivery, civil society is the answer to meeting modern welfare needs.

We examine one of the most pressing welfare challenges of the twenty-first century: adult social care (ASC). Reflecting this volume's central theme of the uncertainties of the age, it examines the evidence on ASC delivery before and during the COVID-19 pandemic of 2020–21. It uses a comparative case study approach focusing on policy and practice in the four nations of the UK. This aligns with a burgeoning literature that has sought to analyse the decentralisation of the welfare state (Borghi and Van Berkel 2007; Chaney 2021). It is appropriate because devolution has created a natural experiment in welfare mixes. The analysis is based upon two WISERD ESRC-funded studies 2018–2021. The dataset comprises over one hundred interviews with civil society policy actors and other stakeholders, complemented by analysis of parliamentary proceeding, policy documents and the 'grey' literature of civil society organisations. The core research questions are: according to the views of key stakeholders, how do the different territorial welfare mixes on ASC in the four nations of the UK compare in their effectiveness? Did the four mixed economy models provide an effective response to ASC delivery in the pandemic? Does the evidence presented in the chapter exacerbate civil inequalities and social stratification? Last, can non-governmental organisations (NGOs) beneficially replace or complement the work of state ASC providers?

The term adult social care refers to non-medical support – including provision of social work, personal care, protection or social support services – to adults in need, typically arising from old age, disability and illness. Our focus is ASC in the community. This is non-institutional care and refers to the situation where care workers visit care-users' homes to help with personal care tasks such as washing and dressing. This also includes a range of support in community settings, including day care, advice and information services.

ASC is a suitable field to explore new approaches to welfare pluralism because an ageing population coupled with austerity presents considerable challenges in meeting rising demand (Meier and Werding 2010). Of late, this is often framed in terms of what the UK prime minister has dubbed a "crisis in social care"[1] (see also, Ogden 2017). A global demographic shift means we live in an era when, for the first time, the number of older people (60+ years) will exceed younger people. For example, the period 1998–2025 is expected to see a doubling of the world's older person population (ages 65 and above) (United Nations 2019). In the UK, in 1998, one-in-six people were aged 65+ years (15.9 per cent), this is projected to reach around one-in-four people (24.2 per cent) by 2038 (ONS 2020).

The remainder of this chapter is structured in two parts. Following a summary of the research context, the first part explores the contrasting legal and policy frameworks on third sector ASC delivery in the four nations. As noted, this is complemented by analysis of policies designed to aid welfare delivery in the context of the pandemic. In the second part of the chapter, the discussion outlines policy actors' views of the strengths and limitations of the different territorial approaches to ASC, as well as the response to the pandemic. The conclusion highlights the contrasts and commonalities between the four nations, their significance and wider implications for the mixed economy of welfare in the twenty-first century.

Research context

Following devolution in 1998/9 principal responsibility for ASC policy lies with the governments and legislatures in each of the four nations. Patterns of need and welfare state capacity vary between polities. With a population of 56,286,961, 13.4 per cent of whom are aged 70+ years, England has the highest absolute level of need. There are key variations in relative need based on the proportion of older people in each nation. Of Scotland's population of 5,463,300, 13.6 per cent are aged 70+ years, compared to 15.2 per cent of the Welsh population (3,152,879) and 11.9 per cent of Northern Ireland's population of 1,893,667 (ONS 2020). As noted in Chapter 1, 80 per cent of the UK's 134,000 voluntary organisations are based in England (NCVO

2020). There are 25,000 charities in Scotland (SCVO 2020a), 32,286 third sector organisation (TSO) in Wales (WCVA 2020) and 4,836 voluntary and community sector organisations in Northern Ireland (NICVA 2020). Across polities, social services (including ASC providers) remain the largest subsector in terms of both number of organisations and total income. Recent data indicate that there are 32,258 social services organisations, which make up 19 per cent of all organisations in the sector and generate an income of £12bn (NCVO 2020).

Currently, there is wide variation in *per capita* public expenditure on social care across the four nations. England is the least generous, spending on average £303 per head, compared to £428 in Scotland, £396 in Wales and £461 in Northern Ireland (Oung et al 2020: 4). England has the highest proportion of self-funders (that is, those not eligible for state support). Estimates suggest self-funders represent approximately 30 per cent in the domiciliary care sector in England, 25 per cent in Scotland, 21 per cent in Wales and 7 per cent in Northern Ireland (Oung et al 2020: 11).[2] The contrasting models of welfare pluralism in ASC delivery across the four nations are discussed further in the findings section below. The costs associated with the current and projected patterns of need for domiciliary ASC are striking and underline why ASC is, and will remain, at the forefront of politicised welfare issues. This is illustrated by Wales, the country with the highest proportion of older people. In 2015/16 the cost of ASC was £1.3 billion. Analysis predicts that ASC will require an extra £1.0 billion by 2030/31 (Watt and Roberts 2016).

Given the financial challenges of meeting the projected increase in demand for ASC, many governments internationally and in the UK have embraced welfare pluralism. This is a descriptive label which refers to the situation whereby service contributions by the voluntary and private sectors complement state welfare delivery (Beresford and Croft 1983). The involvement of the third sector has long-standing links with political attempts to recast public service provision (Beveridge 1948 [2015]), yet in recent decades emphasis on encouraging voluntarism and harnessing the contribution of the sector has heightened (Hanlon et al 2007). Prior to 2007/08, the devolved governments' policy discourse on mixed economy approaches to welfare was often driven by more expansive visions of welfare (compared to Westminster). Post-recession, they are increasingly shaped by the administrations' differing responses to austerity – as well as the COVID-19 pandemic, thereby giving added impetus to policy divergence. This economic dimension to welfare pluralism is certain to accelerate in future years owing to the greater size (proportionate to population compared to England) of the public sector(s) in the devolved nations (with inherent vulnerability to downsizing as part of ongoing austerity measures); and the devolution of significant taxation and borrowing powers to Scotland and

Wales. Policy divergence and the rise of territorial welfare mixes in the four UK nations is also driven by electoral politics (Chaney 2021). Specifically, government policy on ASC is shaped by the contrasting party mixes, voting traditions, dominant ideological standpoints and party pledges in each polity. Compared to Westminster, where neo-liberal oriented, Right-of-Centre Conservative administrations have held office for extended periods, since devolution in Wales and Scotland, government has always been by Left-of-Centre socialist and civic nationalist parties (while in Northern Ireland government has been by a consociationalist form of power sharing).

As noted, the present discussion also examines the UK's contrasting mixed economy approaches to ASC in the context of the COVID-19 emergency. As Humphries and Timmins (2021: 6) observe, 'The coronavirus pandemic has for once, though in unwelcome ways, thrown social care into the spotlight. To paraphrase the words of one social care leader, "the penny has dropped that social care matters"'. The UK was hit hard by the pandemic and internationally it is seventh-ranked in terms of the highest numbers of COVID-19 deaths (a total of 153,734 at the time of writing).[3] UK-wide, charities have been particularly affected and are estimated to have lost 24 per cent of their total income following the outbreak. In order to address the crisis, the Coronavirus Act (2020) gave wide-ranging powers to the four governments. Extant work on the earlier, though less extensive SARS-Cov-2 pandemic (Breznau 2021) tells us that when state welfare capacity is compromised through austerity and/or pandemic, the ability of third sector providers to complement state provision is pivotal in public risk perception as well as welfare outcomes.

Legal and policy frameworks: exploring the mixed economies of welfare in ASC in a devolved UK

Attention now turns to examine the four territorial mixed-economy approaches to ASC prior to and during the pandemic (see Table 4.1).

Wales

As Table 4.1 indicates, circa 2016 there was little difference in the extent of private sector involvement in welfare mix in ASC delivery between Wales and England. The private sector predominates in both countries (and accounts for 64.9 and 64.8 per cent of Full Time Equivalent (FTE) ASC domiciliary staff, respectively). This is unsurprising, as prior to devolution in 1999 both countries largely shared the same legal and policy framework (although, post-1999 there is a marked difference between the countries in the level of state provision of domiciliary ASC: 17.9 per cent in Wales, compared to only 3.3 per cent of FTE staff. The cause is neo-liberal policy

Table 4.1: Summary of the four mixed economy models of adult social care provision in Wales, Scotland, Northern Ireland and England (c. August 2021)

	Wales	Scotland	Northern Ireland	England
Type of ASC delivery model	Marketised/ mixed system Legal duty to promote third sector provision	Marketised/ mixed system	Marketised/ mixed system	Marketised/neo-liberal system
Welfare-mix indicator: (FTE domiciliary ASC staff, by sector)	FTE staff by sector domiciliary care (c.2016): public sector 3,000 (17.9%); private sector 10,900 (64.9%); voluntary sector 2,900 (17.3%)[1]	FTE staff by sector domiciliary care (c.2016): public sector 11,300 (22.9%); private sector 15,300 (31%); voluntary sector 22,800 (46.2%)[2]	FTE staff by sector domiciliary care (c.2016): public sector 3,400 (30.1%); private sector 5,300 (46.9%); voluntary sector 2,600 (23%)[3]	FTE staff by sector domiciliary care (c.2016): public sector 10,100 (3.3%); private sector 201,200 (64.8%); voluntary sector 99,100 (31.9%)[4]
Governing party/ orientation	Welsh Labour Party/ Left-of-Centre	Scottish National Party/ Left-of-Centre	Consociationalist cross-party power sharing	Conservative and Unionist Party/ Right-of-Centre
Legislative framework	Composite, overarching Act	Fragmented, series of statutes	Fragmented, series of statutes	Fragmented, series of statutes
Structural relationship with health service	A partnership approach	A partnership approach	Structurally integrated[5]	A partnership approach
Legal and policy framework subject to review c.2021?	Yes. Reform initiated in January 2021 Government published White Paper[6]	Yes. Reform initiated in September 2020	Yes. Reform initiated on 9 June 2020	Yes. Reform initiated – Health and Care Bill published February 2021[7]
Per capita public expenditure on social care (c.2019/20)[8]	£396	£428	£461	£303
Govt. social care expenditure p.a.	£1,102m[9]	£2,238m[10]	£878m[11]	2019–20, local authorities spent £16.5 billion commissioning care[12]
Legal incorporation of care users' (human) rights?	Yes. Under Human Rights Act 1998 – compels devolved bodies not to act in contravention of the ECHR[13]	Yes. Under Human Rights Act 1998 – compels devolved bodies not to act in contravention	Yes. Under Human Rights Act 1998 – compels devolved bodies not to act	Yes. Under Human Rights Act 1998 – compels public bodies not to act in contravention of the ECHR

Table 4.1: Summary of the four mixed economy models of adult social care provision in Wales, Scotland, Northern Ireland and England (c. August 2021) (continued)

	Wales	Scotland	Northern Ireland	England
	(incorporated into Government of Wales Act, 1998) In addition, UN Convention on the Rights of Older People incorporated into Section 7.1 of SSWB(W)A 2014[14]	of the ECHR (incorporated into Scotland Act 1998, Section 100). Carers (Scotland) Act 2016 S.36 also conveys rights in the Carers' Charter set by ministers[15]	in contravention of the ECHR (incorporated into Northern Ireland Act, 1998, see Sections 68–71)[16]	

Sources: ICF Consulting (2018a, b, c, d); Welsh Government 2021; Department of Health and Social Care 2021; Oung et al 2020; Scottish Government 2018; Public Health Agency 2020a; NAO 2021a.

[1] ICF Consulting (2018d), p 7, Table 2.4, https://socialcare.wales/cms_assets/file-uploads/The-Economic-Value-of-the-Adult-Social-Care-Sector_Wales.pdf

[2] ICF (2018c),p 8, Table 2.4, https://skillsforcareanddevelopment.org.uk/wp-content/uploads/2019/03/11-_-2018-The-Economic-Value-of-the-Adult-Social-Care-sector-Scotland.pdf

[3] ICF (2018b), p 8, Table 2.2, https://www.skillsforcare.org.uk/Documents/About/sfcd/The-econo mic-value-of-the-adult-social-care-sector-Northern-Ireland-4.pdf

[4] ICF (2018a), p 6, Table 2.4, https://www.google.co.uk/url?sa=t&rct=j&q=&esrc=s&source= web&cd=&cad=rja&uact=8&ved=2ahUKEwj1zpK-3_vvAhVbi1wKHSf1CioQFjAEegQIAxAD&url= https%3A%2F%2Fwww.sssc.uk.com%2F_entity%2Fannotation%2F653460f8-ef55-cc16-a743-d64742c23de4&usg=AOvVaw0hvCT9ePJR6tPsPWOT1bXl

[5] Critics argue there are continuing shortcomings in this regard.

[6] https://gov.wales/sites/default/files/consultations/2021-01/consutation-document.pdf

[7] https://www.gov.uk/government/publications/working-together-to-improve-health-and-soc ial-care-for-all

[8] Oung et al (2020).

[9] Public Health Agency (2020b), p 17, Table 4.1, https://socialcare.wales/cms_assets/file-uploads/The-Economic-Value-of-the-Adult-Social-Care-Sector_Wales.pdf

[10] Scottish Government (2018), p 5, Figure 3, https://www.gov.scot/binaries/content/documents/govscot/publications/advice-and-guidance/2018/10/scottish-government-medium-term-health-social-care-financial-framework/documents/00541276-pdf/

[11] Public Health Agency (2020a), p 17, Table 4.1, https://www.skillsforcare.org.uk/Documents/About/sfcd/The-economic-value-of-the-adult-social-care-sector-Northern-Ireland-4.pdf

[12] National Audit Office, https://www.nao.org.uk/press-release/the-adult-social-care-market-in-england/#:~:text=In%202019%2D20%2C%20local%20authorities,within%20which%20lo cal%20authorities%20operate.

[13] https://www.echr.coe.int/Documents/Convention_ENG.pdf

[14] https://www.legislation.gov.uk/anaw/2014/4/contents

[15] Unlike Wales which incorporates UN treaty into Welsh law, this does not incorporate UN human treaties into Scots law but sets out performance related duties, https://www.gov.scot/publicati ons/carers-charter/

[16] https://www.equalityhumanrights.com/en/advice-and-guidance/human-rights-health-and-soc ial-care

reforms in England that eschewed state ASC provision). It is in this context that the Social Services and Well-being (Wales) Act (SSWB(W)A), 2014 (effective from April 2016) is a singular piece of legislation introduced to change the prevailing welfare mix and transform care delivery. It is significant because Section 16 of the Act states that local government must promote: the development of social enterprises, co-ops and TSOs to provide care and support and preventative services; and involve service users in the design and running of services. The legislation effectively conveys new rights to care users and TSOs: both can expect local government support. Furthermore, the Act requires that service providers uphold the United Nations Convention of the Rights of Older People. Support for 'not-for-profits' is thought to be an imaginative idea in that such enterprises are able to use all their income to develop a quality service without having to divert profits to shareholders. In this way the ambition of the Act resonates with the collectivist ideology of the electorally dominant Welsh Labour Party that has governed Wales since the outset of devolution in 1999 (Chaney and Drakeford 2004). It is likely that an increasingly distinctive approach will emerge in future years. At the outset of 2021, the Welsh government published its White Paper ('Rebalancing care and support: A consultation on improving social care arrangements and strengthening partnership working to better support people's well-being').[4] Just five years on from the SSWB(W)A – which was supposed to be a transformational Act, the White Paper effectively signals its partial failure to reconfigure the social care landscape from a profit driven market to a not-for-profit one.[5] It articulates critical areas where focused action is needed to deliver improvement, including 'refocusing the fundamentals of the care market – away from price towards quality and value' and securing the 'reorientation of commissioning practices – towards managing the market and focusing on outcomes'.

In the light of the COVID-19 pandemic in 2020–21, one Welsh government minister said: 'The pandemic has made more apparent the sector's fragility' (Welsh Government 2021: 7).[6] Several policy reforms have been introduced to help TSOs and those delivering ASC in the community. These were part of the £24 million overarching Welsh Government Third Sector COVID-19 Response made up of separate funds including the Third Sector Resilience Fund, Voluntary Services Emergency Fund, Third Sector Infrastructure Enabling Fund and the Voluntary Sector Recovery Fund.[7]

Scotland

Of the four nations, it is in Scotland that the not-for-profit sector has the greatest role in delivering domiciliary ASC. It has a total income of over

£1.2bn and provides just over a third of all registered social care services and supports more than 200,000 people and their families (CCPS Scotland 2020: 1). The proportion of voluntary sector staff delivering domiciliary ASC (as opposed to residential care) is even higher, providing 46.2 per cent of the FTE staffing in ASC (Table 4.1). The current Scottish mixed economy model of ASC provision is set out in a complex raft of enactments, including the Community Care and Health (Scotland) Act 2002 that introduced free personal care for adults, regardless of income or whether they live at home or in residential care.[8] The Social Care (Self-Directed Support) (Scotland) Act 2013 is a further key element in the current mixed economy model of ASC.[9] It requires the 31 Integration Authorities, which have responsibility for commissioning health and social care services, to promote the personalisation of social care through the expansion of direct payment and individual budgets. As Cunningham et al (2019: 17) note, this has promoted the marketisation of care that has proved highly problematic for third sector ASC providers (these will be discussed in the second part of the chapter).

In the face of evident policy complexity, in September 2020 the Scottish Government announced a review of the present model of ASC provision.[10] Its vision for the successor system underlines a mixed-economy approach whereby, 'People organising and delivering social care work together [including] communities, community workers, mental health practitioners, GPs, nurses, hospitals, therapists, housing services, transport services, and others' (Scottish Government 2019: 5). The stated aim for systems, processes and decision making is one in which 'the relationship between public, independent and third sector health and social care organisations is trusting and collaborative' (Scottish Government 2019: 14). To date, the Scottish Government has failed to provide precise details on inter-sectoral collaboration and the commissioning of private and TSOs. However, a recent Independent Review report (Scottish Government 2021) provides a few indicators:

- Recommendation: 'A National Care Service for Scotland should be established in statute along with, on an equal footing, NHS Scotland, with both bodies reporting to Scottish Ministers' (p 105).
- 'Third sector organisations should be more involved in collaborative approaches to planning, commissioning and procuring social care support services' (p 11).
- 'A national approach [should be developed] – without nationalisation itself – [this] is needed to resolve these unacceptable features of current employment arrangements [low pay for care workers], without removing the unquestionable value added by the diversity and specialism of the third sector in particular, and without dismantling organisations that are already doing a good job' (p 43).

Following the COVID-19 outbreak, policy reforms were introduced to support the work of TSOs, including those delivering ASC. The principal measure announced by the Scottish Government was a £350 million fund to support the welfare and well-being of those most affected by the coronavirus pandemic.[11] The funding was open to councils, charities, businesses and community groups. The Communities Secretary said the stated aim was to "be focused on delivery, not bureaucracy or red tape. Local authorities, local businesses, community groups and the third sector know and understand the support needs of their communities the best". She continued, "Where people and organisations have solutions or ideas, I want to hear them".[12] Specific strands of the emergency government funding included: a £70 million Food Fund to address issues of food insecurity, especially for older people; a £50 million Wellbeing Fund to help charities and others who require additional capacity to work with at-risk people who may be worst affected by the crisis; a £40 million Supporting Communities Fund to support community efforts at a local level; and a £20 million Third Sector Resilience Fund, to immediately address organisations that were at high risk due to lockdown (Scottish Government 2020: 3).

England

The Care Act (2014)[13] says it will promote well-being and prevention as guiding principles for ASC. It also emphasises the need for local government to build on the resources of local communities, offer joined-up services, and create a market of providers for care and support. To further these aims the Act placed a range of duties on the 151 local authorities responsible for arranging care services. The latter are either provided by social service departments or, in most cases, commissioned from 14,800 registered providers in the independent (private and voluntary) sectors. In 2019–20, local authorities spent a net £16.5 billion on commissioning care.[14] At its outset, the English Act was predicted to result in a significant increase in the privatisation of social care provision because Section 79 enables local authorities to delegate nearly all their functions to the private sector, including assessments. Notably the Act (Section 5) refers to, 'Promoting diversity and quality in provision of services' with reference to 'markets' ('A local authority must promote the efficient and effective operation of a market in services for meeting care and support needs').

As Clements (2017: 11) notes: 'the problem [with the English statute] of course is not merely that [it may result in] driving down standards as cost reductions are required, but [also] of driving out smaller providers as only the larger corporations are able to compete on cost'. Revised statutory guidance covering England issued in 2017,[15] required that local authority commissioning procedures, 'must encourage a variety of different providers and different types of services' (para. 4.37), such as 'voluntary and community-based organisations, including user-led organisations, mutual and small businesses' (para. 4.38). However, data show that the English model of ASC remains dominated by the private sector. Expenditure on private providers is recorded as £14,212 million compared to £251 million paid to voluntary organisations.[16] Recent estimates suggest that approximately 75 per cent of staff (975,000 people) work for private sector independent employers contracted to deliver social care, compared to 25 per cent in voluntary organisations (ICF/Skills for Care 2018a: 30).

Curry et al (2019: 6) offer a bleak assessment of the current system, describing it as:

> unfair, complex, confusing, and failing to meet growing care needs in the population. A decade of austerity has seen government funding for local authorities halve in real terms ... which has led to councils tightening the eligibility criteria for care ... estimates of unmet need go as high as 1.5 million [people]. A restrictive means test, which has not been adjusted since 2010, means that people with property, savings and income in excess of £23,250 must meet the entirety of their care costs alone – and for many these can be catastrophic.

The result is that in the wake of the 2014 Care Act, 'the system has increasingly become a safety net for those with the very highest needs and the very lowest means' (Curry et al 2019: 6). In February 2021, the government acknowledged the current failings and published legislative proposals for a new Health and Care Bill, incorporating duties to review and assess local authority performance.[17]

The Westminster government's principal policy response to the pandemic, designed to support the third sector, was a £750 million package of financial support (DCMS and Office for Civil Society 2020). Of this, £360 million was initially allocated by central government departments to charities in England based on evidence of service need and £310 million to smaller, local voluntary organisations, including the £200 million Coronavirus Community Support Fund. Ultimately, the DCMS distributed £513 million to voluntary, community and social enterprise organisations (DCMS and Office for Civil Society 2020: 10).

Northern Ireland

As with other policy areas, over the past decade the development of social care policy has been held back by political *impasse* and the reintroduction of periods of direct rule from Westminster. Health and social care in

Northern Ireland are structurally integrated. This contrasts with the other systems in the UK and explains the distinctive welfare mix in the province. It has the highest percentage of FTE staff working in the domiciliary care sector employed by the public sector (30.1 per cent) (Table 4.1). The system is currently undergoing reform. Presently, the Northern Ireland Executive has eschewed means-testing and ASC is available to any eligible person who requires assistance. Alongside state provision, a significant proportion of ASC is delivered by voluntary sector organisations. This is estimated to save the local economy around £4.4 billion every year.[18] Thus, the five regional Health and Social Care Trusts commission health and social care services using a mix of statutory, voluntary or private providers. A recent survey found that the statutory sector provided 27 per cent of domiciliary care contact hours, with 73 per cent provided by the independent sector.[19]

In June 2020, in a statement to the Northern Ireland Assembly, Robin Swann MLA, Minister of Health, set out his approach to the rebuilding of health and social care services to respond to the initial wave of the COVID-19 pandemic. He announced that a new 'Strategic Framework for Rebuilding Health and Social Care Services'[20] would provide a basis on which to stabilise and restore service delivery over a two-year period. In the meantime, the Northern Ireland Executive has extended £16.2 million in emergency funding to charities to support unavoidable costs and eliminate deficits accumulated because of the pandemic (O'Neill and NICVA 2021).

Policy actors' views of the strengths and limitations of the different territorial approaches to welfare pluralism in ASC

Wales: pre-pandemic

A range of civil society actors highlighted the merits of the SSWB(W)A and praised its ethos and aspirations. Yet domiciliary care workers, managers and commissioners also highlighted a series of shortcomings in the Welsh mixed-economy model of ASC. They noted how the Act, far from promoting collectivism, had led to marketisation. They underlined widespread use of spot contracts and brokerage systems. Moreover, they referred to the instability that these create, not only for service users but also commissioners. Often service providers could 'hand back' contracts that they found were unduly onerous or uneconomic. Care packages were also found to remain on brokerage systems for lengthy periods, often because of labour shortages (Atkinson et al 2016: 2). A further failing was insufficient funding and competition for contracts to deliver ASC. This prevented third sector and private organisations from paying staff sufficiently. In turn, this caused staffing shortages and 'considerable employment insecurity and work intensification ... resulting in many working "full-time hours for part-time money"' (Atkinson et al 2016: 3). The malaise was compounded by payment for contact time only, and non-payment for travel time, resulting in what can only be described as 'commissioning-led income insecurity' which also had a 'negative impact on interactions with service users' (Atkinson et al 2016: 3). Some of these issues were subsequently addressed through the Welsh government's adoption of a trade union's Residential Care and Ethical Care Charter.[21]

Further policy failings included the complicated institutional structures associated with ASC delivery under the 2014 Act. This complexity undermined the transparency of the system and, in turn, levels of third sector trust in the new arrangements. The new structures centre on Regional Partnership Boards (RPBs)[22] designed to promote welfare pluralism and bring together health boards, local authorities and the third sector to 'ensure effective services, care and support are in place to best meet the needs of their respective populations'.[23] In practice, the level of the third sector's involvement in RPBs was found to be highly variable. In some areas there was thorough-going engagement, yet in others non-engagement meant that TSOs were effectively excluded from shaping local ASC delivery. In such instances, RPBs effectively became a 'rubber stamping' exercise. One reason for TSOs' non-engagement was that they lacked the resources and capacity to engage with the new implementation structures and deliver ASC services, as envisaged by the Act.

Under the new arrangements the commissioning of services was also found to be problematic. Many local authorities were unprepared, had limited capacity and contrasting understandings of their new role in promoting TSOs' delivery of ASC. In some instances, stakeholders spoke of how the relationship between local authorities and TSOs was managed primarily through the procurement of services. As one interview noted:

'I mean to be honest ... commissioning and contracting with the third sector in some ways is no different to commissioning and contracting with the private and independent sector, in as much as we have a statutory responsibility to provide a service for a great number of people who are vulnerable in the borough, but we can't do it all ourselves.' (Local Authority Officer)

In contrast, in other instances, commissioning was understood to be part of the development of a holistic preventative strategy to reduce demand for ASC in which TSOs played a key role in both identifying needs and delivering service innovations. Here strategic commissioning was viewed as part of a collaborative process in which TSOs were a significant partner.

This approach created opportunities for more thoroughgoing dialogue about the strengths, limitations and possibilities of TSOs' role in the delivery of welfare services. As demonstrated by this local authority commissioner:

> 'So, we took what was working well and we said, "okay look how can we start to develop this jigsaw?" We were getting more pieces of it, that were starting to come together, pulling in public health and we made a bid for LEADER [EU] funding. So, we started to get more organisations involved in growing our preventative model ... We shifted resources from the local authority into third sector to fund some of the project.' (Local Authority Officer)

These differences highlight how the roles of TSOs are directly impacted by wide geographical variations in local commissioning practices across the 22 local authorities in Wales. This had a significant impact on the way local authorities exercised their 'duty to promote' and the capacity of TSOs to successfully respond to local needs within a given area. Often, stakeholder accounts revealed how the anticipated collaborative approach set out in the Act was undermined. Instead, the new practices were found to be creating a quasi-market, not just between the for-profit and not-for-profit sectors, but between TSOs. This created relations shaped by competition and cost–cutting that sought economies of scale that risked undermining the role of community and smaller TSOs. Thus, as noted, it promoted the marketisation of ASC instead of delivering the collectivist, mixed economy vision of the legislation. Our research participants also highlighted a raft of issues around the monitoring and enforcement of the new statutory framework on civil society organisations' welfare delivery. They identified a lack of clarity about how local authorities will be required to report on and be held to account for, their (Section 16) actions to promote the third sector. Strikingly, in the Regulation and Inspection of Social Care (Wales) Act 2016 no reference is made to the statutory duty to 'promote' the sector (and how this will be measured/assessed). There appears to be a paradox here: the Welsh government has created a prescriptive legislative instrument (the Section 16 Duty to promote TSOs' role in ASC delivery) but has yet to identify how it will ensure and monitor its effectiveness.

Wales: pandemic response

Policy actors' views on the Welsh approach to welfare pluralism in ASC in the context of the pandemic revealed several core strengths, challenges and weaknesses. The partnership structures between government and the third sector set out in the devolution statutes were seen as a key strength.

As one interviewee explained, "It is notable that through the pandemic [the Welsh government] has continued to work through these existing structures, strengthening but not replacing them" (Welsh Parliament/ *Senedd Cymru* 2021a: 11). Partnership working has been established over many years and this was praised:

'What we've heard, going onto COVID in a sense, is how at a Wales level, we do know each other across different organisational boundaries. ... I've heard organisations say it's been amazing, when the crisis happened that you could pick up a phone to your Welsh government official and there's been an almost "sod organisational boundaries" [attitude], there's something that needs to be done and people have worked quite closely together.' (Interviewee – National infrastructure organisation)

Others underlined how the voluntary sector played an invaluable role in sharing essential messages with communities and the people they support, particularly at the outset of the pandemic. Among the challenges and shortcomings identified was the need for stronger links between funders and the 'resilience community' (that is, ASC care providers and allied services). Others spoke of how 'the issue of co-ordination of volunteers appeared to be particularly acute' (Welsh Parliament/ *Senedd Cymru* 2021b: para. 89). For its part, in terms of timing, the representative body of the third sector in Wales highlighted how the coincidence of a number of reform agendas and the pandemic had compounded the challenges: 'leaving the EU ... transforming service models, including in health and social care and adapting to digitally driven change ... all had a significant impact as well' (Welsh Parliament/ *Senedd Cymru* 2021b: para. 160). Others identified issues of 'race' equality and 'that a key priority for the sector in the recovery, will be to tackle the high levels of isolation and loneliness within [ethnic] communities ... loneliness has been exacerbated' (Welsh Parliament/ *Senedd Cymru* 2021b: para. 170).

Rich testimony also detailed the limits of the third sector's resilience and the need for government support. One care network manager said, "I think there is an enormous amount of trauma in the sector". She continued:

'Obviously, we're a sector that needs to keep running, keep caring for our most vulnerable citizens. The sector, as you know, was already in a vulnerable situation, with difficulties in recruiting and retaining staff, widely recognised as underfunded, and we've gone into this crisis in that situation. ... We are obviously seeing the [additional staff costs for] cover for people self-isolating, people shielding ... very little, if any, of that money [Welsh government emergency aid] so far has made it to the front line ... people have resorted to crowdfunding just to keep going and to reward staff for keeping going.'[24]

Scotland: pre-pandemic

A manager of a third sector carers' network explained how it 'strive[d] to maintain its basic proposition of a supportive relationship [with public sector providers] within the confines of the prevailing institutional and public policy] architecture'. She concluded that, 'Some of it is helpful, some of it less so (rigid service categories, time and task specifications, transfer of financial risk through contractual conditions)' (CCPS 2020: 2). In particular, the civil society discourse was critical of the bureaucratisation, commodification and marketisation of ASC under Scotland's current mixed economy model. One stakeholder noted that:

> We have, arguably, reached a point where the commodification has in effect become the service, now described as 'adult social care' ... we have opted to put those services in place through a market mechanism which describes people's care and support arrangements as 'packages'; we divide groups of people with support needs into 'client groups' and bundle them into 'lots', to be tendered on the market. (CCPS 2020: 3)

As Cunningham et al (2019: 17) note, the Self-Directed Support (Scotland) Act (2013) promoted the marketisation of care that has proved highly problematic for third sector ASC providers. It has threatened the sustainability of third sector ASC providers because it has led to the proliferation of smaller packages of individual services being commissioned, rather than larger block contracts that contain large volumes of work. This matters, principally because the personalisation and greater user choice introduced by the legislation may exacerbate recruitment and retention problems for third sector providers of social care. They find it 'highly problematic to staff services where working time is characterised by intangibility. ... Constant recruitment and retention problems can erode narrow surpluses negotiated in contracts by providers requiring them to draw from their financial reserves and threaten their sustainability' (Cunningham et al 2019: 17).

Third sector managers also alluded to an implementation gap and a lack of joined-up policymaking. A key issue was that the development and introduction of self-directed support (SDS) was intended to change service delivery towards a discussion about 'outcomes', and the things that people would like to be supported to achieve. However, as one interviewee observed, "self-directed support has not had the transformational impact we hoped for: that is partly the result of poor implementation, but we believe it is also because the system architecture has remained largely unchanged, rendering SDS the proverbial square peg in a round hole" (CCPS 2020: 7).

Scotland: pandemic response.

Speaking at the 'Valuing the Third Sector' debate at the Scottish Parliament in December 2020, Ruth Maguire MSP said:

> 'We must embrace the adversity of the pandemic and seize it as an opportunity to do things differently. We must learn from innovative practice shown by some funders and the third sector during the pandemic. The COVID crisis has shone a light on the issues impacting the sector and on inequality in our society.'[25]

Third sector stakeholders concurred. One Chief Executive said, "Reform of social care in Scotland is long overdue. The COVID-19 pandemic has exposed fault lines which require radical overhaul and long-term change. It has also revealed what can be achieved when obstacles are removed in a crisis."[26]

Others alluded to the challenging experience of the pandemic:

> Social care providers ... have found themselves on the frontline as never before. Almost all have had to struggle with stress and uncertainty, inadequate staffing, inadequate funding, no or inadequate personal protective equipment (PPE), and increasing demand. They have by and large overcome these challenges. Social care bodies now want to ensure that the current recognition of carers as highly skilled and essential workers is reflected in how they are paid and valued post-emergency, and that the flexibility and openness that has been shown by public sector funders and procurement staff is not lost – can we use hard lessons learnt during COVID-19 to value social care more, and find new ways of supporting and valuing our most vulnerable citizens? (SCVO 2020a: 5)

The Scottish Government's Independent Review of ASC also highlighted the key staffing issues that were exposed by the pandemic: 'There is currently no national oversight of workforce planning for social care in Scotland. ... Experience during COVID-19 has shown us how difficult it is to deploy appropriate staff quickly when there is an urgent priority to meet' (Scottish Government 2021: 83). Almost half (42 per cent) of voluntary organisations surveyed during the pandemic said they needed government financial aid to get through the crisis. Moreover, our findings reveal how the pandemic challenged conventional wisdom on voluntary sector financial sustainability. One national infrastructure organisation commented:

> Pre-COVID the chat around us, the best model to be sustainable was to have like a sort of portfolio of different sources of income, so don't be too heavily dependent on government income and make sure that you've got a bit from trading and a bit from funders, and the organisations that had that patchwork are the organisations that found it the most difficult as soon as COVID hit. (Scottish Government 2021: 86).

Notwithstanding the Scottish Government's £350 million emergency grant fund, TSOs reported several issues, including communication failings. One in 10 said that they had not heard of the Third Sector Resilience Fund (TSISN 2020: 22). Moreover, the SCVO, the representative body of the sector in Scotland, highlighted that even with government aid many TSOs were struggling to survive: 'Voluntary sector finances have always been precarious, and we now face even deeper and more complex financial issues, and there is no silver bullet that will deliver sustainability. ... Many voluntary organisations face real and grave threats to their future.' The SCVO reported that a quarter of charities had furloughed staff (up to 30 per cent of all third sector staff, or 32,000 people) (SCVO 2020a: para. 34).

Stakeholders also alluded to shortcomings in the government's emergency scheme and its impact on third sector ASC delivery:

> Voluntary organisations relying on their reserves have not been eligible for immediate crisis funding in Scotland and are finding their resilience diminished at a time when their reserves and existing funding sources dry up. ... These are long-term issues for the voluntary sector, we need consistent, core investment for the long term and strong, positive relationships with the public Sector. (SCVO 2020a: para. 44)

Others concluded that: 'The lessons for improvement are really about joining-up the [different third sector support] funds to enable them to speak to and reach into pockets of the sector and joining-up the delivery of new and on-going support' (Scottish Parliament, Local Government and Communities Committee 2020).

A further key finding was the inability of the prevailing Scottish mixed economy model of ASC delivery to respond with sufficient speed to the developing health crisis of the pandemic. For example, one inquiry (2021) heard that 'from mid-March [2020 – the first outbreak of the pandemic] care at home packages were removed or severely reduced almost overnight from older people across Scotland'. Another charity said it recognised social care providers faced challenging decisions, however, it believed 'providers did not sufficiently consider whether families could provide the care that was being withdrawn' (Scottish Parliament Equalities and Human Rights Committee 2021: 27). The statistics on the impact of the pandemic make grim reading. Analysis reveals that excess deaths of people with dementia during the peak months of lockdown were 24.5 per cent higher than the previous five-year average (Age Scotland 2021: 22). A disabled people's organisation reported that over 800 disabled people responded to its survey in April 2020 to share what they were living through: 'From losing vital social care support and being left unable to get out of bed, to fears about involuntary "do not resuscitate" notices and job losses, people told us they were "being pushed to the brink". People told us they felt suicidal' (Inclusion Scotland 2020: 2).

A manager with a carers' organisation, interviewed in our study, reflected on the early days of the crisis:

'It started off with fear. The calls we were getting were about fear, "What am I going to do about this? Should I be going to work? What am I going to do without money if I don't go to work? How are we going to get food?" All of these things, it started with that fear part of it. But then it became, "What am I going to do without any support?" Because local authorities and partnerships stepped back. Carers felt abandoned. And that is what our calls were full of, it was, "I feel abandoned, I don't know what to do. I'm already at breaking point". And as we worked through some of those things, our immediate reaction was about how do we find information for people about what they need around access to food, and these sorts of things. And that stuff popped up really quickly. We could help enable that, you know, put in money, put in support for that to be able to happen'. (Care Organisation Manager)

England: pre-pandemic

Recent analyses offer a withering critique of systemic ASC failings in England. One account said, 'social care is on the cusp of [crisis]' (Brindle 2015). In part, the cause is incrementalism and policies shaped around electoral cycles and governing parties' calculation of political gain: 'Short-term funding and the lack of a long-term vision has hampered planning, innovation and investment in ASC. The current accountability and oversight arrangements are ineffective for overseeing the care market' (National Audit Office 2021a: 6). A major failing relates to institutional oversight and inadequate legal powers. The Department of Health and Social Care does not know how effectively local authorities commission care and neither does it have full information on their performance and the outcomes achieved. Strikingly, it has no legal powers to intervene or hold individual authorities to account. The scale of the pathologies is notable. Critics explain that:

> The Department has not met previous commitments to tackle recruitment and retention challenges for the 1.5 million people who work in care. [Moreover,] it has not produced a workforce strategy since 2009, despite committing to do so in 2018. … For 2019–20, the Department assessed that most local authorities pay care providers below a sustainable rate for care. Around 24 per cent of adults aged 65 and over have unmet care needs. (NAO 2021: 3)

Spending by councils on social care services commissioned from external providers has risen by £1.4 billion since 2015. Recent research notes that: 'This spending has had only limited impact: local authorities continue to report [private sector] companies handing back contracts [by local authorities to deliver ASC] or going out of business, and service users report difficulties in finding the care they need' (King's Fund 2020: 1). A key issue is the complex and fragmented nature of the current system: carers and voluntary workers have had to fill in gaps in care, which is not sustainable as it has a physical and emotional effect on them. The inability to access appropriate care meant that 'some people had lost trust in these [private-contracted and statutory] services and felt forced to turn elsewhere for support, such as voluntary sector organisations' (King's Fund 2020: 88).

England: pandemic response

Among 1,008 TSOs surveyed by government, almost half said they had accessed government support packages (including the Coronavirus Job Retention scheme allowing organisations to furlough employees).[27] When asked about the effectiveness of the emergency aid, almost half of respondents (43 per cent) gave negative replies (DCMS and Office for Civil Society 2021). One civil society organisation working for older people said its staff headcount had dropped from 118 to 52 in two years. It added:

> The COVID-19 crisis has come from the left field [and] may tip over the charity. We are fighting hard to avoid this outcome [… we have suffered a] loss of 70 per cent of our volunteers who are now self-isolating; and a loss of 90 per cent of our income over night.[28]

Another said, 'The crisis is biting us hard. Even with us doing everything we can (such as furloughing staff, applying for business support, paid staff voluntarily cutting their wages, etc.) we will not be able to continue beyond the next few months if nothing substantial changes'.[29]

Equalities and human rights organisations raised several concerns about the Westminster government's COVID response. For example, referring to the emergency legislation (the Coronavirus Act 2020),[30] one said, 'Our members have particular concerns about how the Act will operate in practice, potentially resulting in significant reductions in social care, support and legal protection for older people and disabled adults'.[31] The NCVO was critical of the government's pandemic response, highlighting that many charities' financial models precluded them from taking on additional debt in emergency situations such as the pandemic. It noted that:

'put simply, the government's intervention will not be enough to prevent good charities around the country from closing their doors. Many of the charities which do survive will look very different in a few months' time, with severely reduced capacity to provide support that people rely on at a time when their contribution to recovery will be vital'.[32]

Others alluded to the unprecedented pressure the pandemic has placed on the third sector:

'I think [its] not just organisational, but I think we're very concerned ... in terms of the exhaustion, and the burnout ... the evidence is showing of people who have just worked relentlessly, as others have, through this, but I think there is a greater toll that is being taken that will take us a long time to deal with.' (National infrastructure organisation)

During the pandemic, stakeholders reported how charities and voluntary sector organisations were subject to significantly higher levels of public trust compared to other organisations. Notably, central government's role in ASC was trusted by only 7 per cent of respondents (Charities Aid Foundation 2020: 7).[33]

Northern Ireland: pre-pandemic

Prior to the pandemic, the Expert Advisory Panel Report on Adult Care and Support concluded: that 'fundamental reform of adult care and support is required to avoid a total collapse of the system with all the implications this would have for those in need. This requires both leadership and ownership across the whole system of care and support' (Kelly and Kennedy 2018: 6). A key point made by the panel is: 'that the current mechanisms have not been successful in creating or enabling a mixed economy of service provision'. In response it hints that reforms favouring the third sector may be introduced (as per the Welsh model): 'A move to a more community-based approach to adult care and support also has a part to play. … This may mean building into procurement procedures the means to stimulate parts of the market, such as the community and voluntary sector, that have not yet been adequately developed' (Kelly and Kennedy 2018: 48).

These points were also made to the Northern Ireland Affairs Select Committee Inquiry which concluded:

> The independent social care sector is struggling with competition from the low wage sector, particularly hospitality and retail, and a competitive relationship with the statutory sector. High quality social care requires a skilled and valued workforce, but social care workers are often on low wages and have little scope for career development and progression.[34]

Stakeholder interviews support this view. A manager with an older peoples' organisation said, 'the system isn't fit for purpose and also the workforce system isn't fit either because those who we most value to deliver, are the ones that have no career path, no career progression and are not valued in terms of a recognised pay scale either'.

Thus, in Northern Ireland (as in the other UK nations), a key failing of the current system is the sectoral inequality in wages. In the public sector, wages and employment conditions for care work are fairer. In contrast, in the private and voluntary sectors pay is often at minimum wage rates and service conditions have declined. Because most of paid care work is now provided by these sectors, there are significant inequalities. Kelly and Kennedy (2018: 54) explain why this situation has arisen:

> There is some odd thinking. Under the guise of saying, 'we can reduce the cost of care by outsourcing to the independent sector because they are more efficient', we've actually created a commissioning model that forces providers to compete almost exclusively on price. Such that we get a 'race to the bottom'. By far the largest cost for any care provider is the cost of staff. The only way a provider can effectively keep the price of their services low is through pressing down on wages and staff costs. And in our view, there is collusion with this impoverishment in the way that care and support services are commissioned.

As one TSO observed, it is 'vital that the role of community and voluntary organisations is recognised and that services should be provided by a skilled, competent and valued workforce, with decent salaries, stable working conditions and manageable workloads, along with opportunities for continuous learning and improvement' (Age Northern Ireland 2018: 5). The regulator, the Northern Ireland Social Care Council (2017: 11), notes how the prevailing problems are compounded by the lack of comprehensive data on social care. This impedes workforce planning at a system-wide level. Other shortcomings identified by stakeholders included excessive bureaucracy and short-term contracts issued to voluntary sector care providers. As one noted, 'budgets are having a particularly negative impact on social care, with year-on-year uncertainty impeding the ability of providers to plan for the future and develop service innovations'.

Northern Ireland: pandemic response

In June 2020, the Minister for Health and Social care set out her plan to the Northern Ireland Assembly for rebuilding health and social care services to respond to the COVID-19 pandemic. The consultation responses to the plan from external stakeholders highlighted that detailed consideration should be given to the role that the independent sector can play in rebuilding efforts. They also said that the government's plan gave insufficient attention to partnership working and co-production between sectors. Furthermore, they noted that in the past there had been a lack of genuinely independent expertise to help shape welfare delivery and there was a need for reforms to address economic inequality and promote human rights in ASC (Northern Ireland Executive Department for Health 2020: 9–12).

Three further themes emerged from the study data about ASC providers in Northern Ireland during the pandemic. First, community organisations repeatedly emphasised their battle for survival and that they were fighting to keep themselves afloat in the face of a range of challenges including: a loss of funding owing to reduced donations (because of lockdown and furloughed workers having less disposable income, as well as the scaling back of public awareness campaigns designed to raise money), and staff redundancies because of declining revenue. As one interviewee said:

> 'You've got a mixture of people trying to respond on the ground, and also people trying to survive, you know, organisations trying to survive, and that's just been top of the list for most of the time. The key message here is that for adult social care providers the pandemic has affected every aspect of organisational life – funding, staffing, volunteers, delivery capacity, and ability to operate.'

Second, voluntary sector adult care providers are the front line of service providers for the vulnerable. As one interviewee noted of the COVID-19 crisis,

> 'The community sector came to the fore in ways that other sectors couldn't and wouldn't and I think the status of the community sector

has been enhanced considerably in that it's not just about what you did for us or what they did for the wider community, it's the fact that they exist and that they naturally stood up to the plate when lockdown came in and services were required. I mean, half, if not three-quarters of the public sector was at home.'

This is reflected in data showing that public trust and confidence in charities is higher in the province: 71 per cent of Northern Ireland respondents reported trusting charities; 12 per cent higher than in Great Britain, and 14 per cent higher than the Republic of Ireland (Charity Commission for Northern Ireland 2020). The CCNI said, 'it's important to remember just how vital the public are to charities – and the role that trust and confidence plays in running a successful charity, even during a pandemic. A charity that does not have the public's trust and confidence may find it struggles to ... fulfil its charitable objectives' (NICVA 2020: 14).[35]

The third theme is the beneficial effects of government suspension of bureaucracy/red-tape during the crisis. For example, a study participant noted: "there was definitely an instant flexibility and rolling forward of funding arrangements for the next 12 months – you know, without too much scrutiny". Another observed that,

'To varying degrees, government at all tiers, has demonstrated itself to be flexible and capable of responding to an emergency situation. What is unclear, at this stage, is whether this has been done because of a recognition of the value and contribution of third sector and community groups or because government did not have a choice in the face of emergency-levels of demand for social care services'.

At a government–third sector conference, Carál Ní Chuilín MLA, Minister for Communities reflected on the positive response to the pandemic from the voluntary and community sector:

'It is important to continue this new way of working after COVID-19. Against the backdrop of a society that is facing increasing pressures compounded by the uncertainties presented of Brexit, a restrictive overall budget, decades of inequality and poverty, and poor mental health, it is important to continue the collaborative way of working demonstrated over the last few months.'

She proceeded to describe 'three key pillars' under which she believes the current work can continue: partnership and collaboration; co-design and co-production; delivery of real improvements and real outcomes.[36]

Discussion

Against the backdrop of this volume's central theme of the uncertainties of the age and their impact on civil society, this chapter has examined ASC delivery in the four nations of the UK before and during the COVID-19 pandemic. This is appropriate because along with healthcare, domiciliary care was in the frontline of the welfare response to the global COVID-19 emergency. Four core research questions were addressed. The first asked, according to the situated knowledge of stakeholders, how do the different territorial welfare mixes on ASC in the four nations of the UK compare in their effectiveness? Our analysis found key contrasts and commonalities across territories. All nations have marketised, mixed economy ASC systems based on a combination of state provision and external commissioning of domiciliary care. Territorial politics have resulted in marked variations in the welfare mixes. Successive Westminster governments' neo-liberal economic policies have resulted in the dominance of private sector ASC providers in England and a residual state sector (almost two-thirds and just 3 per cent of the ASC workforce, respectively). In Wales, the political aspiration of reforms introduced since 2016 have been to boost the third sector. This reflects the governing Welsh Labour Party's eschewing of privatisation of welfare. It is captured in the Welsh government statement (2014: 7):

> Demand and expectations are increasing, and public funding is under continuing pressure. ... We recognise that quality of life cannot be delivered by the state alone. ... We believe that the Third Sector can help to transform the way that public services meet present and future demands, by treating people and communities as assets and equals in the design and delivery of services.

Yet the legacy of pre-devolution 'England and Wales' policies, combined with shortcomings in the implementation of new laws, means the private sector also dominates in ASC provision in Wales, although, unlike England, the state sector remains a significant provider. In contrast, in Scotland, almost half of ASC staff are in the voluntary sector. Northern Ireland presents something of a paradox. It is the only nation where health and social care is structurally integrated, yet it is not the public but voluntary sector that predominates.

This study has also shown that, currently, in all four nations, 'mixed economy' models effectively mean market-based models. These tend to follow the crude market logic of competition on price. This means that relations between TSOs are shaped by competition and tendering, with smaller, community-focused TSOs often being directed by commissioners to work in formal collaborations with larger TSO partners in preference to local community groups. The overall result is a capitalist race to the bottom, with contracts awarded to the cheapest tender. This results in low pay and lower quality care and short-term contracts undermining the resilience of TSOs, especially in the face of emergencies such as the pandemic. This leads to what one stakeholder called "commissioning-led income insecurity" which has negative impacts on interactions with service users. Special mechanisms are required to counter these tendencies, such as those seen in the Welsh model where an interventionist government has placed a legal duty on local government to promote TSOs in ASC delivery through commissioning and other means. However, the Welsh experience provides a cautionary tale. It reveals a series of shortcomings and underlines that interventionist measures need to be designed and implemented with care and precision to deliver an effective mixed economy approach to ASC.

According to stakeholders, did the four mixed economy models provide an effective response to ASC delivery in the pandemic? The simple answer here is 'no'. Neither of the models had the resilience and responsiveness to deal with the pandemic in an effective way. Policy actors did acknowledge positive aspects, such as the over-riding of bureaucratic rules and regulations to expedite their response to care in the context of COVID-19. Also, in different ways and with contrasting levels of generosity, the four governments extended economic aid to TSOs and did so swiftly. However, there were manifold shortcomings and emerging lessons identified in stakeholders' accounts. One was that the aid template (including the law on charities) meant TSOs almost had to fail financially to be eligible for aid. Those struggling along on their reserves were ineligible. It was only when TSOs ran out of funds that they could access emergency payments. This was a major flaw evident in each polity. A key outcome of the pandemic was the way it confirmed the need for systemic reform in ASC delivery in each nation.

Earlier work on the SARS pandemic revealed how it led to social deficit (Basco et al 2021). The evidence presented in this chapter shows that the COVID-19 emergency has also exacerbated civil inequalities and social stratification. It adds to a burgeoning literature highlighting the unequal social effects of the crisis (Aquanno and Bryant 2020). In part, these stem from the four pre-COVID welfare models and the party politics underpinning them. In short, neo-liberal policies in England are less supportive of those on lower incomes than the socialist and civic nationalist models that apply in Wales and Scotland. This is illustrated by the markedly different entitlement rules applying to ASC eligibility in the four nations. Many people in England with property, savings, and an annual income more than £23,250 must meet the entirety of their care costs alone. For many these can be catastrophic, exacerbating inequalities and civic stratification. In Wales, the governing Welsh Labour Party noted, 'We've already met our manifesto pledge to raise the capital threshold for residential care to £50,000 three years early' (Welsh Labour Policy Forum 2021: 8). Nominally, ASC is 'free' in Scotland and Northern Ireland (although some eligibility criteria do apply). As the foregoing analysis reveals, the pandemic has also increased 'racial' inequalities, with ethnic minorities suffering disproportionately. As stakeholders underlined, this will continue into the post-pandemic recovery phase: 'a key priority for the sector in the recovery, will be to tackle the high levels of isolation and loneliness within communities ... this is a particular issue for Windrush elders, [in consequence there is a need for] ring-fenced funding for tackling loneliness and isolation' (Welsh Parliament/ *Senedd Cymru* 2021a: para. 170).

The fourth question addressed in this chapter asked can NGOs beneficially replace or complement the work of state ASC providers? Here, based on the views of an extensive range of stakeholders, the answer is a resounding 'yes'. However, the policy pathologies in the current mixed economy models are manifold. Short-term funding and lack of a long-term vision have hampered planning, innovation and investment in ASC. Incrementalism in policy development is a core failing shared across polities. Over past decades (pre- and post-devolution), short-term political fixes based on electoral cycles and political calculation of electoral gain and the pursuit of government office have led to flawed policies, badly implemented and inadequately monitored. Reforms necessary to address this require both leadership and political ownership across the whole system of care and support. Without the adoption of new approaches to mixed-economy ASC delivery, the longer-term impact of the pandemic is likely to see an extension of short-term contract funding of third sector and not-for-profit organisations by government. This transfers risk and responsibility to the third sector without securing their longer-term survival (see Dubbeld and de Almeida 2020). As Mok et al (2021) conclude of the pandemic recovery, 'much will depend upon the state–market–family and community configurations in social welfare provision and the power relationship between the state and the third sector'. A key factor that will determine whether the ongoing ASC reforms in each nation are successful is whether politicians and policy-makers to listen to the situated knowledge of civil society providers, as well as the views of service users. In this respect, past evidence does not augur well.

Notes

[1]   UK Prime Minister Boris Johnson, BBC Interview, 14 January 2020, https://www.inde pendent.co.uk/news/uk/politics/boris-johnson-social-care-plan-bbc-breakfast-elect ion-latest-a9282611.html
[2]   https://www.nuffieldtrust.org.uk/news-item/how-much-social-care-does-each-coun try-fund#key-points
[3]   https://coronavirus.data.gov.uk/details/deaths
[4]   https://gov.wales/sites/default/files/consultations/2021-01/consutation-document.pdf
[5]   https://gov.wales/sites/default/files/consultations/2021-01/consutation-document.pdf

6 https://gov.wales/sites/default/files/consultations/2021-01/consutation-document.pdf

7 https://wcva.cymru/funding/voluntary-services-recovery-fund/

8 https://www.legislation.gov.uk/asp/2002/5/contents

9 https://www.legislation.gov.uk/asp/2013/1/contents/enacted

10 https://www.gov.scot/groups/independent-review-of-adult-social-care/

11 https://www.gov.scot/news/helping-communities-affected-by-COVID-19/

12 https://www.gov.scot/news/helping-communities-affected-by-COVID-19/

13 http://www.legislation.gov.uk/ukpga/2014/23/pdfs/ukpga_20140023_en.pdf

14 https://www.nao.org.uk/press-release/the-adult-social-care-market-in-england/#:~:text=In%202019%2D20%2C%20local%20authorities,within%20which%20local%20authorities%20operate.

15 https://www.gov.uk/government/publications/care-act-statutory-guidance/care-and-support-statutory-guidance

16 Health and Social Care Information Centre (2015), p 15, Table 2.1: Summary of adult social care expenditure and income; by primary support reason and service

17 https://www.gov.uk/government/publications/working-together-to-improve-health-and-social-care-for-all

18 http://www.hscboard.hscni.net/our-work/commissioning/#:~:text=The%20Health%20and%20Social%20Care,the%20population%20of%20Northern%20Ireland.&text=The%20HSCB%20also%20commissions%20services%20from%20voluntary%20and%20community%20organisations.

19 Circa September 2020, https://www.health-ni.gov.uk/sites/default/files/publications/health/dcs-adults-ni-20_0.pdf p7.

20 https://www.health-ni.gov.uk/publications/rebuilding-health-and-social-care-services-phase-5-plans

21 https://www.unison.org.uk/content/uploads/2017/03/24230.pdf and https://www.unison.org.uk/news/2018/04/welsh-government-cracks-zero-hour-contracts-homecare/ and; https://www.bbc.co.uk/news/uk-wales-40201678

22 https://gov.wales/regional-partnership-boards-rpbs

23 https://gov.wales/sites/default/files/publications/2020-02/part-9-statutory-guidance-partnership-arrangements.pdf (gov.wales)

24 May Wimbury, *Fforwm Gofal Cymru*/Care Forum Wales, https://record.assembly.wales/Committee/6198#A57763

25 https://www.theyworkforyou.com/sp/?id=2020-12-01.6.0

26 http://www.ccpscotland.org/news/coalition-of-care-andsupport-providers-welcomes-independent-review-of-adult-social-care-in-scotland/

27 https://www.gov.uk/guidance/claim-for-wages-through-the-coronavirus-job-retention-scheme

28 Written evidence submitted by Age UK West Cumbria Ltd to the Digital, Culture, Media and Sport Parliamentary Select Committee – April 2020, https://committees.parliament.uk/work/243/impact-of-COVID19-on-the-charity-sector/publications/written-evidence/?page=2

29 Written evidence submitted by Age UK East Sussex to the Digital, Culture, Media and Sport Parliamentary Select Committee – April 2020, https://committees.parliament.uk/work/243/impact-of-COVID19-on-the-charity-sector/publications/written-evidence/?page=2

30 https://www.legislation.gov.uk/ukpga/2020/7/contents/enacted

31 Written evidence submitted by Equally Ours to the Digital, Culture, Media and Sport Parliamentary Select Committee – April 2020, https://committees.parliament.uk/work/243/impact-of-COVID19-on-the-charity-sector/publications/written-evidence/?page=2

[32] Written evidence submitted by NCVO to the Digital, Culture, Media and Sport Parliamentary Select Committee – April 2020, https://committees.parliament.uk/work/243/impact-of-COVID19-on-the-charity-sector/publications/written-evidence/?page=2

[33] https://www.thirdsector.co.uk/charities-trusted-deliver-social-care-caf-survey-finds/management/article/1674833

[34] https://publications.parliament.uk/pa/cm201919/cmselect/cmniaf/300/30007.htm#_idTextAnchor033

[35] https://www.nicva.org/article/northern-ireland-has-highest-levels-of-trust-in-charities-across-the-uk-and-ireland

[36] https://www.nicva.org/article/nicva-conference-COVID-19-taking-stock-at-the-year-end

References

Age Northern Ireland (2018) *Written evidence to the Northern Ireland Affairs Select Committee Inquiry into 'Funding priorities for the 2018–19 Budget: Health'*. Available at: http://data.parliament.uk/writtenevidence/committeeevidence.svc/evidencedocument/northern-ireland-affairs-committee/funding-priorities-for-the-201819-budget-health/written/92127.html

Age Scotland (2021) *Written evidence to Scottish Parliament Equalities and Human Rights Committee Inquiry on the Impact of the COVID-19 Pandemic on Equalities and Human Rights*, Edinburgh: Scottish Parliament Equalities and Human Rights Committee. Available at: https://sp-bpr-en-prod-cdnep.azureedge.net/published/EHRiC/2021/3/2/1283533c-8aed-4a8c-8034-1ab216baca73-1/EHRiCSO52021R5.pdf

Aquanno, S. and Bryant, T. (2020) 'Situating the pandemic: Welfare capitalism and Canada's liberal regime', *International Journal of Health Services* (online first), https://doi.org/10.1177/0020731420987079

Atkinson, C., Crozier, S. and Lewis, L. (2016) *Factors that affect the recruitment and retention of domiciliary care workers and the extent to which these factors impact upon the quality of domiciliary care: Interim findings summary, Department: Knowledge and Analytical Services*, Cardiff: Welsh Government. Available at: https://gov.wales/sites/default/files/statistics-and-research/2019-07/160118-factors-affect-recruitment-retention-domiciliary-care-workers-interim-en.pdf

Basco, S., Domènech, J. and Rosés, R. (2021) 'The redistributive effects of pandemics: Evidence on the Spanish flu', *World Development*, 141. https://doi.org/10.1016/j.worlddev.2021.105389

Beresford, P. and Croft, S. (1983) 'Welfare pluralism: The new face of Fabianism', *Critical Social Policy*, 3(9): 19–39.

Beveridge, W. (1948/ 2015) *Voluntary Action: A report on methods of social advance*, London: Routledge.

Borghi, V. and Van Berkel, R. (2007) 'New modes of governance in Italy and the Netherlands: The case of activation policies', *Public Administration*, 85(1): 83–101.

Breznau, N. (2021) 'The welfare state and risk perceptions: The Novel Coronavirus Pandemic and public concern in 70 countries', *European Societies*, 23(sup1): S33–S46.

Brindle, D. (2015) Social care is on the cusp of a crisis, *The Guardian*, 14 October. https://www.theguardian.com/social-care-network/2015/oct/14/social-care-cusp-crisis

CCPS Scotland (Coalition of Care and Support Providers in Scotland) (2020) *Independent review of Adult Social Care, submission from CCPS – Coalition of Care & Support Providers in Scotland*, Edinburgh: CCPS.

Chaney, P. (2021) 'Exploring the politicisation and territorialisation of adult social care in the UK: Electoral discourse analysis of state-wide and meso elections 1998–2019', *Global Social Policy* (online first), https://doi.org/10.1177/14680181211008141

Chaney, P. and Drakeford, M. (2004) 'The primacy of ideology: Social policy and the first term of the National Assembly for Wales', *Social Policy Review*, 16: 121–142.

Charities Aid Foundation (2020) *CAF UK Giving coronavirus briefing: How charities and donors are reacting to COVID-19*, London: CAF.

Charity Commission for Northern Ireland (2020) *NICVA COVID-19 Impact Survey 2020*, Belfast: CCNI.

Clements, L. (2017) *Care Act Overview*. Available at: http://www.lukeclements.co.uk/wp-content/uploads/2017/01/0-Care-Act-notes-updated-2017-01.pdf

Cunningham, I., Baluch, A., James, P., Jendro, J. and Young, D. (2019) *Handing back contracts: Exploring the rising trend in third sector provider withdrawal from the social care market*, Edinburgh: CCPS/University of Strathclyde Business School.

Curry, N., Hemmings, N., Oung, C. and Keeble, E. (2019) *Social care: The action we need*, London: Nuffield Trust.

DCMS (Department for Digital, Culture, Media & Sport) and Office for Civil Society (2020) *Financial support for voluntary, community and social enterprise (VCSE) organisations to respond to coronavirus (COVID-19)*, London: DCMS. Available at: https://www.gov.uk/guidance/financial-support-for-voluntary-community-and-social-enterprise-vcse-organisations-to-respond-to-coronavirus-COVID-19

DCMS and Office for Civil Society (2021) *Survey data on how the United Kingdom's third sector has been impacted by and responded to the ongoing coronavirus pandemic in June 2020*, London: DCMS. Available at: https://www.gov.uk/government/publications/dcms-coronavirus-impacts-third-sector-survey

Department of Health and Social Care (2021) *Integration and innovation: Working together to improve health and social care for all*, London: DHSC. Available at: https://www.gov.uk/government/publications/working-together-to-improve-health-and-social-care-for-all

Dubbeld, B. and de Almeida, F. (2020) 'Government by grants: The post-pandemic politics of welfare', *Transformation*, 104(1): 55–66.

Edmiston, D. (2017) 'Welfare, austerity and social citizenship in the UK', *Social Policy and Society*, 16(2): 261–270.

Gamble, A. (2016) *Can the Welfare State Survive?* Cambridge: Polity Press.

Hanlon, N., Rosenberg, M. and Clasby, R. (2007) 'Offloading social care responsibilities: Recent experiences of local voluntary organisations in a remote urban centre in British Columbia, Canada', *Health and Social Care in the Community*, 15(4): 343–367.

Health and Social Care Information Centre (2015) *Personal Social Services: Expenditure and unit costs England 2014–15*, London: Health and Social Care Information Centre.

Humphries, R. and Timmins, N. (2021) 'Stories from social care leadership: Progress amid pestilence and penury', London: King's Fund. Available at: https://www.kingsfund.org.uk/publications/social-care-leadership

ICF/Skills for Care (2018a) *The economic value of the adult social care sector – England: Final report*, London: ICF.

ICF/Skills for Care (2018b) *The economic value of the adult social care sector – Northern Ireland: Final report*, London: ICF.

ICF/Skills for Care (2018c) *The economic value of the adult social care sector – Scotland: Final report*, London: ICF.

ICF/Skills for Care (2018d) *The economic value of the adult social care sector – Wales, Final report*, London: ICF.

Inclusion Scotland (2020) *Rights at risk: COVID-19, disabled people and emergency planning in Scotland*, Edinburgh: Inclusion Scotland.

Kelly, D. and Kennedy, J. (2018) *Expert Advisory Panel Report on Adult Care and Support: Proposals to reboot adult care & support in N.I.*, Belfast: NIA. Available at: https://www.health-ni.gov.uk/sites/default/files/publications/health/power-to-people-full-report.PDF

King's Fund (2020) *A fork in the road: Next steps for social care funding reform*, London: King's Fund. Available at: https://www.kingsfund.org.uk/publications/key-challenges-facing-adult-social-care-sector-england

McKevitt, D. and Lawton, A. (eds) (1994) *Public Sector Management: Theory, critique and practice*, London: SAGE.

Meier, V. and Werding, M. (2010) *Ageing and the welfare state: Securing sustainability*, CESifo Working Paper, No. 2916, Munich: Center for Economic Studies and ifo Institute (CESifo). Available at: https://www.econstor.eu/bitstream/10419/30705/1/618100946.pdf

Mok, K., Ku, Y. and Yuda, T. K. (2021) 'Managing the COVID-19 pandemic crisis and changing welfare regimes', *Journal of Asian Public Policy*, 14(1): 1–12.

National Audit Office (2021a) *The adult social care market in England*, London: NAO.

National Audit Office (2021b) *National Audit Office's report into government funding for charities during the COVID-19 pandemic* (March 2021), London: NAO.

NCVO (National Council of Voluntary Organisations) (2020) *The UK Civil Society Almanac 2020*, London: NCVO. Available at: https://ncvo-app-wagtail-mediaa721a567-uwkfinin077j.s3.amazonaws.com/documents/ncvo-uk-civil-society-almanac-2020.pdf

NICVA (Northern Ireland Council for Voluntary Action) (2020) *Profile of the sector*, Belfast: NICVA.

Northern Ireland Executive Department for Health (2020) *Department of Health – Temporary amendment of the Health and Social Care Framework Document for the period June 2020 to May 2022: Consultation document*, Belfast: Northern Ireland Executive Department for Health.

Northern Ireland Social Care Council (2017) *Workforce review: Social care matters*, Belfast: Northern Ireland Social Care Council.

Ogden, J. (2017) 'Rising cost of dementia care risks social care funding crisis', *Progress in Neurology and Psychiatry*, 21(1): 5–25.

O'Neill, S. and NICVA (2021) *Communities Minister announces release of £7.5 million to support charities*, 10 March 2021. Available at: https://www.nicva.org/article/communities-minister-announces-release-of-75-million-to-support-charities

ONS (Office for National Statistics) (2020) *Population estimates for the UK, England and Wales, Scotland and Northern Ireland, provisional: mid-2019*, Newport: ONS. Available at: https://www.ons.gov.uk/peoplepopulationandcommunity/populationandmigration/populationestimates/bulletins/annualmidyearpopulationestimates/mid2019

Oung, C., Schlepper, L. and Curry, N. (2020) *How much social care does each country fund?* Nuffield Trust. Available at: https://www.nuffieldtrust.org.uk/news-item/how-much-social-care-does-each-country-fund

Public Health Agency (2020a) *Annual report & accounts for the year ended 31 March 2020 – Northern Ireland*, London: PHA. Available at: https://www.skillsforcare.org.uk/Documents/About/sfcd/The-economic-value-of-the-adult-social-care-sector-Northern-Ireland-4.pdf

Public Health Agency (2020b) *Annual report & accounts for the year ended 31 March 2020 – Wales*, London: PHA. Available at: https://socialcare.wales/cms_assets/file-uploads/The-Economic-Value-of-the-Adult-Social-Care-Sector_Wales.pdf

Rueda, D. (2014) 'Welfare, austerity and social citizenship in the UK', *Socio-Economic Review*, 12: 381–407.

Scottish Government (2018) *Scottish Government Medium Term Health and Social Care Financial Framework*, Edinburgh: Scottish Government.

Scottish Government (2019) *Social care support – An investment in Scotland's people, society, and economy: Programme Framework – A partnership programme to support, local reform of adult social care*, Edinburgh: Scottish Government.

Scottish Government (2020) *The Third Sector Resilience Fund (TSRF): Analysis of applications and awards (March–September 2020)*, Edinburgh: Scottish Government.

Scottish Government (2021) *Independent review of adult social care in Scotland*, Edinburgh: Scottish Government.

Scottish Parliament Equalities and Human Rights Committee (2021) *Report on the impact of the COVID-19 pandemic on equalities and human rights*. Available at: https://sp-bpr-en-prod-cdnep.azureedge.net/published/EHRiC/2021/3/2/1283533c-8aed-4a8c-8034-1ab216baca73-1/EHRiCSO52021R5.pdf

Scottish Parliament, Local Government and Communities Committee (2020) *Scottish Parliament evidence on the pandemic and the third sector*, 20 June 2020, Edinburgh: Scottish Parliament. Available at: https://archive2021.parliament.scot/parliamentarybusiness/report.aspx?r=12726

SCVO (Scottish Council for Voluntary Organisations) (2020a) *Submission to the House of Lords: Lessons from coronavirus*, Edinburgh: SCVO. Available at: https://storage.googleapis.com/scvo-cms/wp-content/uploads/2020/07/SCVO-submission-lessons-from-coronavirus-House-of-Lords-Select-Committee-on-Public-Service-July-2020.pdf

SCVO (2020b) *Coronavirus and its impact on the Scottish voluntary sector: What do we know so far?* Edinburgh: SCVO.

TSISN (Third Sector Interface Scotland Network) (2020) *Corona Virus Survey Report*, Edinburgh: TSISN.

United Nations (2019) *World population prospects 2019*, New York: United Nations. Available at: https://population.un.org/wpp/

Watt, T. and Roberts, A. (2016) *The path to sustainability: Funding projections for the NHS in Wales to 2019/20 and 2030/31*, London: The Health Foundation.

WCVA (Wales Council for Voluntary Action) (2020) *The voluntary sector in Wales*, Cardiff: WCVA.

Welsh Government (2014) *Third Sector Scheme*, Cardiff: Welsh Government.

Welsh Government (2021) *Rebalancing care and support: A consultation on improving social care arrangements and strengthening partnership working to better support people's well-being*, Cardiff: Welsh Government, White Paper Number: WG41756.

Welsh Labour Policy Forum (2021) *Welsh taxes, finance & Brexit: Second stage consultation document*, Cardiff: WLP.

Welsh Parliament/Senedd Cymru (2021a) *Equality, Local Government and Communities Committee Inquiry: Impact of COVID-19 on the voluntary sector*, Cardiff: Welsh Parliament/Senedd Cymru.

Welsh Parliament/Senedd Cymru (2021b) *Health, Social Care and Sport Committee Inquiry into the impact of the COVID-19 outbreak, and its management, on health and social care in Wales*, Cardiff: Welsh Parliament/Senedd Cymru.

5

The contemporary threat to minority languages and cultures: civil society, young people and Celtic language use in Scotland and Wales

Rhys Jones, Elin Royles, Fiona O'Hanlon and Lindsay Paterson

Introduction

Since the 1960s, academics and policy-makers alike have become increasingly aware of the threats facing minority languages and cultures, speaking not only of language shift but also of language endangerment and language death (see for example, Fishman 1991; Crystal 2000). Language shift illustrates the challenges facing minority languages, in particular the reduction in overall numbers of speakers, the breaking down of intergenerational transmission, and a downturn in the use of minority languages both in everyday settings and in different areas of life (Baker 2011: 72). It is reckoned, for instance, that around half of the estimated 6,800 languages spoken today will have disappeared by the end of the twenty-first century (Crystal 2000; Nettle and Romaine 2000), largely as a result of a process of language shift, as the speakers of minority languages choose, instead, to speak 'majority' languages. Globalisation is considered to be one of the most powerful dynamics contributing to weakening minority languages, resulting in language shift and loss (Laponce 2004). In a similar vein, many authors have drawn attention to the impact of globalisation on the various cultural forms practised by various 'minorities' and to the interrelationships between cultural loss, identity change and language decline (for example, Fishman 2001: 21).

It is largely as a result of such threats that civil society activists, academics and policy-makers began, especially from the 1960s onwards, to advocate and formulate efforts to respond in creative and practical ways to the challenges facing minority languages and cultures, to halt and reverse their decline, and to promote their revitalisation. For instance, increasing the status of regional or minority languages through political constitutions and legal systems has been the focus of considerable language activism, with attempts being made in a variety of countries to promote equal rights for minority cultures (Lewis 2017). A number of contributors to the language revitalisation literature place a substantial emphasis on the nature of 'the government's language policy' (Tsunoda 2005: 54), and the need for policy programmes to promote and support the continued acquisition and use of the target language (see also Giles et al 1977; Ó Riagáin 2000). Within such policy programmes, the education system has been considered as a key social domain to address language and culture shift in different geographical settings (Ferguson 2006; Baker 2011). The media has also been viewed as another crucial social domain for the promotion of minority language use, with the traditional print, radio and television media (Cormack and Hourigan 2007), and latterly digital media (Cunliffe 2007; Crystal 2011), being particular areas of concern.

Such broad trends have been mirrored in Scotland and Wales, the two countries that form the immediate empirical focus for this chapter. Both Welsh and Scottish Gaelic are members of the broader family of Celtic languages and represent the two main regional minority languages spoken in the UK today. In each case language shift has occurred as the influence of English has increased. Language shift has affected the Scottish Gaelic language in far-reaching ways. McLeod (2004) notes such language shift to have been ongoing since the late Middle Ages, with historic economic and political factors resulting in the geographical association of the Gaelic language with the Highlands and Islands of Scotland in the north-west of the country from the fourteenth century. In relation to more recent language shift, MacKinnon (2010: 129) notes that Scottish Gaelic has experienced 'over a century of demographic decline' since the 1891 census showed 6.8 per cent of the Scottish population (254,415 people) to be Gaelic speaking. This is evidenced in census figures which show decreases in Gaelic-speaker numbers every 40 years – to 136,135 (3 per cent of the population) in 1931, to 88,415 (1.8 per cent) in 1971 and 58,000 (1.1 per cent) in 2011. However, such demographic decline is also reflected in the density of Gaelic speakers within 'traditionally' Gaelic-speaking areas of the Highlands and Islands (Withers 1984). For example, while MacKinnon noted there to be 70 per cent plus Gaelic speakers in all of the Hebridean Islands and western coastal civil parishes in 1891, by the 2011 census, only seven civil parishes (of 871 in Scotland) had over 50 per cent of Gaelic speakers (National Records of Scotland 2015). Such a decline in density of Gaelic speakers has implications for the use of Gaelic as the predominant language of communication in local community life. The decline in the number and density of Gaelic-speakers in traditional communities is related to myriad socio-economic, political and cultural factors, including out-migration of Gaelic-speakers from the agrarian Highlands and Islands of Scotland abroad or to the industrial lowlands (where large groups of Gaelic-speakers now reside), the World Wars, and a reduction in the intergenerational transmission of Gaelic from parents to children in the home (McCullough 2018). However, as noted above, from the 1960s, civil society actors have worked with government bodies to try to stem such linguistic decline – with a key area of work being education due to its ability to create new speakers of Gaelic, and thus compensate for the decline in family- and community-based intergenerational transmission of the language. Since the mid-1980s, efforts in Scotland have focused on education through the medium of Gaelic (rather than bilingual models or the teaching of Gaelic as a subject in English-medium education), as Gaelic-medium education has been found to be most effective in building bilingual competence in Gaelic and in English among children living in Anglicised homes and/or communities (Mitchell et al 1987, Robertson 2003). Gaelic-medium educational provision has developed across Scotland since 1985, with its national scope reflecting efforts by civil society activists since the 1960s to 'restore Gaelic as a language for the whole of Scotland' (Gebel 2002: 200). In the 2019–20 school year, there were 5,152 pupils being educated in Gaelic-medium primary and secondary schools across Scotland, 0.7 per cent of all pupils (BnG 2020). In terms of geographical location, just over half of these pupils (55 per cent) live in the Highlands and Islands and 45 per cent live in the Lowlands, and in terms of home-language, a maximum of one in 10 of Gaelic-medium pupils across Scotland have Gaelic as their 'main home language' (Scottish Government 2020). The impact of such educational initiatives on the number of Gaelic speakers is not as marked as in the Welsh context (discussed below), but Gaelic-medium education has contributed to the slowing of the rate of decline of Gaelic since 1991, and, between the 2011 and 2011 censuses, there was an 8.6 per cent increase in the number of Gaelic-speakers between the ages of three and 24, in line with language policy aims (BnG 2018).

The Welsh language has followed a similar trajectory in Wales. The nineteenth century and early twentieth century was a period when the fortunes of the Welsh language began to change dramatically. Between 1801 and 1891 the percentage able to speak Welsh fell from an estimated 95 per cent to 54.5 per cent, before falling further to 49.9 per cent in 1901 and 44.6 per cent in 1911 (Jones 1998: 225). Moreover, during the same period there was a drastic decline in the percentage of monolingual Welsh speakers, falling from 30.4 per cent of the population in 1891 to 15.1 per cent in 1901 and 8.7 per cent by 1911 (Jones 1998: 225). A particularly alarming trend for the long-term sustainability of the language was that between 1901 and 1931 the age profile of Welsh-speakers became increasingly skewed towards older generations (Aitchison and Carter 2000: 40–42). The ageing of the Welsh-speaking population reflected substantial levels of outward-migration as a result of the industrial recession and agricultural restructuring that occurred during the interwar period (Thomas 1987). However, it also highlights an increasing tendency on the part of Welsh-speaking parents to decide against transferring the language to their children. During the second half of the twentieth century the decline of the Welsh language, both in numerical and percentage terms, continued. Indeed, during the 1951–71 period it appeared as if the language was entering a period of 'inexorable decay' (Thomas 1956, cited in Aitchison and Carter 2000: 45). However, in the 1960s, Welsh language civil society activists successfully campaigned for state support for the extension of Welsh-medium educational provision to English-first language pupils in Anglicised areas, provision which was recommended by the Gittins Committee in 1967 in order to safeguard the Welsh language and culture as a core part of Welsh national identity. By 2019–20, there were 96,651 pupils being educated in Welsh-medium primary and secondary schools across Wales, 23 per cent of all pupils (StatsWales 2020). The clear impact of such educational initiatives on the number of Welsh speakers is reflected in 2011 census figures, which report 35 per cent of 3–19 year olds in Wales to be Welsh-speaking (some 212,401 people), as compared with 19 per cent for all people aged 3+, and which show an overall increase in the number of Welsh speakers over a 20-year period – from 504,000 in 1991 to 562,000 people in 2011 (Statistics for Wales 2012). The continued growth in Welsh-medium statutory education forms the key aspect in the statistical projections underlying the *Cymraeg 2050* plan, which aims to increase the number of Welsh speakers from 562,000 in 2011 to 1,000,000 by 2050 (Welsh Government 2017).

When conceived in relation to the notion of threat, the current predicament of the Scottish Gaelic and Welsh languages thus paints a somewhat contradictory picture. The idea of 'threat' is suggestive of someone or something that is actively threatening someone or something else. In this regard, one could suggest that the formal or institutional subjugation of the Scottish Gaelic and Welsh languages, respectively, is far less apparent nowadays than it was during the nineteenth and early twentieth centuries. There are few explicit attempts actively to promote the majority language of English at the expense of Scottish Gaelic and Welsh. Moreover, there is now a relatively long history of efforts to promote the prospects of both languages (see for example, Jenkins and Williams 2000; McLeod 2020). Whereas revitalisation efforts since the 1960s have arguably been more prominent and far reaching in Wales, important developments for Gaelic took place during this period, particularly in the fields of education and broadcasting (Paterson et al 2014: 430). (For a review of Scottish language policy over the past 50 or so years, see McLeod (2020); for a similar review of Welsh language policy, see Jones and Lewis (2019).) In both cases, changes in governance owing to the establishment of devolved government in Wales and Scotland from 1999 onwards has been a catalyst for a new period as activist-led efforts have been increasingly bolstered by more sustained institutional support in favour of both languages by both sub-state governments (Lewis and Royles 2018). Key advancements include the Gaelic Language (Scotland) Act 2005, which established a statutory language planning agency, Bòrd na Gàidhlig, and created a framework for Scottish public bodies to create Gaelic language plans. In Wales, additional steps taken post-devolution include passing the Welsh Language (Wales) Measure 2011, which accorded the language official status for the first time (Dunbar 2007; Williams 2015). A further important feature common to both cases, which we will explore in more detail below, is the publication by the respective sub-state governments of national language strategies that set key targets and define priority areas for intervention.

Such a reduction in institutional threat has been mirrored, to a large extent, by a reduction in public antipathy towards both languages. Recent surveys in both countries, for instance, have shown public support for both languages. Evidence from a survey of public attitudes to Gaelic conducted in 2021 suggests that Gaelic is increasingly treated as a symbol of Scottish distinctiveness, with 79 per cent of the 1,365 people surveyed viewing the language as important to Scottish heritage (Dean et al., 2022). Within the same survey, 7 in 10 of those surveyed supported the current level of Scottish Government spending to promote the learning and use of Gaelic (£29m in 2021). In the most recent survey data on attitudes towards the Welsh language in Wales (2017–18), 86 per cent of the population viewed the Welsh language as something to be proud of and 67 per cent thought more effort needed to be put into supporting the language (Welsh Government 2018). In this sense, the more historical association between minority languages and social and cultural divisions within civil society – particularly in Wales – has changed. Rather, minority languages such as Welsh are being increasingly viewed as having the potential to create positive social and cultural bonds within their respective civil societies. Indeed, some academics have contested that minority languages can act as a vehicle for otherwise excluded and disenfranchised groups, such as migrants, to engage with and become members of civil society (Higham 2020; compare Chapter 8 of this volume). Similarly, Welsh government policy is clear in its Race Equality Plan (Welsh Government 2021: 116) when it states that Welsh is 'a language for all and a way of uniting people from different backgrounds'. In practical terms, the Welsh government seeks to ensure equality of access for more individuals from black and minority ethnic communities across Wales both to Welsh-medium education and activities and events occurring through the medium of Welsh (Welsh Government 2021: 116–118).

And yet, despite the reduction in an active hostility towards the Scottish Gaelic and Welsh languages (whether institutionally or among the public at large), and despite the success of Welsh-medium and Gaelic-medium education in increasing the number of young people able to speak Welsh and Gaelic, it is clear that both languages are still in a precarious demographic and sociolinguistic position (Lewis and Royles 2018). A key contemporary threat to the ongoing vitality of both languages is the low levels of social usage of Welsh and Gaelic by Welsh-medium and Gaelic-medium educated young people, particularly among peers – a sociolinguistic phenomenon which has been noted by policy-makers, educationalists, researchers and civil society actors in both Wales and Scotland over the past 20 years (WAG 2002; BnG 2007, 2012, 2018; Morris 2007; Stiùbhart 2011; Thomas et al 2011; Cunliffe et al 2013; NicLeòid 2015; Welsh Government 2015; O' Giollagáin et al 2020). The lack of consistent transfer of school-based language use into social language use poses a key threat to the success of language planning measures which aim to use education as a means to create a new generation of Welsh and Gaelic speakers who will use the language in their social lives into adulthood (Welsh Government 2017; BnG 2018). Within a context of increasing recognition across a number of international cases of the consequences of over-reliance on the education system in language revitalisation efforts (Ò Riagàin et al 2008; Pujolar and Gonzàlez 2013; Vila et al 2018), this chapter will consider the ways in which out-of-school activities might make a distinct contribution in encouraging language use and in creating more positive psychological effects with respect to pupils' identification with the language and their views of its status or prestige. Specifically, we will explore pupils' experiences of the National Eisteddfod and the National Mòd – each annual eight-day large-scale minority language and culture events – in relation to peer language use, identity and ideology, in order to consider the potential impact of such intensive but periodic minority language events. The chapter is structured as follows. In the next section, we present the rationale for our focus on national festivals in relation to social use of Welsh and Gaelic among young people, and then present our theoretical framing, which draws on the work of Billig (1995) to consider the role of 'hot' contexts such as the Eisteddfod and Mòd (as opposed to 'banal' contexts such as education) in relation to minority language identity development, and on the work of Puigdevall et al (2018), whose work on 'linguistic mudes' considers the impact of participation in 'intensive' minority language experiences from a linguistic perspective. Subsequently, we outline the methodological basis of our cross-national comparison and then present details of our sample and of the methods employed to collect and analyse the data. Two empirical sections follow. In the first we examine the significance of the Eisteddfod to peer-language use and attitudes among Welsh-medium educated young people in Wales. In the second, we similarly explore the significance of the Mòd for Gaelic-medium educated pupils in Scotland. This is followed by our conclusions and recommendations for policy and research.

National festivals and minority language use in social contexts

The importance of minority language use in informal contexts by pupils educated through the medium of a lesser used language is underlined by

Fishman (1991), who emphasises the importance of such social contexts for pupils' identification with the minority language and culture and for pupil language use during, and beyond, the school stage. Such an emphasis on social contexts for minority language use has been mirrored in post-devolution Welsh and Scottish language planning (WAG 2003, 2010; BnG 2007, 2012, 2018; Welsh Government 2017), on the shared assumption that 'a language which is confined to the educational sector is not a living language' (WAG 2003: 7). As a result, government strategies have aimed to ensure that opportunities were extended for children and young people to use Welsh and Gaelic in leisure and social situations, with funding provided to civil society partners enabling this type of activity, including the National Eisteddfod, Urdd Gobaith Cymru (the main Welsh-language youth organisation) and the Mentrau Iaith in Wales, and to the National Mòd, Fèisean nan Gàidheal (the main Gaelic-language youth arts organisation), and Comann na Gàidhlig (who run Spòrs Gàidhlig and the Iomairtean Gàidhlig community initiatives in Scotland) (WAG 2003; Welsh Government 2014; BnG 2018). These institutions work at national, community and local (school-linked) levels, and aim to support the language practices of young people in a range of informal situations – relating to culture, music, sport and drama. Within these, the most recent Welsh and Gaelic language strategies, *Cymraeg 2050* (Welsh Government 2017) and the *National Gaelic Language Plan* (BnG 2018) signal a growing emphasis on larger events and festivals for the reproduction of the Celtic language and in providing opportunities to use the languages (Welsh Government 2014: 18; BnG 2018: 28). The present chapter will thus focus on young people's experiences of two such national festivals – the Eisteddfod Genedlaethol Cymru – an eight-day annual Welsh language and culture festival which attracts 160,000 visitors per year and aims to 'promote the culture of Wales and safeguard the Welsh language, Welsh history and traditions in a diverse modern society' (National Eisteddfod 2012), and Am Mòd Nàiseanta Rìoghail – an eight-day annual Gaelic language and culture festival which attracts around 3,000 visitors per year, which aims to 'support and develop all aspects of the Gaelic language, culture, history and heritage' and to 'promote the use of the language in everyday community life' (ACG 2020). In terms of youth provision, in addition to competitions, the National Eisteddfod has run Maes B, an award-winning late-night Welsh language rock and pop festival for those aged 16+ since 1997. This is the hub for Welsh-speaking young people at the festival and includes a separate youth camping area. The National Mòd similarly both provides competitions and organises 'Fringe' events for all ages, including performances from Gaelic-language bands, but this has not been developed into a specific 'youth festival' as in the Welsh context. Rather, the National Mòd notes that its 'focus' is the competition side (ACG 2020). Specifically, we will explore both Celtic-speaking young people's perceptions of the national festivals in providing them with an intensive opportunity to use Welsh or Gaelic socially, and any ongoing impact of participation in this event on young people's identities or everyday Welsh or Gaelic language use. In so doing, we provide empirical data to begin to fill an important gap in current research evaluations of the Eisteddfod and Mòd which tend to focus on attendee numbers and the economic impact of these national festivals – as peripatetic events – on the communities where they are held in a particular year (for example, see National Eisteddfod 2003, cited in Welsh Government 2013; Welsh Government 2013; Glamis Consultancy and STR 2020).

In terms of theoretical framing, our study draws on a number of themes. First, we are influenced by the work of Billig (1995). His ideas, and those of others following in his wake, focus on the social construction of 'nationalism' as a personal and group identity by means of repeated and iterative engagement with nationalism in both 'banal' or mundane and 'hot' or occasional contexts (Billig 1995; Özkırımlı 2000; Jones and Merriman 2009). We build on this work by suggesting that young people's engagement with the Welsh or Gaelic languages has the potential to socialise them into a minority language community and into civil society more broadly. We are particularly concerned here with the significance of the 'hotter' or more occasional and periodic events in the reproduction of minority languages and cultures, and the relationship(s) between them and the ongoing, more banal cultural experiences of individuals and groups that speak minority languages. Second, we draw upon the theoretical work on 'linguistic changes' (Pujolar and Gonzàlez 2013) which explores the question of how longer term changes in language use emerge from participation in such 'hot' – in the sense of atypical and intensive – linguistic or cultural experiences. Puigdevall et al (2018: 446) note mudes to be 'a change in the way one organises language choice in everyday life', and note them to be dependent on a 'complex interaction of situational, motivational and ideological factors' (p 448), where the third category incorporates identity. Third, our work is informed by previous work that has examined the socialisation of young people and, in particular, the role of various institutions in facilitating this process of identity formation (see Brent 2009; Mills 2021). In particular, we draw on research that has examined the role played by institutions in using minority languages to inform youth identity (Jones and Royles 2020a).

In the following discussion, we will explore young people's reports of their feelings of personal or group identification with Welsh or Gaelic in relation to their participation in the National Eisteddfod or Mòd, and whether such participation is associated with a linguistic mude, particularly in relation to ongoing language use in social contexts with peers. Although work on linguistic mudes has tended to focus on second language speakers of minority languages, we extend its scope to include first language speakers whose choice to use Welsh/Gaelic with peers would still constitute a linguistic change away from an English-language norm.

Cross-national comparison, data and methods

Our study is framed within the 'home international' (Raffe et al 1999) approach to cross-national comparison, which compares different nations of the UK. The data presented in this chapter aim to explore a 'common policy concern' across the Welsh and Scottish contexts – namely, low levels of peer social minority language use among Celtic-medium educated adolescents – and aims to observe 'how similar approaches' to addressing this policy concern 'work in different contexts' (Raffe 2005: 4). As noted above, civil society provision for social language use through large-scale national festivals such as the Eisteddfod and the Mòd have been proposed as a key approach to addressing the policy concern in both Wales and Scotland. In terms of the comparison, we have seen that although the Welsh and Scottish contexts are similar in their use of minority language education to try to stem the decline in the Celtic languages, there is a key difference between the contexts in terms of the size of the Celtic-medium education sector, and the size of the language communities overall, with Welsh-medium education having 19 times as many pupils as Gaelic-medium pupils, and the Welsh language having 10 times as many speakers as Gaelic. There is also a different historical relationship between language and national identity in the two contexts – with Welsh acting as a key ethnic marker of national identity (Paterson and Jones 1999) and Gaelic playing a more peripheral role, with Scottish national identity rather centred on civic administrative structures, such as the education and legal systems (Devine 2000). However, the more recent development of Welsh civic institutions and the greater acceptance of Gaelic as a key aspect of national heritage may be eliding this distinction (Paterson and Jones 1999; Royles 2007). The data presented in this chapter are drawn from interviews with 32 Welsh-medium secondary and college students, and 45 Gaelic-medium secondary pupils, between 14 and 18 years of age, with the four education settings in Wales and six in Scotland drawn from a range of sociolinguistic contexts (from the most Welsh/Gaelic speaking areas of Wales and Scotland to those in Anglicised areas with low proportions of the local population able to speak Welsh/ Gaelic). The research was conducted in the 2016–17 academic year as part of an ESRC-funded WISERD Civil Society Research Centre project which examined the link between education, language and identity in Scotland and Wales. The interviews explored pupils' experiences of minority language education, their language use, identities and their patterns of participation in extra-curricular activities such as hobbies and civil society events, including the Eisteddfod and the Mòd.[1] The interviews were conducted in Welsh and Gaelic, and were analysed using thematic data analysis using NVivo (Silverman 2004; Spencer et al 2013a). Following Spencer et al (2013b), emergent themes were derived from the respondents' data, our theoretical focus and research aim. Quotations within this chapter are provided in both the original language (Welsh/Gaelic) and in an English translation.

The Welsh language and the Eisteddfod

A number of interviewees in our study placed a strong emphasis on the experience of going to Welsh-language festivals and the annual National Eisteddfod festival in particular. They reflected on their engagement with the 'Maes B' hub for young people at the festival – the location of the late-night performances by the main Welsh-language bands, with a youth camping area. Interviewees described these spaces as ones that possessed a significant potential to facilitate the forging of social networks and ones, moreover, that were predicated on the use of the Welsh language. A pupil from a Welsh-speaking household in Cardiff noted:

'Oeddwn i a ffrindiau fi ym Maes B yn yr haf, a just yn union pryd ti yno, ti just teimlo fel ti'n cysylltu gyda phawb yn hawdd. Mae'n hawdd neud ffrindiau. Mae pawb yn fel relatio gyda'i gilydd, ac mae just, mae pawb yn siarad Cymraeg, so mae'n teimlo fel teulu mawr, yr iaith Cymraeg. … Just pawb just yn mynd lan at ei gilydd, yn siarad Cymraeg. Ti byth yn gweld hwnna yng Nghaerdydd. Mae fe bach fel od i weld fel tro cynta' ni. Ie, oedd o'n eitha' od ond neis yr un pryd.'

'Me and my friends were at Maes B in the summer, and just when you're there, you just feel like you connect easily with everybody. It's easy to make friends. Everybody can relate to one another, and just, everybody speaks Welsh, so it feels like a big family, the Welsh language … Just everybody going up to one another, speaking in Welsh. You never see that in Cardiff. It was a bit odd to see it that first time. Yes, it was a bit odd, but nice at the same time.'

The above quote illustrates the significance of the embodied experience of Welsh-language periodic events such as the Eisteddfod to young Welsh speakers. This event can be classified as a 'hot' event for this pupil both in terms of group identity and belonging – where she notes that 'it feels like a big family, the Welsh language' – and in terms of her experience of a peer-initiated use of the Welsh language among young people. This student, like some others in our sample, perceived this use of the Welsh language to be similar to that which would exist in areas of high density of Welsh speakers. The unusualness, or 'marked' nature of this linguistic practice in relation to the pupil's everyday experience living in an Anglicised area of Wales is underlined by the respondent's reflection: 'You never see that in Cardiff.' In the remaining paragraphs of this section, we draw out two key themes relating to the impact of Maes B as a 'hotter' or periodic event in encouraging identification with, and use of, the Welsh language. The first theme relates to first-language and second-language Welsh pupils' experiences of the Eisteddfod and the second relates to pupils' perceptions of the possibilities and obstacles to extending such Welsh-language use into everyday life.

In relation to the first theme, our findings show that events such as the Eisteddfod and Maes B had an equally positive effect on pupils, regardless of their home language. Some of our interviewees argued that events such as the Eisteddfod were particularly important for young people whose parents spoke Welsh. In such cases, these 'hot' events were seen to affirm and normalise their Welsh language use practices and attitudes. Indeed, one interviewee felt that having Welsh-speaking parents meant that the Eisteddfod and music festivals were more important to them than to friends and fellow pupils who did not speak Welsh at home. For this person, attending the Eisteddfod was viewed as an important part of their 'core' identity as a Welsh person and Welsh speaker, reflecting and reinforcing their sense of Welshness (compare Billig 1995). Nevertheless, the evidence from other interviewees suggested that festivals could equally form an important (if not more important) part of the cultural and Welsh-language socialisation experiences of young people who were not from Welsh-speaking backgrounds and who had learnt the language at school. This was clearest in the case of a young female student whose parents did not speak Welsh. During the period when she attended a Welsh-medium primary school, she reflected that she spoke Welsh but the language and its culture did not really influence her. However, secondary school friends from more Welsh-speaking backgrounds had opened up opportunities to attending these 'hot' events. As a result, the student experienced a significant heightening of her connection with the Welsh language and culture:

'Fi fel arfer yn mynd i Eisteddfod, gwrando ar gerddoriaeth Cymraeg, mynd i wyliau Cymraeg fel y Tafwyl, ble fysaf fi ddim os fi heb 'di cwrdd â ffrindiau sydd wedi cylchynu o gwmpas y Gymraeg.'

'I usually go to the Eisteddfod, listen to Welsh music, go to Welsh festivals like Tafwyl, and I wouldn't be involved in these if I hadn't met friends who are active in Welsh.'

Interestingly, the same student reflected that going to the Eisteddfod and other Welsh-language festivals were essential to her being able to 'follow' Welsh culture, and she reported a 'linguistic mude' (Pujolar and Gonzàlez

2013) as a result of her participation in such 'hot' events, explaining that she now spoke Welsh socially with her friends at school as a result of this.

However, despite using Welsh with peers at the Eisteddfod and Maes B event, some of our respondents – especially those living outside of the Welsh-speaking 'heartland' (Jones and Fowler 2008) – cited geography as having an impact on their ability to use the Welsh language in everyday settings. A number of interviewees across the sample of schools and colleges we researched drew attention to the limitations on their opportunities to use the Welsh language socially in their own areas. The situation was deemed to be stark in some cases. In the words of one interviewee living in a town in the post-industrial area included in the study: "*ond does dim Cymraeg. Dw i'n byw yn xxx, ac mae literally dim byd*" ("but there is no Welsh. I live in xxx, and there is literally nothing").

At the same time, our research captured the involvement of young people in activities to encourage greater social use of Welsh organised by different organisations. For instance, one interviewee whose usage of Welsh had declined and who lived in an area of decreasing levels of Welsh language use was involved with the Urdd and Mentrau Iaith. Through the latter she participated in the activities of a group established to provide opportunities to speak Welsh for young people whose language use was in decline. Nevertheless, a broader finding of the research that Welsh-medium students perceive that lack of opportunity is preventing their social use of Welsh in Anglicised areas is significant to language planning for the Welsh language. The main contrast to limitations on the potential opportunities for young people to use Welsh was the area with a high proportion of Welsh-speakers. The 'banal' opportunities to socialise in Welsh available to young people in this area included attending Young Farmers, the Urdd aelwyd and competing at Eisteddfodau, in addition to Welsh being spoken on the streets and in different contexts in their lives. It is therefore significant that through 'hot' events such as the Eisteddfod and participating in Maes B activities, young people believe that they can experience – however fleetingly – a similar experience to this type of linguistic socialisation.

Scottish Gaelic and the Mòd

The data from the Scottish context show several aspects of similarity, but also key differences, from the Welsh data. In terms of similarities, participation in the National Mòd, like participation in the Eisteddfod, is reported to both reflect and extend first-language speakers' home and community language use and identities, and to provide an extended opportunity for second-language learners of Gaelic to use their Gaelic in social contexts and to deepen their socialisation into the Gaelic language and culture. As in the Welsh context, some Gaelic-medium pupils living in areas with a low density of Gaelic speakers reported challenges in transferring their Gaelic language use with peers at the National Mòd into their everyday life. One upper secondary pupil living in a Lowland town noted that although she spoke Gaelic all week to her friends at the National Mòd (friends she knows through her long-term participation in local and National Mòds), when she is at home:

> '*Chan eil cothroman agam a bhith a' bruidhinn Gàidhlig ri daoine eile ach dìreach nuair a bhios mi sa chlas agus còmhla ri [ainmean nan tidsearan]. Chan eil duine eile agam, chan eil na caraidean agam uile Gàidhlig neo rudan mar sin neo pàrantan Gàidhlig.*'

> 'I don't have any opportunities to speak Gaelic to other people – just when I am in my [Gaelic] class and with [Gaelic teachers]. I have no-one else, not all my friends have Gaelic or anything like that and my parents don't speak Gaelic.

Similarly, to the Welsh pupils described above, this pupil cites situational factors related to limited opportunity as the key factor limiting her social use of Gaelic within her local Anglicised language context. However, an analysis of the pupil's interview in relation to identity and motivation (the other two factors which Puigdevall et al (2018) note to underpin language use) shows these to align with the pupil's *current* Gaelic language use practices – in the school and in 'hot' contexts such as the local and National Mòds – thus highlighting a lack of impetus for any further linguistic mudes. In terms of identity, the pupil reports a compartmentalised identity, where Gaelic is important to her at school and in her music. She notes of the importance of Gaelic in her life:

> '*Tha e anns a' mheadhan, tha e na phàirt mhòr ach tha e na phàirt bheag aig an aon turas. Tha e na phàirt mhòr leis tha mi air a bhith ga bruidhinn bho bha mi beag agus cuideachd tha e anns a' cheòl agam cuideachd, ach chan eil mi a' bruidhinn e ri duine anns an taigh neo duine a tha na caraidean dhomh, agus chan eil e uabhasach mòr dhomh.*'

> 'It is in the middle, it's like a big part but it's a little part at the same time. It's a big part because I have been speaking it since I was little [at school], and also, it is in my music – but I don't speak it to anyone at home, or my friends, and so it's not very big for me.'

Similarly, in terms of motivation, the pupil notes her current Gaelic language use practices in music-related and educational contexts to be linked to her wish to study music and Gaelic at university, and to have a career in Gaelic traditional music.

Although for this pupil the Mòd is a 'hot' Gaelic event (Billig 1995), a key difference between the Welsh and Scottish contexts was that the National Mòd was only still a 'hot' event for a small proportion of our sample (about one in four) by the mid to upper secondary school stage, even though the sample consisted of people who might be expected to treat the Mòd as significant. A key reason given by pupils for lack of participation was the Mòd's focus on a 'competition' format. Although most of the sample reported participation in the Mòd in primary school, with pupils often competing as part of school choirs, or school-supported individual or small group performances, such support with competition preparation was often not available at secondary school, particularly in Anglicised areas. In our sample it was notable that while the three secondary schools in Gaelic-speaking areas had a Gaelic choir, three of the four secondary schools in Anglicised areas did not, with teachers noting issues relating to small numbers of Gaelic-medium pupils (in otherwise English-medium schools) making maintaining Gaelic-specific groups difficult, together with capacity issues of small numbers of Gaelic-speaking teaching staff in secondary schools where only a few subjects are taught through the medium of Gaelic. One secondary Gaelic teacher from an Anglicised area reflected in relation to Mòd preparation:

'*Tha mi dol a dh'fheuchainn, chan e sinne thairis air na bliadhnaichean a bhiodh a' toirt taic dhaibh a dhol chun a' Mhòid. ... tha an fheadhainn anns a' bhun-sgoil tha iadsan a' dèanamh tòrr a thaobh nam Mòdan Ionadail agus tha iad a-nis a' dol chun a' Mhòid Nàiseanta cuideachd. Mar sin tha [ainm tidseir] na Iar-cheannard anns a' bhun-sgoil, tha ise ag ràdh rium "Come on feumaidh sibh beagan a bharrachd a dhèanamh a thaobh taic a thoirt dhaibh" ach 's e dìreach nach eil ùine againn an t-uabhas a dhèanamh. Ach tha ceangal làidir againn a-nis le [àite ionadail] Gaelic Choir agus tha cuid de na sgoilearan a' dol ann an sin don Junior Choir. Tha iadsan a' dèanamh an t-uabhas agus tha iad comasach ... cuideachd tha cothrom a tha seo gu bhith aca ullachadh a dhèanamh airson a' Mhòid còmhla ri tutor tha dol a thighinn a-staigh bhon choimhearsnachd.*'

'I am going to try, it wasn't us over the years who would be helping them with going to the Mòd ... but the ones in the primary school they do a lot concerning the local Mòds and they now go to the National Mòd as well. Because of that xxx who is the Deputy Head Teacher in the primary school has been saying to me "Come on, you must do a little more to support them" but it's just that we don't have much time to do an awful lot. But we now have a strong link with the [local] Gaelic Choir and some of the pupils go there to the Junior Choir. They do an awful lot and they're good ... the pupils also will have this opportunity to prepare for the Mòd along with a tutor who is going to come in from the community.'

This quote shows the importance of coordination and co-working between the school and civil society in creating equality of opportunity for Gaelic-medium secondary pupils across Scotland to access activities such as the National Mòd. However, even when such opportunity is available, some secondary pupils reported having become bored of the Mòd format – for example, one pupil reflected *"Rinn mi e ann an S1 agus an uair sin sguir mi, a chionn 's gun do rinn mi tòrr Mòdan"* ("I did [the National Mòd] in Secondary 1, but then I quit as I had done a lot of Mòds"), while others cited lack of success within the competition format, or a feeling that their musical skills were not 'performance standard' as reasons for non-participation.

Indeed, in the Scottish context, rather than a particular focus on the National Mòd, pupils identified a range of 'hot' events for intensive social Gaelic language use among peers, including (1) the annual Gaelic drama summer school, organised by Fèisean nan Gàidheal, where Gaelic-speaking young people between 13 and 17 years of age work together on short films and drama performances over 6–11 days, living together in hostel or university accommodation, (2) teen Fèisean – which are annual, week-long music, art and drama activities run regionally, (3) Film G – an annual Gaelic-language youth film competition which involves local preparation of a film, and a glitzy awards ceremony for those shortlisted, (4) sports trips – such as a week-long Gaelic-language youth ski-ing trip provided by Comann na Gàidhlig and (5) spending school holiday time in a strongly Gaelic-speaking area where the pupil knows local Gaelic-speaking young people (often by means of a family-heritage link). In best practice, there were opportunities for pupils to use their Gaelic regularly in more 'banal' events (for example, weekly school-based Gaelic-drama club or weekly local Fèis music lessons) that would prepare them for 'hotter' events (such as, the annual national Gaelic drama summer school, or the regional summer teen Fèis event).

Moreover, many pupils reported participating in a *range* of Gaelic-medium activities. For example, a mid-secondary Gaelic-medium pupil living in an Anglicised area whose parents do not speak Gaelic, notes that in the previous year she had participated in school Gaelic drama club, local ceilidhs, the national Gaelic drama summer school, the teen Fèis in her area, the local Mòds, the National Mòd, the Film G competition (including attending the awards ceremony), and had spent time in a strongly Gaelic-speaking area where her Gaelic-speaking grandparents live. She reports that she speaks Gaelic 'all the time' to her friends in her local Anglicised context, and reports strong motivation and personal and group identity rationales for such Gaelic language use. In terms of motivation she notes that she wants to use her Gaelic as she enjoys speaking it and continuing to improve, and in terms of identity, in addition to a personal sense that Gaelic is important to who she is, she feels part of a local 'Gaelic community ... who speak Gaelic and who do things in Gaelic and attend Gaelic events' as well as part of a broader Gaelic-speaking community in her (strongly Gaelic-speaking) area of family heritage. This pupil's Gaelic language use with peers in a mainly English-medium school within an Anglicised area has thus been achieved through the 'complex interaction of situational, motivational and ideological factors' of which Puigdevall et al (2018: 448) speak, with participation in the Mòd being one part of this broader picture. That this pupil attends the same school as the pupil who noted 'I don't get any opportunities to speak Gaelic to other people – just when I am in my Gaelic class', underlines the importance of a holistic exploration of pupils' individual experiences when exploring language use in minority language contexts. Other Gaelic-medium pupils in our sample achieved such peer Gaelic language use and identification through participation in a range of 'hot' events, not including the Mòd, which indicates the need for a larger study on the circumstances which facilitate peer minority language use.

Discussion and recommendations

Our data from the Welsh context have shown the success of Maes B as a Welsh-medium youth festival. It reflects young people's popular culture in Welsh, and thus provides an authentic and meaningful opportunity for Welsh-speaking young people to use Welsh together naturally. Significantly from the perspective of taking 'ownership' of minority language use – within the 'personal paradigm' (Pujolar and Gonzàlez 2013) – it is the young people themselves that define the linguistic practices, instead of teachers, youth leaders or others leading activities for young people. Maes B provides a time-limited and intensive template as to how young people might live and socialise through the medium of Welsh. Our data from the Scottish context have also shown the success of the National Mòd as a 'hot' event for those pupils participating in language and music competitions, who report the existence of a Gaelic-speaking peer community at the Mòd. However, the comparison of the Welsh and Scottish contexts also highlights an area of possible policy learning for Scotland – namely, the creation of a youth hub at the National Mòd that would run in parallel with the 'competition' side, where a greater number of young people could socialise through Gaelic and engage in the 'Fringe' events such as Gaelic-language bands, irrespective of wider participation in competitions of the National Mòd. A challenge to the organisation of a youth living space in the Scottish context would be that the National Mòd often occurs in urban settings where accommodation is typically in local hotels and B and Bs, rather than camping on the Maes (field), but location-specific solutions could be sought on an annual basis.

Gaelic-speaking youth camping areas could also be considered for key Gaelic-related music festivals such as the Tiree Music Festival or HebCelt, which several pupils reported attending. The former festival already has a 'family campsite' and a 'chill out campsite' in addition to a 'main campsite', for example. Such initiatives would align with Bòrd na Gàidhlig's wish, as expressed in the National Gaelic Language Plan 2018–23, to 'develop initiatives to increase the range of, and participation in, attractive activities and sports' through Gaelic for young people (BnG 2018: 41).

A second finding from our data from the Scottish context relates to the relationship between pupil participation in such 'hot' periodic minority language and culture events and Gaelic language use with peers in everyday local contexts. Although there was alignment between existing local minority language use practices with friends and Gaelic language use at such national 'hot' events for some pupils, for others, minority language use with peers at the Mòd marked a shift from their everyday language practices. While some of these pupils reported a longer-term positive impact on their everyday minority language use with peers as a result of participation in such periodic events, others reported challenges in transferring peer minority language use from such 'hot' events into their everyday lives. The exploration of the latter pupils' language use, using Puigdevall et al's (2018) tripartite model of situational, identity and motivational factors, underlined the complexity of youth minority language use, and the challenges of evaluating the impact of pupil participation in such minority language civil society events. Our findings showed that different pupils experience similar opportunities or contexts very differently depending on their identities, attitudes and motivations (for example, the two pupils from the same school in the Scottish context), and that different pupils have different patterns of participation in minority language events, with some participating in one key event (for example, the Mòd) and others participating in a range of events.

Thus, our exploration of the impact of the National Eisteddfod and National Mòd as 'hot' events that may reflect, maintain or modify Celtic-medium pupils' language attitudes and language use has underlined the need for a larger, longitudinal study of Welsh- and Gaelic-medium pupils which would explore the effects of pupils' participation in multiple minority language experiences – nationally, regionally, locally and online – on their agency in relation to their language use over time. Such a focus on pupil language practices 'across space and time' (Hult 2010: 7) reflects a broader shift in the language planning literature to explore the importance of meso- and micro-level contexts in addition to macro-level contexts (Johnson and Ricento 2013), and reflects a growing interest in the contextual and ideological processes involved in speakers of lesser used languages developing the agency to use these languages (Bouchard and Glasgow 2018; Glasgow and Bouchard 2018; Liddicoat and Taylor-Leech 2020). The research would enable us to explore how participation in 'hot' minority language and cultural experiences relate to other 'hot' and more 'banal' minority language experiences – noting that young people will evaluate the relative salience or banality of experiences differently in accordance with their individual interests and circumstances – and would also enable us to explore language and identity investment associated with participation in different 'models' of social language use. For example, young people may participate in Eisteddfods, Urdds, Mòds and other Celtic-language hobbies that have a local to regional to national competition format, in lots of local events and/ or in several national events (for example, large Welsh-language festivals such as Maes B and the Cardiff Tafwyl Festival or smaller national events such as the Gaelic drama summer school and activity camps). The mundane and the extraordinary are likely to combine in different ways for different students, and there is a need to understand the ways in which these inform one another in terms of the development of young people's attitudes, ideologies, identities or language practices in order both to inform future policy and provision for Welsh and Gaelic at local, regional and national levels, and to evaluate the impact of civil society contributions to creating opportunities for social minority language use in Wales and Scotland (Lewis and Royles 2018; Royles et al 2019).

Two broader issues arise in relation to the themes discussed in this chapter. First, we need to reflect on the ways in which potentially negative associations of minority language promotion within different settings is changing. While minority languages may well have contributed in the past to the formation of divisions within civil society, awareness and recognition of their inclusive potential to act as facilitators of social interaction and positive identity formation is growing. Recent policy statements in relation to race equality and minority languages, and recent academic research on such themes, emphasise this positive potential (for example, Jones and Royles 2020b). Consequently, attention should be given in future work to reflecting on initiatives to increase access to the Welsh language by ethnic communities via civil society activities in order to enhance this agenda in Wales and beyond. Second, we need to reflect on the broader potential offered by 'hotter' or occasional events in helping to create positive links within civil society. Much research in this area tends to focus on the importance of the quotidian reinforcement of common sets of experiences: ones that have the potential to lead to common senses of belonging. However, our discussion in this chapter highlights the need to reflect on the significance of 'hotter' and more occasional events in creating social interaction, trust and common identities between different groups of people (compare Closs Stephens 2016). That is not to say that such events should be viewed as silver bullets that can overcome social and cultural divisions within society. Rather, it points to the need to examine their potential in more detail, particularly as ways of reinforcing the daily and more mundane forms of socialisation promoted by other institutions.

Note

[1] The interviews were conducted by Dyfan Powel in the Welsh case and by Kirstie MacLeod in the Scottish case, the two post-doctoral researchers on the project.

References

ACG (An Comunn Gàidhealach) (2020) *An Comunn Gàidhealach: History.* Available at: https://www.ancomunn.co.uk/about/history

Aitchison, J. W. and Carter, H. (2000) *Language, Economy and Society: The changing fortunes of the Welsh language in the twentieth century,* Cardiff: University of Wales Press.

Baker, C. (2011) *Foundations of Bilingual Education and Bilingualism,* Clevedon: Multilingual Matters.

Billig, M. (1995) *Banal Nationalism,* London: SAGE.

BnG (Bòrd na Gàidhlig) (2007) *The National Plan for Gaelic 2007–2012,* Inverness: Bòrd na Gàidhlig.

BnG (2012) *National Gaelic Language Plan: Growth and improvement,* Inverness: Bòrd na Gàidhlig.

BnG (2018) *National Gaelic Language Plan 2018–23,* Inverness: Bòrd na Gàidhlig. Available at: https://bit.ly/3kWvMMO

BnG (2020) *Pupil Numbers in Gaelic Education 2019–20,* Inverness: Bòrd na Gàidhlig.

Bouchard, J. and Glasgow, G. P. (2018) *Agency in Language Policy and Planning: Critical inquiries,* New York: Routledge.

Brent, J. (2009) *Searching for Community: Representation, power and action on an urban estate,* Bristol: Policy Press.

Closs Stephens, A. (2016) 'The affective atmospheres of nationalism', *Cultural Geographies,* 23: 181–198.

Cormack, M. and Hourigan, N. (2007) *Minority Language Media: Concepts, critiques and case studies,* Clevedon: Multilingual Matters.

Crystal, D. (2000) *Language Death,* Cambridge: Cambridge University Press.

Crystal, D. (2011) *Internet Linguistics,* Abingdon: Routledge.

Cunliffe, D. (2007) 'Minority languages and the internet: New threats, new opportunities', in M. Cormack and N. Hourigan (eds), *Minority Language Media: Concepts, critiques and case studies,* Clevedon: Multilingual Matters, pp 133–150.

Cunliffe, D., Morris, D. and Prys, C. (2013) 'Young bilinguals' language behaviour in social networking sites: The use of Welsh on Facebook', *Journal of Computer-mediated Communication,* 18: 339–361.

Dean, L., O'Hanlon, F., Hinchcliffe, S., Scholes, A., Curtice, J., Whitford, R., Wilson, V., Standing-Tattersall, C. and Daniels-Creasy, A. (2022) *Scottish Social Attitudes Survey 2021: Public Attitudes to Gaelic in Scotland*, Edinburgh: ScotCen Social Research.

Devine, T. (2000) *The Scottish Nation 1700–2000*, London: Penguin.

Dunbar, R. (2007) 'Scotland: Language legislation for Gaelic', *Cambrian Law Review*, 38: 39–82.

Ferguson, G. (2006) *Language Planning and Education*, Edinburgh: Edinburgh University Press.

Fishman, J. (1991) *Reversing Language Shift: Theoretical and empirical foundations of assistance to threatened languages*, Clevedon: Multilingual Matters.

Fishman, J. (2001) *Can Threatened Languages Be Saved? Reversing language shift revisited: A 21st century perspective*, Clevedon: Multilingual Matters.

Gebel, K. (2002) *Language and ethnic national identity in Europe: The importance of Gaelic and Sorbian to the maintenance of associated cultures and ethno cultural identities.* Unpublished PhD thesis, Middlesex University.

Giles, H., Bourhis, R. Y. and Taylor, D. M. (1977) 'Towards a theory of language in ethnic group relations', in H. Giles (ed.), *Language, Ethnicity and Intergroup Relations*, London: Academic Press, pp 307–348.

Glamis Consultancy and STR (2020) *Evaluation of the Royal National Mòd Glasgow 2019*, Angus: Glamis Consultancy. Available at: https://bit.ly/2TQOlpw

Glasgow, G. P. and Bouchard, J. (2018) *Researching Agency in Language Policy and Planning*, New York: Routledge.

Higham, G. (2020) *Creu Dinasyddiaeth i Gymru: Mewnfudo Rhyngwladol a'r Gymraeg*, Cardiff: University of Wales Press.

Hult, F. (2010) 'Analysis of language policy discourses across the scales of space and time', *International Journal of the Sociology of Language*, 202: 7–24.

Jenkins, G. H. and Williams, M. A. (2000) *Let's Do Our Best for the Ancient Tongue*, Cardiff: University of Wales Press.

Johnson, D. C. and Ricento, T. (2013) 'Conceptual and theoretical perspectives in language planning and policy: Situating the ethnography of language policy', *International Journal of the Sociology of Language*, 219: 7–21.

Jones, D. (1998) *Statistical Evidence Relating to the Welsh Language 1801–1911*, Cardiff: University of Wales Press.

Jones, R. and Fowler, C. (2008) *Placing the Nation: Aberystwyth and the reproduction of Welsh nationalism*, Cardiff: University of Wales Press.

Jones R. and Lewis, H. (2019) *New Geographies of Language: Language, culture and politics in Wales*, Basingstoke: Palgrave.

Jones, R. and Merriman, P. (2009) 'Hot, banal and everyday nationalism: Bilingual road signs in Wales', *Political Geography*, 28(3): 164–173.

Jones, R. and Royles, E. (2020a) 'The state, civil society and the shadow state: Analysing three vectors of relationality', *Geoforum*, 114: 40–48.

Jones, R. and Royles, E. (2020b) 'Reclaiming authenticity: The spaces and scales of national sincerity', *Environment and Planning C: Politics and Space*, 38: 1091–1107.

Laponce, J. A. (2004) 'Minority languages and globalization', *Nationalism and Ethnic Politics*, 10(1): 15–24.

Lewis, D. H. (2017) 'Normative theory's contribution to language policy research', *Journal of Multilingual and Multicultural Development*, 38(7): 577–583.

Lewis, H. and Royles, E. (2018) 'Language revitalization and social transformation: Evaluating the language policy frameworks of sub-state governments in Wales and Scotland', *Policy and Politics*, 46(3): 503–529.

Liddicoat, A. and Taylor-Leech, K. (2020) 'Agency in language planning and policy', *Current Issues in Language Planning*, 22(1–2): 1–18, doi: 10.1080/14664208.2020.1791533

MacKinnon, K. (2010) 'The Gaelic language-group: Demography, language-usage, transmission and shift', in M. Watson and M. MacLeod (eds), *The Edinburgh Companion to the Gaelic Language*, Edinburgh: Edinburgh University Press, pp 129–145.

McCullough, K. L. (2018) 'Resolving the "Highland Problem": The Highlands and Islands of Scotland and the European Union', *Local Economy*, 33(4): 421–437.

McLeod, W. (2004) *Divided Gaels: Gaelic cultural identities in Scotland and Ireland c.1200–c.1650*, Oxford: Oxford University Press.

McLeod, W. (2020) *Gaelic in Scotland: Policies, movements, ideologies*, Edinburgh: Edinburgh University Press.

Mills, S. (2021) *Mapping the Moral Geographies of Education: Character, citizenship and values*, London: Routledge.

Mitchell, R., McIntyre, D., MacDonald, M. and McLennan, J. (1987) *Report of an independent evaluation of the Western Isles' Bilingual Education Project*, Stirling: Department of Education, University of Stirling.

Morris, D. (2007) 'Young people's social networks and language use: The case of Wales', *Sociolinguistic Studies*, 1(3): 435–460.

National Eisteddfod (2003) *National Eisteddfod of Wales: The Way Ahead. Report produced by Stevens Associates*, Cardiff: National Eisteddfod.

National Eisteddfod (2012) *National Eisteddfod Business Plan 2012–2014*, Cardiff: National Eisteddfod.

National Records of Scotland (2015) *Scotland's Census 2011: Gaelic Report (part 2)*, Edinburgh: National Records of Scotland.

Nettle, D. and Romaine, S. (2000) *Vanishing Voices: The extinction of the world's languages*, Oxford: Oxford University Press.

NicLeòid, S. L. (2015) *A' Ghàidhlig agus beachdan nan sgoilearan: cothroman leasachaidh ann am foghlam tro mheadhan na Gàidhlig*, Slèite: Clò Ostaig.

O' Giollagáin, C., Camshron, G., Moireach, P., O Curnáin, B., Caimbeul, I., MacDonald, B. and Péterváry, T. (2020) *The Gaelic Crisis in the Vernacular Community: A comprehensive sociolinguistic survey of Scottish Gaelic*, Aberdeen: Aberdeen University Press.

Ó Riagáin, P. (2000) 'Irish language production and reproduction 1981–1996', in J. A. Fishman (ed.), *Can Threatened Languages Be Saved? Reversing language shift, revisited: A 21st century perspective*, Clevedon: Multilingual Matters.

Ò Riagáin, P., Williams, G. and Vila i Moreno, F. X. (2008) *Young People and Minority Languages: Language use outside the classroom*, Dublin: Trinity College.

Özkırımlı, U. (2000) *Theories of Nationalism: A critical introduction*, Basingstoke: Macmillan.

Paterson, L. and Jones, R. W. (1999) 'Does civil society drive constitutional change? The cases of Wales and Scotland', in B. Taylor and K. Thomson (eds), *Wales and Scotland: Nations again?* Cardiff: University of Wales Press, pp 169–197.

Puigdevall, M., Walsh, J., Amorrortu, E. and Ortega, A. (2018) ' "I'll be one of them": Linguistic mudes and new speakers in three minority language contexts', *Journal of Multilingual and Multicultural Development*, 39(5): 445–457.

Pujolar, J. and Gonzàlez, I. (2013) 'Linguistic "mudes" and the de-ethnicization of language choice in Catalonia', *International Journal of Bilingual Education and Bilingualism*, 16(2): 138–152.

Raffe, D. (2005) 'Learning from "home international" comparisons: 14–19 curriculum and qualifications reform in England, Scotland and Wales', *Policy Learning in 14–19 Education Seminar*. Available at: https://bit.ly/34UtWXc

Raffe, D., Brannen, K., Croxford, L. and Martin, C. (1999) 'Comparing England, Scotland, Wales and Northern Ireland: The case for "home internationals" in comparative research', *Comparative Education*, 35(1): 9–25.

Robertson, B. (2003) 'Gaelic education', in T. G. K. Bryce and W. Humes (eds), *Scottish Education: Second edition, post-devolution*, Edinburgh: Edinburgh University Press, pp 250–261.

Royles, E. (2007) *Revitalising Democracy: Devolution and civil society in Wales*, Cardiff: University of Wales Press.

Royles, E., O'Hanlon, F. and Jones, R. (2019) 'Evaluation, impact and outcomes in working with children and young people in regional and minority revitalization efforts'. Workshop Briefing Report. Available at: https://bit.ly/386DksB

Scottish Government (2020) *Pupil Census 2019: Supplementary tables*, Edinburgh: Scottish Government.

Silverman, D. (2004) *Interpreting Qualitative Data: Methods for analysing talk, text and interaction*, London: SAGE.

Spencer, L., Ritchie, J., Ormston, R., O' Connor, W. and Barnard, M. (2013a) 'Analysis: Principles and processes', in J. Ritchie, L. Spencer, C. M. Nicholls and R. Ormston (eds), *Qualitative Research Practice*, London: SAGE, pp 269–294.

Spencer, L., Ritchie, J., O' Connor, W., Morrell, G. and Ormston, R. (2013b) 'Analysis in practice', in J. Ritchie, L. Spencer, C. M. Nicholls and R. Ormston (eds), *Qualitative Research Practice*, London: SAGE, pp 295–346.

Statistics for Wales (2012) *2011 Census: First results on the Welsh language*, Cardiff: Welsh Government.

StatsWales (2020) *Pupils by local authority, region and Welsh medium type.* Available at: https://bit.ly/3k3TxB8

Stiùbhart, M. (2011) 'Cainnt nan deugairean', in R. Cox and T. Armstrong (eds), *A' Cleachdadh na Gàidhlig: Slatan-tomhais ann an dìon cànain sa choimhearsnachd*, Slèite: Clò Ostaig, pp 275–282.

Thomas, B. (1987) 'A cauldron of rebirth: Population and the Welsh language in the nineteenth century', *Welsh History Review*, 13: 418–437.

Thomas, E. M. and Roberts, D. B. (2011) 'Exploring bilinguals' social use of language inside and out of the minority language classroom', *Language and Education*, 25(2): 89–108.

Tsunoda, T. (2005) *Language Endangerment and Language Revitalization*, Berlin: Walter de Gruyter.

Vila i Moreno, F. X., Ubalde, J., Brexta, V. and Comajoan-Colomé, L. (2018) 'Changes in language use with peers during adolescence: A longitudinal study in Catalonia', *International Journal of Bilingual Education and Bilingualism*, 23(9): 1158–1173.

WAG (Welsh Assembly Government) (2002) *Bilingual Future: A policy statement by the Welsh Assembly Government*, Cardiff: Welsh Assembly Government.

WAG (2003) *Iaith Pawb: A national action plan for a bilingual Wales*, Cardiff: Welsh Assembly Government.

WAG (2010) *Welsh-medium education strategy*, Cardiff: Welsh Assembly Government.

Welsh Government (2013) *Report and recommendations of the National Eisteddfod Task and Finish Group*, Cardiff: Welsh Government. Available at: https://gov.wales/sites/default/files/publications/2018-12/national-eisteddfod-task-and-finish-group-report-and-recommendations.pdf

Welsh Government (2014) *A living language: A language for living: Moving forward – policy statement*, Cardiff: Welsh Government.

Welsh Government (2015) *Welsh language use in Wales, 2013–15*, Cardiff: Welsh Government.

Welsh Government (2017) *Cymraeg 2050: A million Welsh speakers*, Cardiff: Welsh Government.

Welsh Government (2018) *Cymraeg 2050: Annual report 2017–18*, Cardiff: Welsh Government. Available at: https://gov.wales/sites/default/files/publications/2019-03/cymraeg-2050-a-million-welsh-speakers-annual-report-2017-18.pdf

Welsh Government (2021) *Anti-racist Wales: The Race Equality Action Plan for Wales*, Cardiff: Welsh Government. Available at: https://gov.wales/sites/default/files/consultations/2021-03/race-equality-action-plan-an-anti-racist-wales_2.pdf

Williams, C. H. (2015) 'Cultural rights and democratization: Legislative devolution and the enactment of the official status of Welsh in Wales', in I. Urrutia, J. Massia and X. Irujo (eds), *Droits Culturels et Démocratisation/ Cultural Rights and Democratisation*, Institut Universitaire Varenne, pp 183–203.

6

Digital threat or opportunity? Local civil society in an age of global inter-connectivity

Michael Woods, Taulant Guma and Sophie Yarker

Introduction

Writing in the 1960s, the cultural theorist Marshall McLuhan foresaw the emergence of a 'global village' as technology dismantled the significance of distance (McLuhan 1964). The metaphor of the village not only conveyed the proximity of social and economic relations in the new global age, but also indicated the forging of a new universal space of social consciousness, identity and belonging, and collective action. In the ensuing decades, the advent of digital technologies extending far beyond those envisaged by McLuhan has facilitated the articulation of a 'global civil society' (Keane 2003), underpinned by a growth in global consciousness and a globalisation of values, and mediated by transnational institutions and non–governmental organisations (NGOs) (Arts 2004). Most recently, social media technologies have permitted new forms of transnational social mobilisation that can bypass the mediation of institutions and NGOs, as individuals around the world connect and engage directly and instantaneously, further embedding the 'villageness' of global civil society.

It would be tempting to see the corollary of this rise of global civil society as the diminution of local civil society, with the global and the local pitted against each other in a zero–sum game. Certainly, scholars have documented the erosion of traditional structures of civic engagement and lamented the loss of 'community' in parallel with globalisation. Robert Putnam (2000), for instance, described the erosion of bonding social capital and local civil society structures in American communities in his seminal study *Bowling Alone*, which he attributed in part to the atomisation of society under the spell of television and the mass media, even as digital technology was in its infancy. Charts in the appendix of *Bowling Alone* meticulously detailed the falling membership of conventional civic and local social organisations, but also the expansion of national or international campaigning groups. Other observers similarly noted a shift towards more individualistic, nationally mediated and passive forms of social and political participation, coining terms such as 'armchair activism' and 'cheque-book participation'.

Yet, the popular narrative of the emasculation of the local by the global has long been countered by alternative discourses that have emphasised globalisation-as-hybridisation over globalisation-as-homogenisation (Robertson 1992; Pieterse 2003) and pointed to the relational constitution of localities. From a relational perspective, localities, or places, are not stand-alone bounded territories that exist in opposition to the global. Rather, they are formed by the intersection and entanglement of diverse social, economic, cultural and political relations that extend nationally and internationally (Massey 1991, 2005). Local senses of identity, cultural practices and civil society actions have always been coloured and shaped by influences from elsewhere, as captured in Massey's (1991) phrase 'a global sense of place'. The development of advanced digital technologies, including web 2.0 interfaces that facilitate user-generated content and interaction, and various social media platforms and instant messaging services, has further intensified and accelerated the entanglement of the local with the global. This has, on the one hand, introduced competition for local civil society organisations by creating new virtual realms for social, political and civic engagement and by allowing individuals to identify with and participate in distant sites of collective action; but, at the same time, it has also enabled the 'stretching' over space of communities with participation by individuals resident elsewhere (such as out-migrants), facilitated access to new resources, prompted new forms of organising, and contributed to a reworking of local identities and cultures through 'digital place-making' (Gordon and de Souza e Silva 2011; Halegoua and Polson 2021).

Far from being supplanted by global civil society, local civil society is being reconfigured in globalisation, with potentially new areas of concern, new groups and organisations, and new ways of working and mobilising, but nonetheless an enduring presence and significance. In this chapter we focus in particular on the contribution of digital technologies, especially social media, to these dynamics of reconfiguration of local civil society. Through examining evidence from case studies of local civil society groups in three localities in Wales, UK – Aberystwyth, Cardiff and Swansea – we consider how digital technologies shape the articulation of issues within local civil society by increasing awareness of global events and processes; how digital technologies have impacted on the ways in which local civil society groups operate and organise within their localities; and how digital technologies have enabled local civil society groups to forge connections beyond their locale. This analysis is presented in the latter part of the chapter, followed by a conclusion in which we reflect on the challenges and opportunities for local civil society from digital technologies. First, however, the next section positions the empirical research in the broader context of the international academic literature.

Digital technology and civil society: perspectives from the international literature

The impacts of digital technologies for civil society organisations and movements have been extensively documented in the academic literature. Studies have generally emphasised the positive dimensions of digital technology in expanding the capacity of civil society organisations to extend their reach, network and access to additional resources. The potential for creating new spaces and structures for civil society mobilisation in non-democratic states or countries with constrained or weak civil societies has been especially noted (Harrison 2014; Kumar and Thapa 2015; Faith and Prieto-Martin 2016; Armstrong and Butcher 2018; Dennis and Hall 2020), but research has also explored the augmentation of conventional civil society activities by digital technologies in mature democracies. Thapliyal (2018), for example, documented the use of digital media by grassroots public education advocates in the United States to amplify local campaigning, share knowledge and expertise, and build a collective identity through social media accounts such as Parents Across America and United Opt Out National, as well as Facebook-coordinated school walkouts.

The upscaling of civil society activity and the creation of translocal alliances is a repeated theme. Crepaz (2020) argues that digital technologies facilitated a bottom-up 'Europeanization' of civil society activism during the 'refugee crisis' of 2015, with social media allowing grassroots activists to exchange information and coordinate activities across regions and nations and to directly lobby politicians at different scales, and the internet providing a forum for disseminating alternative discourses that challenged anti-migration representations. Other studies have described the mobilisation of transnational, digital-based campaigns, such as the marshalling of international support behind opposition to a planned military base in South Korea (Schattle 2015), or transnational social media campaigns on animal welfare, environmental and ethical consumption issues (Dauvergne and Neville 2011; Parigi and Gong 2014; Pillay and Maharaj 2015).

While digital technologies equip civil society groups with new capacities and resources, they can also present challenges to the established structure and working practices of civil society organisations, including transnational NGOs. The accessibility of digital tools has empowered a global movement of autonomous activists, who are able to create their own content, make connections and target political leaders, corporations and institutions directly, without mediation by civil society organisations or the conventional media (Parigi and Gong 2014; Pillay and Maharaj 2015; Dennis and Hall 2020;

Haussler 2021; Ozkula 2021). The increasing autonomy of digital activists has, in turn, forced established civil society organisations to rethink their organisational structures, membership models, planning processes and communications strategies, as Ozkula's (2021) study of Amnesty International and Pillay and Maharaj's (2015) study of Greenpeace demonstrate. As the relationship between civil society organisations and individual activists are refashioned, Tatarchevskiy (2011: 298) argues that a new division of labour has been created, in which 'organizational "experts" take care of the mechanics of activism while lay citizens contribute ... "visual labor"', creating representations online that legitimise the organisation's claims. At the same time, online communities and social media platforms provide consumers for the voluminous content produced by autonomous digital activists, creating 'an audience for private actions' (Parigi and Gong 2014: 250) that transforms individual atomised citizenship into collective civil society mobilisation.

There are, however, limitations to the efficacy of digital civil society activism that reflect spatially contingent unequal distribution of resources, institutional structures and power relations in the non-virtual world, which conventional civil society organisations may be best placed to overcome (Harrison 2014; Couldry et al 2014; Schattle 2015; Dennis and Hall 2020). Moreover, for many, online and 'offline' participation with civil society groups are not alternatives but mutually reinforcing activities. Mercea (2012) found that prefigurative engagement with a civil society group online increased the likelihood of participation in 'offline' events, which by definition are grounded in specific spaces and places.

Indeed, rather than presenting a threat to local civil society, there is a strong argument that digital technologies offer opportunities to rejuvenate local civil society by providing tools through which disconnected residents can be engaged, information exchanged and actions planned, external resources enrolled, narratives constructed and shared, and new community identities articulated. Examples documented in recent research include the use of social media to coordinate local volunteer networks in Greece (Theocharis et al 2017), contest narratives around the impacts of AirBnB expansion in Barcelona (Garay et al 2020), and recruit translocal support for a labour dispute at hotels in Texas (Brady et al 2015). Gordon and de Souza e Silva (2011: 108) further observe that:

> There has been rapid growth in the use of locally oriented online social spaces, such as online forums, virtual worlds, and location-aware applications for phones. These online spaces are factoring into everyday life in neighbourhoods and reorganizing the traditional relationships of neighbor to neighbor. ... These new platforms for social interaction reconfigure the way people engage with each other in their local communities.

For Gordon and de Souza e Silva, the role of digital technologies in re-engaging people, and especially younger people, in civil society cannot be divorced from the spatial contexts in which the engagement occurs, or 'the affordances of net localities on civic action' (p 106). One aspect of this is 'digital place-making', in which digital media technologies, practices and infrastructures are harnessed 'to understand embeddedness within urban places and to foster a unique sense of place within rapidly changing urban environments' (Halegoua and Polson 2021: 574). While this may involve the creation and dissemination of representations of place by individuals through social media, it can also encompass more collective social media interactions by neighbours that reform local civil society by creating new local social networks and articulating new senses of place identity, as for example in Facebook- or WhatsApp-mediated mutual support networks during the COVID-19 pandemic (Hardley and Richardson 2021).

At the same time, the literature cautions that digital technologies are not a panacea for frailties in local civil society. Brown and Dustman (2019) and Gordon and de Souza e Silva (2011) both record obstacles to effective use of digital technologies in community organising, including the differential capacities (and willingness) of individuals to use technologies, risks of 'social network burnout', and inadequately designed platforms that fail to recognise the ongoing importance of physical interaction. These are issues requiring further exploration, as are questions around the use of digital technologies by local civil society organisations, rather than by individuals, and the role of digital technologies in bridging local and global civil society, which have only been partially touched on in the existing literature. This chapter aims to address this gap by examining the use of social media and other digital technologies by local civil society groups that explicitly connect local action with issues of global concern.

Case studies and methods

This chapter draws on research on the reconfiguration of local civil society in an age of global connectivity, undertaken as part of the WISERD Civil Society Research Centre. The research focused on three case study localities selected to represent contrasting geographical settings in Wales: the small university town of Aberystwyth, the inner-city neighbourhood of Splott in Cardiff, and the suburban community of Mumbles on the edge of Swansea. Within these case study localities, the research primarily focused on civil society groups involved with issues in areas that we considered represented vectors of interaction between the local and the global: food, the environment and refugees and asylum seekers. Examples of specific groups engaged include food banks, an anti-food waste initiative, community gardening schemes, beach clean groups, conservation groups, a branch of Friends of the Earth, and refugee support groups and centres. In Aberystwyth, the groups engaged tended to be focused on the town, while in Cardiff and Swansea some of the groups had a city-wide reach but were based in or involved significant participation from, the case study districts. Interviews were also conducted with local councillors, civic groups with a broad community remit, and a hyper-local news project in Cardiff.

Semi-structured interviews were completed with a total of 32 participants across 17 civil society organisations, between July 2017 and November 2018, plus a focus group with Friends of the Earth members that included 11 participants. Some were conducted as group interviews and others individually. All the interviews were recorded and transcribed with the informed consent of participants and have been analysed through emic and etic coding. The role of social media and digital technologies was identified as a key theme early in the project from literature review and scoping research and was consequently expressly incorporated into the interview schedule and the coding schema.

Digital media, global consciousness and local civil society engagement

In common with many towns and cities in the UK and internationally, the social dynamics and civil society structures in the three case study localities of Aberystwyth, Cardiff and Swansea have evolved with the deepening of globalisation and other socio-economic changes. All three localities have historically strong civic identities and civil society cultures and, to varying degrees, have long been entwined in transnational flows of trade, migration and knowledge. The tightening of global connectivity, and the advent of new digital technologies in particular, has nonetheless had both positive and negative impacts. One interviewee in Aberystwyth observed that "the whole of west Wales was a bit isolated because we're on the periphery of the UK and the periphery of Europe and perhaps the scene here reflected that, whereas now with globalisation, obviously the internet and everything, it's easier to stay in touch" (Aberystwyth, councillor). Others, however, commented on the perceived weakening of established social networks and sites of engagement within communities, with one Cardiff-based participant lamenting that, "I feel quite heartbroken that the social meeting places are becoming few and far between" (Cardiff, community activist).

The erosion of traditional local civil society structures and spaces in the case study localities pre-dated the arrival of digital technologies and, to a large degree, reflected the wider societal and lifestyle trends identified by Putnam (2000), as well as an upscaling of social and civic engagement from neighbourhood to city-wide networks, especially in Cardiff and Swansea. In this context, some participants saw digital technologies as affording opportunities to rebuild local community identities, through hyper-local platforms. Across the case studies, various Facebook groups, Twitter accounts, online forums and WhatsApp groups had been created at town, neighbourhood or even street level, providing new ways of connecting neighbours and new vehicles for civil society action. Most of the interviewees, though not all, used social media in their everyday lives to communicate with family, friends and neighbours, and this blurred with their use of it in civil society engagement. At the same time, some observed that social media changed dynamics of engagement and participation as well as priorities, especially for younger people. However, while one interviewee expressed concern that social media promoted more atomistic concerns with body image or social standing, rather than wider social or environmental issues, another reflected on how social media interaction had politicised their own children in a recent election.

Both social media and traditional media were regarded as important in increasing global consciousness in the localities and especially in increasing awareness around the issues of the environment, food and refugees on which the case study organisations were focused. A couple of interviewees described their own technology-mediated alertness to global events:

'I get emails every day about Palestine, Syria, politics, and I see them. So that's constantly bringing the world into my home.' (Aberystwyth, refugee action group I4)

'I've got *The Guardian* [newspaper] and the BBC apps on my phone and I get breaking news events, where it used to be I would watch the news at ten o'clock and that would be it. Whereas now I can read the news all day, every day, if I want to, and you just get information overload I think.' (Swansea, refugee action group A I3)

Indeed, the volume and constancy of information about a multitude of global issues transmitted through traditional and social media was recognised as a factor that could deter rather than encourage individual action:

'I think you just become almost numb, don't you? … You try to say to people, you know, even if you only do a little thing it will help, but I think you feel that you won't be able to do big things because it seems to need big solutions.' (Aberystwyth, councillor C2)

'I think in terms of technology maybe bridging the gap between global and local and making things easier to act on, I think that's the case, but then I think the way global issues are communicated through the media and through politics as well, I think it can make things seem overwhelming and too big and leads to people not really doing anything to make a difference.' (Cardiff, environmental group A I1)

Grounding global issues in local concerns and actions can enable individuals to overcome the seemingly insurmountable vastness of the problem and to identify manageable responses. As such, global issues are translated into local civil society actions. For instance, beach clean groups enact a practical and locally grounded way for individuals to respond to concerns about marine pollution triggered by global examples on television natural history documentaries:

'When people see Blue Planet[1] and see plastic pollution on a specific island, then when they go to their beach and they see it happening there, then that's what get's people fired up and doing something about it as well. I don't think one is more important than the other. … Certain people are more locally oriented, and some people think more globally, but to get most people involved and the message across to most people then linking those things up an making it obvious that it's all the same issue, I think is going to get the most people involved.' (Swansea, environmental group A I1)

Several research participants recounted personal biographies that had followed this trajectory, with an affective reaction to global events witnessed over traditional or social media followed up by local civil society engagement. Activists in refugee support groups in both Aberystwyth and Swansea, for example, cited seeing images in social media or on television of Alan Kurdi, a three-year-old Syrian boy photographed lying drowned in the surf on a beach in Turkey in September 2015 after a failed attempt by his refugee family to cross to Greece, as the catalyst for their involvement:

'I started, it was about two and a half years ago now. I saw a picture of Alan Kurdi who was the little boy who got washed up on a beach in Turkey and that deeply affected me, seeing that picture. I've got two little boys. One of them was around the same age and I couldn't imagine how scared I'd have to be to risk that happening to my son … I saw it on Facebook. Then I just knew I wanted to do something to help.' (Swansea, refugee support group B I1)

'It arose out of a group of women, I think … On Facebook during the refugee crisis of 2015 going, oh my God. What can we do? It came from that and they were just going, how do we … and they met each other? I think they actually met each other. None of us actually here, but they met each other through Facebook which tells you about

that. ... There we are. So then they did fundraising. They had events.'
(Aberystwyth, refugee support group I1)

The case of Alan Kurdi, and other evocative images of the 'refugee crisis' in Europe in 2015, hence provides a powerful example of the capacity of digital technologies to connect global and local civil society. Images disseminated through traditional and social media connected individuals in the UK with events in distant parts of the Mediterranean or Eastern Europe, eliciting strong emotional reactions. Yet, faced with distance and the intractability of underlying geopolitics, people responded by seeking local venues for action. Established refugee support groups in Cardiff and Swansea reported surges in donations and offers of help. In Aberystwyth, where no refugee support group existed, the images prompted concerned individuals to come together and form a group, and critically it was Facebook that enabled them to do so. The Aberystwyth group initially focused on fundraising for refugee camps in Calais (with which they were also familiar through media reports), but pivoted to lobbying for and supporting refugee resettlement in Aberystwyth and later directly sponsoring refugee resettlement (see Guma et al 2019).

More widely, digital technologies have not only prompted civil society engagement by raising awareness of global issues, but have also provided the means by which individuals have translated affective responses into action – through researching issues, finding local groups and organisations, or in some cases, accessing the resources and support to convert initial individual actions into collective activities:

'I was still very much on my own. So you would see this sort of sweating, short, Welsh girl at the beach with her Santa sack of rubbish doing it on my own and I thought, right, something has got to give. I have to have help. So I did some internet research and found that the Marine Conversation Society has a structure where they have sea champions ... and that's how I got involved. I asked the local county council for their permission to start organising beach cleans. Then set up social media accounts to let the local public know that this was starting up, and it rolled on from there really.' (Aberystwyth, environmental group A, I1)

Some civil society groups have accordingly deliberately sought to link local and global issues as a strategy for recruitment and raising awareness. Environmental groups in Aberystwyth and Swansea affiliated with the national Surfers Against Sewage (SAS) campaign noted that SAS training materials instructed them to find local examples to ground global issues, while at the same time referring to global issues to frame local actions or to capitalise on the motivational capacity of high-profile international cases.

The connective and interactive character of social media has been central to achieving both these objectives:

> 'We had one of our hashtags as "Protect What You Love" which is asking people, what do you love about Aberystwyth? What do you love about this beach? Not about what do you love about a whole world, sort of thing. It's right here. Right now. So even though they're global issues I think we sort of, in our training manual at least, we're encouraged to make it small for them.' (Aberystwyth, environmental group A, I2)

> 'Social media gives you the ability to be able to take examples of this from India, take examples of this from Australia, North America, wherever. … There's no possible way other than social media conveying the story of a whale that died halfway around the world to the people of Aberystwyth, and then sort of making the connection between this is why we don't want to use single use disposable plastics.' (Aberystwyth, environmental group A, I2)

Use of digital technologies by local civil society groups

Digital technologies have not only raised global awareness and facilitated the mobilisation of local responses to global issues, they have also increasingly been adopted as key elements in the routine operation of local civil society groups. All of the groups researched in the case study localities use digital technology and social media tools to some degree, though with differing emphases and varying levels of enthusiasm. While one environmental group commented that, "we really do rely on it", observing that, "social media has allowed us without spending loads of money to grow our audience, like substantially and quickly and always attracting more new people" (Cardiff, environmental group I1), an interviewee with another environmental group remarked that, "we'll use social media but we're very ambivalent" and suggested that, "if Twitter and Facebook collapsed tomorrow, it would have no impact on our business model, which is exactly how we want it to be" (Swansea, environmental group B, I1).

As Table 6.1 shows, there is significant variation in the specific digital technology tools used by the different groups, which to some degree reflects the age profiles of the key activists. Facebook is the most widely used platform, and arguably the technology with which middle-aged and early retired participants are most comfortable. At least one group observed that they had older members who were not on Facebook, though interestingly they still used a digital technology, email, to communicate with these individuals. Moreover, although one interviewee commented that "if you want to reach youngsters, I'm told you've got to use social media, Facebook" (Aberystwyth, environmental group B, I1), another remarked that Facebook was "getting a bit old school now",

Table 6.1: Use of digital technologies by local civil society groups (at time of interview)

Aberystwyth	Environmental group A	Facebook, Instagram, Twitter
Aberystwyth	Environmental group B	Facebook, website
Aberystwyth	Environmental group C	Facebook
Aberystwyth	Food group A	Facebook, Instagram, website
Aberystwyth	Food group B	Facebook
Aberystwyth	Refugee support group	Facebook, Facebook Messenger, website
Swansea	Community group A	Facebook, Twitter, website
Swansea	Community group B	Facebook, Twitter, website
Swansea	Environmental group A	Facebook, Instagram, Twitter
Swansea	Environmental group B	Facebook, Twitter, website
Swansea	Food group	Facebook, website
Swansea	Refugee support group A	Facebook, website
Swansea	Refugee support group B	Facebook, WhatsApp
Cardiff	Environmental group	Facebook, GoFundMe, Twitter, website
Cardiff	Hyper-local news	Facebook, Instagram, Twitter, website
Cardiff	Refugee support group A	Facebook, Twitter, website
Cardiff	Refugee support group B	Website

but "I don't know what the new thing is" (Swansea, food group A, I1). Groups initiated by younger activists, such as the SAS–affiliated groups in Aberystwyth and Swansea and the Aberystwyth Food Surplus Project, were more likely to use Instagram or Twitter. The relatively maturity of the organisation was also significant in shaping digital engagement. Groups that had been spawned from, or remained connected with, established civil society organisations such as churches were among the most limited users of social media, possibly because they had means of recruiting members, communicating information and organising events through more conventional methods. In contrast, newer initiatives that were essentially 'digital natives' in having started online also made greater use of social media in their everyday operation.

Significantly, many of the interviewees demonstrated relatively nuanced understanding of the different formats and qualities of different social media technologies and their suitability for reaching different audiences and communicating different types of information. This understanding informed decisions about which tools were used by civil society groups and for what purpose:

'Twitter is very organisational and middle class generally speaking, and Facebook is much less organisational and much more, I wouldn't say it's class-based Facebook, I'd say it's more generic. But yes, Twitter is very organisational. I mean you could look at the followers on our Twitter page and the majority would be organisations not individuals. ... We use Twitter for organisational networking and promotion and we use Facebook for members of the public or our participants, so two completely separate platforms.' (Swansea, environmental group B I1)

'For beach clean promotion it is Facebook really. I do do a little bit of Twitter and Instagram. I've found Twitter can sort of help to alert some media or some politicians, but in terms of actually just getting people out it is Facebook.' (Swansea, environmental group A I1)

'I find the audience is very different on Facebook and Twitter and Instagram actually. Facebook is mostly people over 40 responding or teenagers with videos. Posting a video. Then it'll get shared a lot by teenagers. Twitter is like your professional type of demographic. I don't know. Twenty-five to 40 I think, and I'll put exactly the same thing on Facebook and Twitter and I'll have like 25 likes and maybe 12 shares on Twitter for an average run of the mill story. Then on Facebook there will be fairly little activity, and then I'll put something out again, the same thing and Facebook.' (Cardiff, hyper-local news initiative I1)

Instagram, although not widely used by the case study groups, was recognised as a primarily visual medium. As such, it was regarded as useful for creating content that could attract attention and reinforce narratives about place (compare Tatarchevskiy 2011), but less appropriate for organising events:

'Instagram is very visual and it's just really images, isn't it? It's great for showing what the project is doing and where it's going. It's not necessarily a great tool if you want to volunteer, putting out a call like that I don't think it would work very well like that, but it is good ... I don't know. I would connect better with that than I would Twitter say, because I'm quite a visual young person.' (Aberystwyth, food group A I1)

'It is image based. Instagram is a hard thing to measure and make direct impact from, because it doesn't encourage click-through. So you don't necessarily get people doing anything after it. It's typically a conversation on Instagram around that post. So just the way it's set up doesn't suit so well as the whole Facebook setup of having an event and getting people who can share that. Of getting who can be invited to it and invite their friends. People who can say they're going to it. Instagram just doesn't have that going on for it. It can work to do a lot of work around awareness, but I haven't got the time to do that on a local level.' (Swansea, environmental group A I1)

'It's all about the picture first on Instagram. It's all about the picture. They're linking into a story and a message and quite often people get an emotion through with that, but then on Twitter it's more about that quick kind of retweet, maybe it is a picture, maybe it's a link. It's not so. You know, you've got to just get it in a really snappy thing. It's got to get people to retweet it. Then on Facebook it's somewhere in between. You can tell a bit of the story that you might have done in that, but again it's more about getting people to share that event or like that post or engage with it or comment on it.' (Cardiff, environmental group I1)

The potential for the same content to reach different audiences and achieve different impacts on different platforms was further emphasised by the editor of a hyper-local news site in Cardiff. He recalled an attempted mugging that had been foiled by the actions of a passer-by who had subsequently wanted to raise awareness of crime in the community: "I put that out on Twitter, barely blinked. Facebook, I think I had something like 25,000 views and 20 shares. It just kept going and going and going and people were tagging other people because they were concerned about their friends" (Cardiff, hyper-local news initiative I1).

Almost all of the groups maintained a website or a Facebook page as a 'virtual shop front' (Harrison 2014), through which they could be found, yet none actively ran online recruitment campaigns, perhaps relying on the wider media or national organisations to trigger interest. As issue-oriented groups they also tended to be less interested in recruiting members than with attracting participants to events, with social media forming the primary vehicle for event promotion. Several commented that social media had displaced offline advertising:

'I think that's the main way we advertise the events and we also have an email list actually. So website, email list, Facebook page. We have always put up posters in places. Do you look at posters? I don't look at posters anymore. I think I get much more reminded by Facebook. So it has been useful. I don't know how. It seems a long time ago, but before Facebook and email, what would we have done. Sent people letters or leaflets, I suppose.' (Aberystwyth, refugee support group I4)

'To get those kind of people to a beach clean we might or might not put a couple of posters up, but apart from that it's social media. That's how people find out about it.' (Swansea, environmental group A I1)

'We used to do posters. We've stopped doing posters. We've stopped doing any printed media. We'd have to have a really good reason to go back to doing that, and you can see as our workshops are always full at the moment with our capacity we don't need to go outside.' (Cardiff, environmental group I1)

Apart from cost and convenience and the capacity for social media posts to be shared by others, extending reach, social media also enables civil society groups to organise and publicise events quickly. Members of a refugee action group in Swansea gave the example of a vigil held for an asylum seeker who had committed suicide, organised on WhatsApp. "An event like that without WhatsApp would have been really hard", one commented, with another adding, "It would take you at least two days, but through WhatsApp we tell them today, this event. Next day they came, everyone".

The speed of response on social media is also significant in its use by food banks, refugee support groups and others to solicit donations, either financial or material, frequently generating responses within hours or days:

'So in those days it would have been the old personal go out and meet people routine. Whereas now we can get a very instant response just by putting something on Facebook.' (Aberystwyth, food group B I1)

'We meet a new family who the wife is pregnant and the baby is due in three months. They need X, Y and Z. So we'll put a shout out, we call it, on Facebook to say that we've got a family. So within two or three days we got it because people will see it and say, I've got one in the attic or sometimes I'll buy one. I'll drop it off to you. So there's an immediacy there which is great.' (Swansea, refugee support group B I3)

Internal communication within local civil society groups has similarly been accelerated and simplified by Facebook, email, and networking apps such as WhatsApp and Facebook Messenger, as several interviewees testified:

'It's far easier to communicate with people now because you can send off an email. You can put something on Facebook or something on Twitter, and you can reach a lot of people instantaneously. So any messages we want to get out it is the quickest and most efficient way of doing it, because we know that people will get it literally just like that.' (Swansea, community group I1)

'People they don't bother to read letters or emails, but through WhatsApp online because they read it and if they feel to respond straightaway they respond. So it's fast communication and sometimes also they see people, what they might say and they might do.' (Swansea, refugee support group B I1)

'You can tell all the Committee members very easily what happened yesterday ... Just send them an email, but in the past how these groups functioned you relied on the Secretary. I can't remember. You know, how do you call a meeting? Did the Secretary ring everybody up? Send them all a letter?' (Aberystwyth, environmental group B I1)

The agility afforded to local civil society decision-making by digital technologies has been particularly significant for the participation by the Aberystwyth refugee support group in the UK government's Community Sponsorship scheme for refugees:

'We were warned about that, because there's a group ... one of the other groups that is sponsoring a family could not make decisions until all of them got into the same room and had a vote, and that delayed things so much that we were told, make sure that you've got a system of being able to make decisions quickly. So now the three of us can make an important decision without having to ask the rest of them. That happened yesterday. ... We can make decisions online as a Trustee Group within minutes.' (Aberystwyth, refugee support group I1)

The flexibility and alacrity of digital technologies accordingly not only provides local civil society groups with new tools and resources, but also potentially new ways of organising civil society that are less constrained by the formalised structures of older groups and more open to collaboration and interactive participation. The couple of groups studied that did not have their own website or Facebook page had a presence on the Facebook sites of other organisations and linked content is commonplace, as is the sharing or re-tweeting of content such as event publicity, increasing reach. An environmental activist explained that for their participation, "there's no boundaries with regards to whether or not its Aberystwyth Beach Buddies, or Marine Conservation Society, or Surfers Against Sewage, or anybody else ... they're all hashtags" (Aberystwyth, environmental group A I2). The interlocking nature of social media accounts reinforces local–global connectivity, with international content shared locally, and local content picked up nationally and internationally, as the interviewee continued: "[X] would quite regularly take a picture of the marine litter problem here in Aberystwyth, [and] share or hashtag with maybe 20 different campaigns" (Aberystwyth, environmental group A I2).

For refugee support groups, the widespread use of social media by refugees and asylum seekers has helped to forge a relationship that departs from the paternalism of traditional welfare organisations, affording an agency to refugees to influence the group's activities as well as a further conduit for bringing international events into local civil society. In one example, the connectivity of refugees in Aberystwyth led to a grounded action in the town facilitated by the support group:

'The Syrian refugees are quite a lot on their mobile phones, Facebook, checking up what's going on in Syria, and before Christmas ... the Syrian refugees wanted to highlight the plight of Eastern Ghouta, just outside of Damascus. So they decided that they were going to make a soup which they called ... "siege soup", because Eastern Ghouta is under siege. So they made a very simple soup and we stood on the corner [of] Owain Glyndwr Square. We stood on the corner and handed out the soup, and the reception was very good.' (Aberystwyth, refugee support group I2)

The external reach of local civil society

Digital technologies can serve to ground global issues in local civil society, but as implied in some of the examples discussed above, they can also take local civil society concerns and campaigns out to external audiences, beyond the locality. "You've got instant communication and it is worldwide as well", noted one interviewee, "anything you put out is there to be seen by the whole world" (Swansea, community group I1). Another commented that, "if someone ha[s] an idea locally somewhere that's really good ... and if they communicate that effectively ... the project starts in one place and it works really well that can spread to other places" (Cardiff, environmental group I1).

Many of the groups studied had subscribers to their social media content that lived outside the locality, many of them former residents who sought to remain part of a stretched translocal community, but not all. These external contacts can form resources that may be mobilised to support local civil society objectives in several ways. For example, when an environmental group in Swansea was nominated for Best Education Project in the National Lottery Awards, determined by a public vote, it used social media to campaign for support. In another instance, a refugee support group in Swansea has received donations from churches in London who had read about their activities. As a member observed, "social media gets things a lot further" (Swansea, refugee support group B I2).

The external reach of local civil society through social media can also help to amplify local issues and campaigns, make connections to broader national and transnational movements, and attract publicity. When a refused asylum seeker committed suicide in Swansea, an activist in a refugee support group wrote a post on the group's Facebook page detailing the system failings that had led to the tragedy, which went viral:

> 'When [X] died I put on a post to tell people what had happened. I think it got shared three and a half thousand times, and there were loads of messages and things like that that, you could get the truth of a story out more than you could without social media.' (Swansea, refugee support group B I2)

The post alerted the BBC and ITV, who covered the story, and attracted responses from Australia, South Africa and Ethiopia. In another case, the activities of a food surplus group in Aberystwyth were covered by a London-based news website by a writer who had been at school with one of the group's participants, but who had found the story through social media: "That must have been through social media, because I don't talk to her anymore. I don't ever see her. I've not spoken to her in years, but I must have her on Facebook" (Aberystwyth, food group A I3).

More quietly and routinely, social media also allows local civil society activists to connect with other individuals involved with similar groups and campaigns in other places, providing mutual support and countering the potential isolation of seeking to mobilise on specific issues in small communities:

> 'It's a global community of local individuals, but in terms of social media, I'm concentrating on the social media particularly Instagram because I find that it can get quite depleting doing this work, and I find it really helpful to engage with other people who are doing exactly the same thing in their little seaside resorts or their big city resort or wherever. You know, they're doing the same things, and we feed off each other. We relay information with each other.' (Aberystwyth, environmental group A I1).

Limitations of digital technologies in local civil society

Digital technologies have afforded many opportunities to local civil society groups, but there are also challenges and limitations. Several interviewees mentioned the time and effort required to manage social media channels and to stay on top of queries, responses and changing content. Lack of time and expertise was cited by some as reasons for not doing more with social media, and in some groups digital tools were managed by one or two individuals and thus were highly vulnerable to their leaving. Furthermore, while social media was commonly regarded as a low cost means of communication, some participants noted increasing efforts by social media providers to push premium services. Although geographically targeted Facebook ads were praised by one group as a cheap and effective way of publicising activities, another interviewee expressed frustration that "I don't feel like my posts are getting as far as they could do, because … Facebook in particular, is always asking you to pay and boost your post … as a community organisation we're not in the position to do that, plus I don't want to give Facebook money" (Cardiff, environmental group I1).

There can also be frustration at the depth of engagement online, with some interviewees questioning how many new participants in activities were really recruited through social media, one observing that, "if we organise an event … 50 or 60 people sign up on the events page on Facebook saying yes, they will attend, and [I] get there and ask for a show of hands of how many people have come through Facebook, in this one particular incident, I can see no one" (Aberystwyth, environmental group C I1). As the same participant commented, the aspatial character of social media can give a false perspective of local support: "You kind of automatically think we've got 100, 200 people interested, but you know 200 people aren't coming to meetings and they could be anywhere."

At the same time, over-reliance on social media can exclude members of local communities that are not online, especially elderly residents. Even more technically attuned community members can miss out on events and activities that are only advertised digitally if they do not check the right Facebook pages or subscribe to the right Twitter accounts or WhatsApp groups, reflecting Gordon and de Souza e Silva's (2011) warning of a new digital 'participation gap' 'where it is no longer a matter of simply having the technology, but knowing what to do with it' (p 111; after Jenkins 2006). The ephemerality of online organisation, lacking a physical presence in a community, can also be problematic, with the Aberystwyth food surplus group deciding to move from an initial digital existence to securing a café premises in the town:

> 'I think that … would be more beneficial than Facebook because it's something that's present and it's visual and it's engaging. Whereas I think on the Facebook if we were to carry on with the pop-up style of things I think it's quite … You can feel quite distant from something in your own town maybe, and … you could easily not go to something that's on Facebook, but if you're walking past it on the day and you think, oh I'm going to go there later, I feel that's much more engaging than just being online.' (Aberystwyth, food group A I3)

Finally, social media can expose local civil society groups in ways not encountered historically. Several interviewees reported experiences of trolling online, with refugee support groups in particular targeted with racist and xenophobic abuse. "I think that it's easier for people online to say things that they would never say to your face", one reflected. "People have said awful things. So now I don't read it. If there's a story in the newspaper and they'll print my name or something, I won't read any of the comments underneath, because I did once and it was awful" (Swansea, refugee support group B I2). As the anonymity afforded by social media extends to location as well as personal identity, civil society groups cannot be certain whether criticism comes from within the community, or from outsiders, with or without links to the locality. One interviewee noted how a post about refugee support work on a councillor's Facebook page had attracted critical comments, but observed, "Apparently a lot of people follow his Facebook page who don't even live in Aberystwyth. They just come here on holiday. I don't know" (Aberystwyth, refugee support group I4). As a consequence, some of the groups have become cautious about what they post online and how they engage with traditional and social media, in some cases moving to closed Facebook and WhatsApp groups.

Conclusion

The development of digital technologies has contributed significantly to the reconfiguration of local civil society in the age of global connectivity. Yet, fears that increased global awareness, mobility and interaction, with the accompanying rise of global civil society, would accelerate the diminution of local identities and local civil society action have not been realised. As Halegoua and Polson (2021: 574) argue, 'instead of depleting a sense of place, the ability to forge attachments to digital media environments and through digital practices enables people to emplace themselves and others'. By examining the engagement of different civil society groups with a range of different digital technologies across three case study localities, this research has obtained a broader perspective than many previous studies, yet its findings both chime with and extend arguments in the international literature.

Digital technologies have raised consciousness of global issues and distant events, yet many individuals respond to the enormity of such problems through grounded actions in their own localities, reconnecting with local civil society organisations or forming new groups oriented around issues such as environmental change, food and refugees. Moreover, digital technologies enable individuals to make these connections and reinforce local–global connections by allowing local civil society actors to access external resources and amplify their concerns to translocal audiences. At the same time, digital technologies have also introduced new ways for civil society groups to mobilise within communities, enhancing the agility of local civil society.

However, the opportunities afforded by digital technologies to local civil society have been accompanied by challenges: demands on time and expertise, ambivalent online contacts, exposure to abuse and criticism, and risks of a new digital participation gap, with engagement in local civil society fragmented by uneven access to technology and information. These are the real 'digital threats' to local civil society. To ensure that the benefits of digital technologies outweigh the threats, civil society groups and the organisations that support them need to be alert to the challenges and develop responses. Attention should be given to the skills and competences of civil society actors and to building sustainable technological capacity within groups, to enhancing understanding of the potential and limitations of specific tools and platforms, and to raising awareness of dangers such as online abuse and trolling, as well as to the need to continue to engage residents who are not digitally connected. Indeed, it should be remembered that the greatest asset of local civil society is that it is embedded in real places and that, as such, digital technologies are most effective and empowering when they are used to reinforce and not replace the physical coming together of community members.

Note

[1] An acclaimed BBC television wildlife documentary series, presented and narrated by Sir David Attenborough.

References

Armstrong, C. and Butcher, C. (2018) 'Digital civil society: How Nigerian NGOs utilize social media platforms', *International Journal of Politics, Culture and Society*, 31(3): 251–273.

Arts, B. (2004) 'The global-local nexus: NGOs and the articulation of scale', *Tijdschrift voor Economische en Sociale Geografie*, 95: 498–510.

Brady, S. R., Young, J. A. and McLeod, D. A. (2015) 'Utilizing digital advocacy in community organizing: Lessons learned from organizing in virtual spaces to promote worker rights and economic justice', *Journal of Community Practice*, 23(2): 255–273.

Brown, M. E. and Dustman, P. A. (2019) 'Identifying a project's greatest 'hits': Meaningful use of Facebook in an underserved community's development and mobilisation effort', *Journal of Social Work Practice*, 33(2): 185–200.

Couldry, N., Stephenson, H., Fotopoulou, A., McDonald, R., Clark, W. and Dickens, L. (2014) 'Digital citizenship? Narrative exchange and the changing terms of civic culture', *Citizenship Studies*, 18(6–7): 615–629.

Crepaz, K. (2020) 'Overcoming borders: The Europeanization of civil society activism in the "refugee crisis"', *Journal of Ethnic and Migration Studies*, early access, doi: 10.1080/1369183X.2020.1851471

Dauvergne, P. and Neville, K. (2011) 'Mindbombs of right and wrong: Cycles of contention in the activist campaign to stop Canada's seal hunt', *Environmental Politics*, 20: 192–209.

Dennis, J. and Hall, N. (2020) 'Innovation and adaptation in advocacy organizations throughout the digital eras', *Journal of Information Technology and Politics*, 17(2): 79–86.

Faith, B. and Prieto-Martin, P. (2016) 'Civil society and civic engagement in a time of change', *IDS Bulletin*, 47(2A): 137–144.

Garay, L., Morales, S. and Wilson, J. (2020) 'Tweeting the right to the city: Digital protest and resistance surrounding the Airbnb effect', *Scandinavian Journal of Hospitality and Tourism*, 20(3): 246–267.

Gordon, E. and de Souza e Silva, A. (2011) *Net Locality*, Chichester: Wiley-Blackwell.

Guma, T., Woods, M., Yarker, S. and Anderson, J. (2019) ' "It's that kind of place here": Solidarity, place-making and civil society response to the 2015 "refugee crisis" in different localities in Wales, UK', *Social Inclusion*, 7(2): 96–105.

Halegoua, G. and Polson, E. (2021) 'Exploring "digital placemaking"', *Convergence*, 27(3): 573–578.

Hardley, J. and Richardson, I. (2021) 'Digital placemaking and networked corporeality: Embodied mobile media practices in domestic space during Covid-19', *Convergence*, 27(3): 625–636.

Harrison, K. H. (2014) 'Virtual shop fronts: The internet, social media and Caribbean civil society organisations', *Globalizations*, 11(6): 751–766.

Haussler, T. (2021) 'Civil society, the media and the internet: Changing roles and challenging authorities in digital political communication ecologies', *Information Communication and Society*, 24(9): 1265–1282.

Jenkins, H. (2006) *Convergence Culture: Where old and new media collide*, New York: New York University Press.

Keane, J. (2003) *Global Civil Society?* Cambridge: Cambridge University Press.

Kumar, R. and Thapa, D. (2015) 'Social media as a catalyst for civil society movements in India: A study in Dehradun city', *New Media and Society*, 17(8): 1299–1316.

Massey, D. (1991) A global sense of place? *Marxism Today*, June: 24–29.

Massey, D. (2005) *For Space*, London: SAGE.

McLuhan, M. (1964) *Understanding Media*, New York: Ginko Press.

Mercea, D. (2012) 'Digital prefigurative participation: The entwinement of online communication and offline participation in protest events', *New Media and Society*, 14(1): 153–169.

Ozkula, S. M. (2021) 'The unmaking of collective action: Changing organizing logics in civil society organizations through social media activism culture', *International Journal of Communication*, 15: 1984–2002.

Parigi, P. and Gong, R. (2014) 'From grassroots to digital ties: A case study of a political consumerism movement', *Journal of Consumer Culture*, 14(2): 236–253.

Pieterse, J. N. (2003) *Globalization and Culture: Global mélange*, Lanham, MD: Rowman and Littlefield.

Pillay, K. and Maharaj, M. (2015) 'The restructuring and re-orientation of civil society in a Web 2.0 world: A case study of Greenpeace', *International Journal of Cyber-Warfare and Terrorism*, 5(1): 47–61.

Putnam, R. (2000) *Bowling Alone*, New York: Simon & Schuster.

Robertson, R. (1992) *Globalization: Social theory and global culture*, London: SAGE.

Schattle, H. (2015) 'Testing the possibilities and limits of global and national public spheres: Lessons learned from the campaign to stop a military base in South Korea', *Globalizations*, 12(2): 149–183.

Tatarchevskiy, T. (2011) 'The "popular" culture of internet activism', *New Media and Society*, 13(2): 297–313.

Thapliyal, N. (2018) '#Eduresistance: A critical analysis of the role of digital media in collective struggles for public education in the USA', *Globalisation, Societies and Education*, 16(1): 49–65.

Theocharis, Y., Vittoratou, S. and Sajuria, J. (2017) 'Civil society in times of crisis: Understanding collective action dynamics in digitally-enabled volunteer networks', *Journal of Computer-Mediated Communication*, 22(5): 248–265.

7

Democratic decline? Civil society and trust in government

Alistair Cole, Ian Stafford and Dominic Heinz

Trust (and its corollary mistrust) lies at the heart of contemporary debates regarding governance and democracy. There is an extensive literature focused on conceptualising trust, and more specifically political trust, and exploring the potential consequences of the perceived decline or erosion in the latter for democracy (Cook 2001; Rothstein and Uslaner 2005; Torcal and Montero 2006; van Deth et al 2007). Problems of democratic deficit, of the misfit between politics and policy, of political corruption apparently undermine trust in politicians and underpin the emergence in most EU polities of forms of national Populist Party responses (Schmidt 2006). There is a strong and growing demand for more diverse and effective forms of citizen and civil society engagement to increase levels of trust and engage an increasingly diverse, busy and complex urban population; hence the linkage between trust and concepts like co-production and co-creation (Fledderus 2015).

The chapter addresses the related themes of trust and mistrust, co-production or co-creation and democratic confidence. It draws on comparative analysis drawn from the UK, France and Germany as part of the WISERD 'Building Trust? Institutions and interactions of multi-level governance in the UK, Germany and France' project. The chapter is divided into three sections. The first section provides a brief overview of debates around the conceptualisation of trust and, in particular, the forms of 'political trust' that are frequently utilised in debates around the crisis of democracy. The second section analyses contemporary arguments around the decline of trust in the three countries included in the project. This analysis draws on a range of data sources, including the 2016 YouGov survey carried out as part of the project. The final section examines the shape and role of civil society actors within the three different national contexts in relation to wider debates around trust in government.

The existential threat to democracy and democratic institutions presented by the decline in political trust has become a well-worn path ventured down by politicians, journalists and academics in recent decades (Lenard 2005; van der Meer 2017). Evidence for the perceived crisis in trust and democratic decline is frequently provided by national and international surveys: for example, in his essay accompanying the 2021 Edelman Trust Barometer, Richard Edelman argued that the survey's results illustrated that the COVID-19 pandemic had 'accelerated the erosion of trust' (Edelman 2021). Similarly, a range of potential remedies have been offered to counter this deepening malaise in trust. The then director-general of the BBC, Tony Hall, for example, remarked in a speech to the Global Business Summit in March 2020 that in the UK "the big story is clear: trust in democratic institutions has plummeted" and that a renewed emphasis on integrity in journalism could strengthen democracy (Hall 2020). It is perhaps symptomatic of our times that Hall's call to arms was significantly undermined by the Dyson report's damning assessment of his own conduct around Martin Bashir's interview with the Princess of Wales in 1996 (BBC 2021). However, Hall was not alone in prescribing this type of remedy, for example, the Edelman 2020 Trust Barometer (Edelman 2020: 8), emphasised the importance of competence and ethical behaviour – 'being honest, having a vision, being purpose-driven and being fair' – in rebuilding trust.

The COVID-19 pandemic which engulfed the world from early 2020 sparked further interest in trust-related research, as Devine et al (2021: 276) note, both in terms of the impact of the presence or absence of trust on government responses to the pandemic but also the impact of the pandemic itself on trust. A wide-ranging literature emerged across multiple disciplines exploring a wide range of areas, including the relationship between trust and compliance with COVID-19-related measures (Bargain and Aminjonov 2020; Ayalon 2021; Plohl and Musil 2020), public discourse and information around the pandemic (Depoux et al 2020; Newton 2020; Nutbeam 2020; Xiao et al 2021), trust in experts and healthcare systems (Baker 2020; Bennett 2020; Cairney and Wellstead 2021; Harris and Sandal 2021), and the impact of COVID-19 on trust in political institutions (Bol et al 2020; Falcone et al 2020; Goldfinch et al 2021; Schraff 2020; Weinberg 2020; Jennings et al 2021). Although Jennings (2020) noted an initial 'rally-round-the-flag' effect of the crisis, trust has steadily been eroded. This was reflected in the 2021 Edelman Trust Barometer which noted that the COVID-19 pandemic created a 'trust bubble' characterised by an increase in trust in government, but this bubble had already appeared to have burst in the UK, shrunk to a smaller degree in Germany, and actually grown between May 2020 and January 2021 in France. This highlights a key theme that will be explored in this chapter; the extent to which trust, and trust-building processes vary between and within states.

The potential solutions for restoring political trust and reversing the perceived decline of democracy that have emerged from the academic literature have moved far beyond the integrity-based prescriptions provided above. A wide range of alternative solutions have been proposed, from the argument that 'greater transparency fosters greater trust in government'

(Porumbescu 2015: 520) to the adoption of more diverse and effective forms of citizen engagement to increase levels of trust and engage an increasingly diverse, busy and complex urban population (Fledderus 2015). However, exploring the potential role that mechanisms such as enhanced transparency or the co-production or co-creation of public services can play in rebuilding trust is fraught with challenges. First, we are faced with the challenge of defining precisely what is meant by 'trust'. For example, Grimmelikhuijsen et al (2013: 577) note that 'across and even within disciplines, a myriad of definitions, concepts, and operationalizations are being used in research'. Indeed, given the breadth of literature and variety of forms and causes attributed to trust, this challenge can often feel insurmountable. Second, concepts such as transparency, co-production and co-creation are just as contested and multi-dimensional as trust. Brandsen and Honingh (2016), for example, identify four different types of co-production based on the extent to which citizens are involved and proximity of this citizen engagement to the core services being provided. Similarly, Ansell and Torfing's (2021: 2) contribution to a recent special edition of *Policy and Politics* sought to clearly distinguish co-creation from co-production in order to avoid 'unwarranted concept-stretching'. Finally, once the core concepts have been delineated, we face the challenge of evaluating the potential impact that measures around transparency or co-production have on trust. For example, Fledderus et al (2014: 439) argue that there is 'absolutely no reason to take for granted that the co-production of service delivery automatically leads to more trust' and seek to identify the conditions that need to be present for trust-building to take place.

This chapter explores the related themes of trust and mistrust, co-creation and democratic confidence, drawing on comparative analysis drawn from the UK, France and Germany as part of the WISERD 'Building Trust? Institutions and interactions of multi-level governance in the UK, Germany and France' project. Although the project was primarily focused on the potential role of transparency in building trust between actors, themes related to co-production and co-creation were quite prominent. The aim of this chapter is to examine the extent to which the development of trust within civil society has varied as much within as between our three states, and whether there are any processes which might be characterised as co-production or co-creation.

Defining trust and co-production

Any academic journal article, chapter in an edited volume or monograph which directly or indirectly engages with questions of trust is relatively incomplete without a section devoted to what we mean by trust. Fledderus (2015: 551), for example, draws on Offe's (1999: 47) definition of trust as 'the belief that others, through their action or inaction, will contribute to my/our well-being and refrain from inflicting damage upon me/us' and operationalises trust in relation to co-production by characterising it as 'the extent to which people say they trust organizations or other people'. This characterisation draws on core assumptions that Lane (1998: 3) argues are shared by many conceptualisations of trust: (1) a degree of interdependence between the trustor and trustee; (2) trust provides a way to cope with risk or uncertainty in exchange relationships; and (3) the vulnerability resulting from the acceptance of risk will not be taken advantage of by the other party in the relationship. However, Lenard (2005: 365) distinguishes between two contrasting approaches to thinking about trust. The first emphasises 'the strategic risk-taking elements of trust' or what Hardin (2006: 16) characterises as an 'encapsulated interest' account grounded in an 'assumption that the potentially trusted person has an interest in maintaining a relationship with the truster'. The second conception identified by Lenard suggests that 'we ought to think of it (trust) as a generalised attitude towards others', so that trust is seen as a moral commitment or social-psychological predisposition, highlighted in Uslaner's (2002) conception of 'moralistic trust'. Lane (1998: 1) offers an alternative 'cognition-or-expectations-based trust' that is operationalised across a wide range of research, including phenomenology (Zucker 1986), systems theory (Luhmann 1979) and structuration theory (Giddens 1984). Lane (1998: 15) argues that this approach shifts the focus away from interpersonal sources of trust, such as familiarity and a common history, to 'formal, socially produced and legitimated structures which guarantee trust'. These contrasting conceptualisations highlight the multidimensional nature of trust as a concept and the way that it has been operationalised in contemporary research.

In addition to different conceptions of the basis for trust, we can also explore different sources or ways of generating trust that are key to understanding the potential trust-building benefits of processes such as co-production or co-creation. Zucker (1986, cited in Fuglsang and Jagd 2015: 26), for example, identified three potential sources of trust: characteristic-based trust driven by shared social similarities, process-based trust drawing on past experiences or exchanges, and institutional-based trust, which can be based on the creation of rules and formal structures. These differing bases for trust are reflected in the distinction within the literature related to different forms of trust or levels of analysis, perhaps most notably between types of social and political trust. 'Particular social trust' or 'thick trust' is characterised as being inter-personal, described by Putnam (2000: 136) as 'embedded in personal relations that are strong, frequent and nested in wider networks'. In contrast, generalised social trust or 'thin trust' is centred on more general information about social groups and situations (Newton 2007). These two forms of inter-personal trust contrast with the characterisations of political trust. Hooghe and Zmerli (2011: 3) draw on Easton's (1965) idea of diffused support to characterise political trust as a 'very thin form of trust' characterised by a 'kind of general expectation that on the whole, political leaders will act according to the rules of the game as they are agreed upon in a democratic regime'. Therefore, whether this expectation is experience-based does not make a significant difference. The distinction between different forms of trust and levels of analysis are key to understanding contemporary research on the dynamics of interpersonal and institutional trust, and processes of building trust. Khodyakov (2007: 118) challenges the assumption that he identifies in Fukuyama's work (1995, 1999) that 'if there is no interpersonal trust, institutional trust is impossible' and instead argues that the relationship between different forms of trust flows in both directions. Thus, institutional forms of trust may be explained as much by the effective performance of institutions as the overall level of thick (particular social trust) or thin (general social trust) forms of trust.

The process of building or generating 'particular social trust' or 'thick trust' is characterised by interpersonal face-to-face contacts, and therefore is often time consuming to build (Nooteboom, 1996). In contrast, 'thin' forms of trust do not require the same kind of face-to-face interactions as, on the one hand, 'generalised social trust' may be dependent on characteristic-based sources of trust, and, on the other, 'institutional trust' may be generated by impersonal mechanisms. Bachmann and Inkpen (2011: 282), for example, note that this may be via 'institutional safeguards' which enable two actors to develop trust 'without having any prior personal experience in dealing with one another'. However, it is important to note that these different forms of trust are not necessarily mutually exclusive, and there is a wide-ranging literature which explores the importance of social interaction and sensemaking within the context of the institutional-based trust (Zaheer et al 1998; Sydow 2006; Fuglsang and Jagd 2015). A variety of strategies have been proposed for building trust within both the interpersonal and institutional settings. Zand (1972), for example, stresses the importance of three factors in reducing uncertainty and building trust at the interpersonal or micro-level:

1. Information: Disclose more accurate, relevant, and complete data about the problem, one's thoughts and one's feeling.
2. Influence: Accept more influence from others in selection of goals, choice of methods, evaluation of progress.
3. Control: Accept more interdependence with others. Impose less procedure to control others. Greater confidence others will do what they agree to. Greater commitment to do what one agreed to.

At the institutional level, Bachmann and Inkpen (2011) identify a similar range of factors designed to reduce uncertainty and risk between organisations: (1) legal regulation; (2) reputation; (3) certification of exchange partners; and (4) community norms, structures and procedures. However, a common thread which runs through the literature focused on building trust is that the process is often time consuming and with little guarantee of success (Huxham and Vangen 2005; Edelenbos and Klijn 2007). This brings us back to the central question of the potential role that co-production or co-creation can play in building or rebuilding trust within the contemporary context.

The academic literature around citizen or community engagement in the co-production or co-creation of public services and public policy is by no means new. The work of Elinor Ostrom and colleagues such as Roger Parks in the 1970s and 1980s is frequently cited as the starting point for co-production research within contemporary reviews of the concept (Parks et al 1981; Ostrom 1996). However, as Alford (2009: 4, cited in Loeffler 2021: 1) notes, 'co-production is (back) in fashion'. This renewed interest is perhaps unsurprising given the potential benefits that co-production and co-creation appear to potentially offer. For example, Brandsen and Honingh (2016: 427) cite one report which stated that co-production could deliver:

> greater ability to get to the root of issues and develop tailored solutions; increased innovation and efficiency of services when they are built around the users' needs; greater user satisfaction; creation of more cohesive communities with greater sense of local ownership; building confidence and capacity of individuals and communities; better use of public resources. (Trades Union Congress 2013: 7)

However, as co-production and co-creation have become increasingly prevalent across the academic literature, so too have the concerns around concept-stretching and growing confusion around how these concepts can be defined. Brandsen and Honingh (2018: 9) observed that the confusion has been exacerbated by the multi-disciplinary interest in co-production and co-creation, and that while interest from sociologists, economists, political scientists, public administration, marketing and management researchers should be celebrated, 'it has also made the original definitions of the terms less suitable and on some points less clear'. Therefore, before exploring how co-creation or co-production can be utilised as a potential mechanism for rebuilding trust and addressing democratic decline, it is first necessary to attempt to clearly define what they mean.

The original definition of co-production frequently identified within the academic literature is, unsurprisingly, inspired by the work of Ostrom et al:

The mix of activities that both public service agents and citizens contribute to the provision of public services. The former are involved as professionals, or 'regular producers,' while 'citizen production' is based on voluntary efforts by individuals and groups to enhance the quality and/or quantity of the services they use. (Parks et al 1981, cited in Brandsen et al 2011: 1)

However, there have been recent efforts to revise the concept to provide greater clarity. For example, Brandsen and Honingh (2016: 431) attempt to identify the core elements of the concept and put forward a revised definition of co-production as 'a relationship between a paid employee of an organization and (groups of) individual citizens that requires a direct and active contribution from these citizens to the work of the organization'. Furthermore, they note that there may be varieties of co-production depending on whether citizens are involved in both design and implementation, and the proximity of these tasks to the core services of the organisation in question. As the concept has increased in popularity and the literature has broadened, the dividing lines between co-production and related concepts, notably co-creation and collaborative governance has become more blurred (Voorberg et al 2015). For example, Ansell and Torfing (2021: 2) note that co-production 'increasingly involves not only users and citizens but also communities, organised stakeholders and private enterprises' (see Table 7.1). In their definition, co-creation lies much closer to collaborative governance, and therefore is more relevant than co-production for the analysis in the final section of this chapter, which centres on building trust within civil society.

In addition to the perceived benefits promised by co-production outlined above, it has also been characterised by Fledderus (2018: 258) as being 'associated with positive effects on the trust relation between citizens and public institutions, and on trust in society in general'. Fledderus (2015: 550) characterises the growth of concepts such as co-production and co-creation as being part of a wider shift to 'New Public Governance' defined by 'inter-agency cooperation, partnerships with non-governmental agencies, decentralization and a role for users as co-producers in the delivery of activation services'. The explicit focus of Fledderus' analysis of trust and co-production is on the relationship between users and service staff, but it notes that third sector organisations perform a key function in fostering voice and supporting co-production by minimising or eliminating opportunistic behaviour (Fledderus 2015: 551). This chapter draws on these observations, and the earlier arguments around building trust, to provide a comparative analysis of the state of trust and the role of civil society across sub-national territories within the UK (North West England, Wales), France (Brittany, Auvergne-Rhône-Alpes) and Germany (Hesse, Saxony-Anhalt).

Table 7.1: Comparing definitions of co-production and co-creation

	Co-production	Co-creation
Definition	'A basically dyadic relation between private service users and public service providers that allows both parties to make good use of their experiences, competences and resources in the service-delivery process'	'The process through which a plethora of public and private actors are involved – ideally on equal footing – in a collaborative endeavour to define common problems and design and implement new, better, yet feasible, public solutions'
Scope	Public service production and delivery focusing on the creation of value for users (small scale)	Design of service systems, planning solutions, societal problem solving, policy-making and public value creation (grand scale)
Actors	Public service producers and service users (perhaps also user organisations and volunteers)	Relevant and affected actors from state, market and civil society
Power relation	Highly asymmetrical vertical relation between professional service providers and users without specialised knowledge and expertise, but with valuable experiences and expertise on own needs	Horizontal relations between interdependent actors who are formally equal but may have unequal power resources
Outcomes	Efficient delivery of pre-designed services tailored to individual needs and aiming to enhance user benefit by drawing on user experience (accidental innovation)	Development of new and better solutions through innovation and continuous improvement (task accomplishment is default)
Examples	Users write the postal code on letters to enhance efficiency, fill out their tax returns to reduce errors, do post-surgical knee training for fast recovery, and help their kids with their homework to stimulate learning	Public and private actors, including citizens, volunteers and civil society organisations, collaborate to design local recycling programmes, enhance traffic safety and fight child obesity

Source: Ansell and Torfing 2021.

The decline of trust? Comparing the UK, France and Germany

The context for our case studies lies in the common process of state reconfiguring that has been identified as part of a European-wide trend, which, it is argued, has led to the redistribution of authority upwards to supranational organisations, most notably the EU and downwards to regional and sub-national territories (Rodriguez-Pose and Gill 2003). The contrasting governance arrangements in our three states can be illustrated by utilising the Regional Authority Index (RAI) originally developed by Hooghe et al

Table 7.2: Regional Authority Index: self-rule dimensions

	Institutional depth	Policy scope	Fiscal autonomy	Borrowing autonomy	Representation	Self-rule
France: Régions	2.0	2.0	1.0	2.0	3.0	10.0
Germany: Länder	3.0	3.0	2.0	3.0	4.0	15.0
UK: Mayoral Combined Authorities	2.0	1.0	1.0	1.0	3.0	8.0
UK: Wales	3.0	3.0	2.0	1.0	4.0	13.0

Source: Updated RAI scores. Available at: https://garymarks.web.unc.edu/data/regional-authority/

Table 7.3: Regional Authority Index: shared-rule dimensions

	Law-making	Executive control	Fiscal control	Borrowing control	Constitutional reform	Shared rule
France: Régions	0	0.0	0.0	0.0	0.0	0.0
Germany: Länder	2	2.0	2.0	2.0	4.0	12.0
UK: Mayoral Combined Authorities	0	0.0	0.0	0.0	0.0	0.0
UK: Wales	1.5	1.0	0.0	0.0	4.0	6.5

Source: Updated RAI scores. Available at: https://garymarks.web.unc.edu/data/regional-authority/

(2010) but which has since been updated and revised (Hooghe et al 2016; Shair-Rosenfield et al 2021). Hooghe et al (2016: 23) measure regional authority by evaluating levels of self-rule, defined as 'the authority that a subnational government exercises in its own territory', and shared rule, defined as 'the authority that a subnational government co-exercises in the country as a whole'. The French case provides a relatively clear example of a unitary state, with the Régions having a degree of self-rule but with shared rule non-existent. The UK case provides a fragmented picture which has evolved considerably over the last 20 years, with the coalition government launching Mayoral Combined Authorities in England, and devolved institutions in Wales evolving from their introduction in 1999. The latter is highlighted by Wales' initial self-rule score of 8.0 in 1999 and its increase to 13.0 in 2018 (Tables 7.2 and 7.3). The German case is notable in the strength of the Länder in both the self-rule and shared rule domains, reflecting the 1949 Basic Law of the German Federal Republic and 2006 reforms which broadened their legislative powers (Swenden 2006; Behnke and Benz 2008). It is within the context of these contrasting governance structures that we explore the state of trust and the role of civil society across sub-national territories within the UK (North West England, Wales), France (Brittany, Auvergne-Rhône-Alpes) and Germany (Hesse, Saxony-Anhalt). However, before we explore the potentially contrasting pictures at the sub-national level, we need to get a sense of the state of trust across our three states.

Across the UK, France and Germany there has been renewed interest in the analysis of political trust and related factors, such as perceptions of the integrity and competence of government, the impact of bad behaviour by politicians and the rise of populist movements, such as the UK Independence Party/the Brexit Party, National Front and Alternative für Deutschland (Mayer and Perrineau 1989; Pattie and Johnson 2012; Allen and Birch 2015; Whiteley et al 2016; Jennings et al 2016; Jennings et al 2017; Jennings and Lodge 2019; Reinl and Schäfer 2020; Weisskircher 2020; CEVIPOF 2009, 2014; Cheurfa and Chanvri 2019). At the national level, the picture of political trust in the UK, France and Germany provided by secondary data largely matches the dominant narrative around the decline of trust. The Eurobarometer data on trust in national government, for example, highlights that although all of our countries have experienced some fluctuations over the past two decades, the general trend over recent years is that the gap between France and the UK, and Germany has grown (Figure 7.1). If we explore more recent data, as noted above, the Edelman Trust Barometer illustrated the growth of a 'trust bubble' related to COVID-19. However, this bubble appears to have burst in the UK and Germany with a return to almost pre-COVID-19 levels, but trust in government has continued to grow more steadily in France (see Table 7.4). The extent that these trends continue is clearly dependent on perceptions of government performance in responding to the pandemic as it continues to evolve, but they appear to

Figure 7.1: Trust in national government

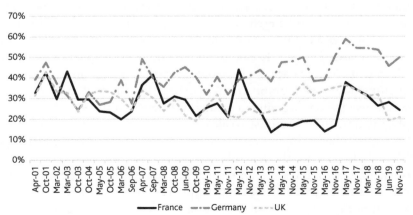

Source: Eurobarometer

Table 7.4: Edelman Trust Barometer: trust in government (percentage of respondents saying they trust government)

	January 2020	May 2020	January 2021	May 2021	January 2022
France	35	48	50	51	53
Germany	45	64	59	55	47
UK	36	60	45	53	42

Source: Edelman Trust Barometer 2020–22

Table 7.5: Now thinking about the national government, how satisfied are you with the way it is doing its job? (Percentage of respondents giving Low Satisfaction scores 0–3)

	2002	2004	2006	2008	2010	2012	2014	2016	2018
UK	36.2	36.9	41.1	52	36.8	41.2	37.8	29.3	46.2
Germany	58.2	53.8	50	39	47.1	26.8	24	25.7	37.5
France	36.1	33.9	42.8	44.3	49.9	49.5	63.2	58.2	49.1

Source: European Social Survey

illustrate, at least in the case of the UK, that 'rally-round-the-flag' effects on public trust in government can disappear as quickly as they appear.

If we narrow our focus and consider the different elements of political trust, such as levels of satisfaction as a proxy for a national government's perceived competence, perceptions of the perceived benevolence of government and the integrity of politicians, the picture tends to reinforce the overall trend towards distrust, but with notable variations across our states. Tables 7.5 and 7.6 collate responses to the European Social Survey question, 'Now thinking about the national government, how satisfied are you with the way it is doing its job?', with scores of 0–3 aggregated as 'low satisfaction' and 7–10 as 'high satisfaction'. Notably in France we can see recent high levels of distrust in terms of perceptions of competence, perhaps illustrating the broad-brush rejection of politics and political organisations and the rejection of the left–right cleavage in favour of alternatives, such as the 2018–19 Yellow Jersey movement (Bedock 2019; Cole 2019; Tran 2021). Indeed, for the last decade, the low satisfaction (0–3) in France has been around 50 per cent and above, and remarkably, in 2014, over 17 per cent of respondents scored the national government 0 out of ten. If we look at the range of measures that can act as a proxy for perceived benevolence, we also see a very negative set of the results. The 2018 European Social Survey question asking the extent to which respondents agreed with the statement 'the Government takes into account the interests of all citizens' also reflected these trends. In France, 21 per cent of respondents stated 'not at all' – significantly higher than both the UK (9.3 per cent) and Germany (4.4 per cent) (Figure 7.2). Finally, if

Table 7.6: Now thinking about the national government, how satisfied are you with the way it is doing its job? (Percentage of respondents giving High Satisfaction scores 7–10)

	2002	2004	2006	2008	2010	2012	2014	2016	2018
UK	18.7	18.5	14.8	11.7	19.3	16.3	20.1	23.5	14.2
Germany	5.7	8.3	10.7	14.6	10.9	22	26.9	26.4	17.4
France	14.3	15	9.1	15.2	10.6	8.2	4.8	6.1	9.4

Source: European Social Survey

Figure 7.2: The government takes into account the interests of all citizens (percentage of respondents in each country)

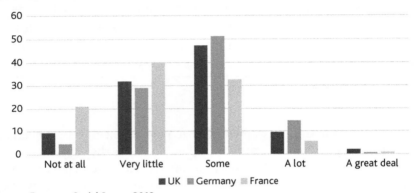

Source: European Social Survey 2018

we utilise the Transparency International Corruption Perceptions Index, based on the perceptions of experts and business executives, as a measure of the perceived integrity of national governments, the UK, Germany and France achieve scores of 77, 80 and 69 respectively. These equate to global rankings of 11th, 9th and 23rd on Transparency International's 2020 Index (Transparency International 2020).

A central aim of the 'Building Trust? Institutions and interactions of multi-level governance in the UK, Germany and France' project was to explore whether trust varies as much within states as between them. However, in comparison to data on trust at the national level, data focused on the sub-national level in all three of our states was relatively scare and therefore analysing political trust at this level was challenging. In France, the CEVIPOF Trust Barometer and a YouGov survey carried out in our project illustrated that scale was a factor in terms of public trust, for example, the latter finding that it was the municipality level (28 per cent) which was most often seen as most representing the needs and concern of the population. However, notably the level of government which followed the municipality level, was the national level (16 per cent), followed by the regional level (14 per cent), highlighting that although scale does appear to be a factor, it is frequently not a straightforward dynamic. Comparable data in Germany and the UK were patchy at best but, in the latter, we seem to see the broad trend that the public generally perceived levels of government which are closer to them, whether it be at the local or regional level, to be more likely to have their interests at heart. For example, the Welsh Election Survey 2016 found that almost 60 per cent of respondents trusted the Welsh government to work in Wales' interests 'just about always' or 'most of the time', whereas the figure for the UK government was just over 21 per cent. The most consistent comparable data source is the Eurobarometer question on trust in regional and local authorities, which although somewhat vague, provides a picture in stark contrast to the national-level data previously discussed (Figure 7.3).

Overall, the picture provided by the existing data on trust paints a relatively stark portrait of 'thin' political trust being in generally poor health at the national level across our three states. Although there have always been variations, most notably in response to government actions on COVID-19, if we view trust in terms of perceptions of competence, benevolence and integrity the picture is particularly bad in France, and marginally better in the UK and Germany. However, there is a potentially more positive picture provided by the admittedly relatively sparse data at the sub-national level, which seems to offer some hope for the rebuilding of political trust. Jeffery (2014: 4) notes that over the past few decades regional decision-making authorities in advanced democracies have exercised an increasingly wide range of policy responsibilities and therefore 'regions now matter much more directly to voters, parties and interest groups'. Therefore, if the sub-national

Figure 7.3: Trust in regional and local public authorities (percentage of respondents in each country that said 'Tend to trust')

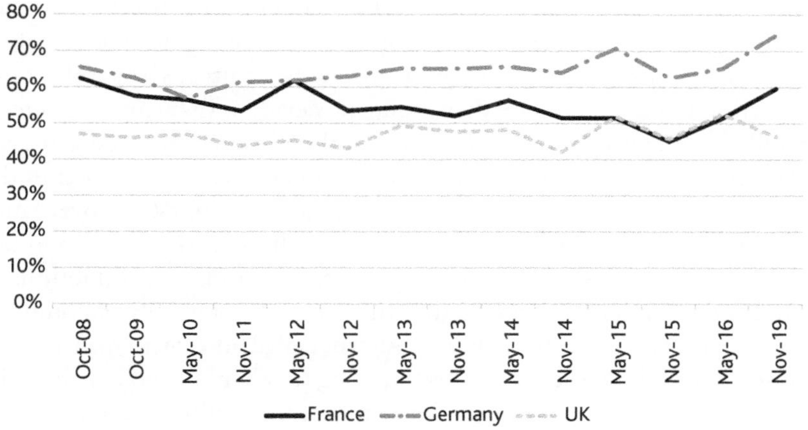

Source: Eurobarometer

145

level can be seen as delivering higher levels of trust, then it may be possible to provide a more optimistic picture of the future of political trust. For example, Denters (2002) notes in his comparison of local and national levels in Netherlands, Norway and the UK that trust in local officeholders was generally higher, and at times considerably higher, than trust in national officeholders. However, the wider literature focused on size and scale provides a somewhat mixed picture (Nielsen 1981; Denk 2012; Welling Hansen 2013). The final section of this chapter examines these themes in relation to the shape and role of civil society actors within the three different national contexts and in six territories at the sub-national level.

A role for civil society?

The process of state rescaling and restructuring that has been to an extent a feature across all three of our states, has been perhaps most influentially characterised through the concept of multi-level governance (Hooghe and Marks 2003; Piattoni 2010). As part of these processes, the role of civil society has evolved over recent years. For example, Passey and Tonkiss (2000: 50) note that the traditional characterisation of civil society as being differentiated from the state and the economy has broken down through the increased role of civil society organisations in delivering public services and as a 'crucial arena for state legitimacy'. Similarly, as noted above, Ansell and Torfing (2021) highlight how civil society organisations potentially play a core role in the co-creation of public policy and delivery of public services in the contemporary context. A key theme within this context has been the central role played by trust in enabling collaboration and partnership within these complex governance settings (Ring and Van de Ven 1994; Lane and Bachmann 1998; Sullivan and Skelcher 2002; Huxham and Vangen 2005; Edelenbos and Klijn 2007; Edelenbos and Eshuis 2012; Klijn and Koppenjan 2016). Huxham and Vangen (2005: 66), for example, note that the 'common wisdom' suggests that trust is 'a precondition for successful collaboration' but that the 'common practice' appears to be that mutual suspicion is often the starting point. Therefore, they argue, it is evident that trust needs to be carefully built and maintained for successful collaboration to be achieved. Although the literature on co-production and co-creation emphasises that these processes are distinct from collaboration and collaborative governance, in a similar way trust can be characterised as both a necessary pre-condition and potential positive outcome of co-creation and co-production. In addition, the building of trust within this context potentially encompasses a variety of forms of trust, including interpersonal and institutional forms. This section explores the context for building trust within and between civil society actors in the two sub-national territories within the UK (North West England and Wales), France (Brittany, Auvergne-Rhône-Alpes) and

Germany (Hesse and Saxony-Anhalt), before exploring overarching themes from across the fieldwork.

A key feature of state rescaling or restructuring within the UK has been the asymmetrical forms of devolution introduced since 1999. Therefore, the context for questions around building trust via co-creation and the potential role of civil society unsurprisingly varies considerably across Wales and the city-regions of North West England, primarily Liverpool and Greater Manchester. From a starting point of relative weakness, civil society organisations in Wales have increased their capacity over the two decades and more of devolution, partly facilitated by the funding and partnership-based approach provided by successive devolved administrations (Entwistle 2006; Bristow et al 2009; Rumbul 2016a). Although we might characterise this process as the maturing of civil society, there have been concerns raised regarding whether this environment has favoured some organisations over others and whether the high dependency on Welsh government funding and small size of policy communities has created a degree of timidity and 'groupthink' in terms of engaging with government policy (Hodgson 2004a, 2004b; Rumbul 2016b). In contrast, a key challenge for civil society in North West England has been simply adapting and responding to the shifting governance arrangements adopted by the UK government. For example, the New Labour government's emphasis on nine Government Office Regions led to the creation of Voluntary Sector North West in the late 1990s to provide support for the voluntary, community and social enterprise sector (VCSE). When the regional architecture was abandoned by the coalition government in 2011 and replaced with a patchwork of different sub-regional governance arrangements, notably Combined Authorities, we saw the creation of bodies such as the Greater Manchester Voluntary, Community and Social Enterprise Devolution Reference Group and VS6 in the Liverpool City Region. Beel et al (2018: 254) argue that these initiatives epitomised 'a joint effort on the part of local civil society actors to exert agency at city-regional level, and influence the process'. Although civil society organisations have responded to devolution in both Wales and North West England, the extent of public engagement is perhaps more open to question.

The context in the two French regions, Auvergne-Rhône-Alpes and Bretagne, has some similarities but also important contrasts with the cases in the UK. It is important to note that the French State has historically been less tolerant towards autonomous groups than in comparable countries (Mény 1986). The State sets itself above special interests, but it recognises the need for dialogue with social partners. Through subsidising voluntary associations, trade unions and professional associations, public authorities (central and sub-national government) bring social organisations into their public policy orbit. A range of perspectives have attempted to capture state–society relations in France, including the close ties between civil servants and the professions

(Muller 1984; Jobert and Muller 1987; Page 2012). Drilling down to the sub-national level, on the one hand the French region of Bretagne can be characterised as having a history of trusting relationships and trans-partisan territorial advocacy; while on the other hand, Auvergne-Rhône-Alpes was created in 2015 as part of the wider reform of the regional level in France and has been marked by political conflicts and administrative turf wars. Traditionally, a key feature of discussions of the former has been the central role provided to the Breton model (for example, Créhange 2019; Lucas 2011). Cole and Pasquier (2015: 54–55) note that this is commonly characterised as being based on 'cross-partisan consensus and regional advocacy' and shaped by high levels of 'institutional inter-connectivity and social and cultural capital, embodied by traditions of inter-communal co-operation, close informal relationships between regional politicians and representatives of the state field services, a vibrant associative life, strong electoral participation and robust social networks'. However, the extent to which this model stills holds in the contemporary setting is contested. In contrast to the fragmentation of relatively artificial administrative regions in England, the territorial reforms of French regions in 2015 was marked by a move from 22 to 13 regions. This process of redefining the regional map manifestly lacked transparency and territorial actors complained of not having been consulted.

In contrast to both the UK and France, despite its formal constitutional status as a federal state, German society can be characterised as highly nationally integrated. Gunlicks and Lees (2003) provide an overview of the complex process by which the German Länder have emerged and constraints within which territorial governance operates within the German context. They argue that an influential concept used to characterise the territorial governance of Germany has been the seemingly contradictory idea of 'unitary federalism' reflecting that 'the requirement of uniform or equivalent living conditions is not only a constitutional requirement, it is also a reflection of the value Germans hold for equality' (Gunlicks and Lees 2003: 388). Sturm (2018) describes Germany as lacking 'a federal culture' and that recent territorial reforms have been driven by functional, top-down agendas rather than bottom-up pressures. Furthermore, the character of German federalism has a direct consequence for civil society and the potential of co-creation for the rebuilding of trust. Sturm (2018: 20) notes that German civil society organises in reference to the Länder but that this is 'not an expression of a wish for regional autonomy. ... It simply reflects the administrative divisions of Germany'. Similarly, he argues that 'what has no influence on decision-making in Germany is proximity to the promise federalism makes, namely more regional autonomy, bringing politics closer to the people, regional participation, accountability and transparency' (p 44). Nevertheless, despite being part of this national political culture, the Länder explored in our research, Hesse and Saxony-Anhalt, have distinct histories, party configurations and place-specific dynamics that provide important contextual features. Institutional continuity is much greater in the case of Hesse, which was established in 1949 but has deeper roots, than in Saxony-Anhalt, which was created in 1990 following unification and has experienced almost permanent institutional reconstruction.

The brief overviews of our three states highlights that a key starting point for our analysis is understanding the political environments and wider context for the fieldwork in each of our states. For example, civil society actors were given a central role in both North West England and Wales, and there was a clear emphasis on partnership and collaboration between civil society actors themselves and with government institutions. To an extent this can be seen as almost an inevitable consequence of the impact of austerity measures, but this underestimates the long-term commitment to partnership-working and shared commitment for delivering for their respective localities. In contrast, in the two German Länder considered in our research, the key factor shaping the trust relations at the sub-national level was the importance placed on the law and legal norms, and there was less emphasis placed on partnership and collaboration. In France, the fieldwork emphasised the central role of public authorities and the historic scepticism regarding the potential role of civil society actors or associations. The analysis of the key factors which shaped processes of building and maintaining trust between civil society actors at the sub-national level within the wider context of increasingly complex forms of multi-level governance identified four overarching themes within and between our cases.

The first of these themes across our cases, and perhaps the strongest similarity across the three states, was the comparison between territories with a strong history of institutional continuity and close interaction between government and civil society actors, and territories with a more recent history and with variable levels of past cooperation at various sub-national scales. In the territories characterised by a stronger sense of territorial identity, and with a longer history of cooperation and partnership working, there were stronger foundations for building trust. North West England provided an interesting case where this dynamic was illustrated in contrast between the different parts of the region. On the one hand, the Greater Manchester Combined Authority drew on the shared history of the Association of Greater Manchester Authorities, established in 1986 and which one interviewee described as "a collaborative venture before devolution was even a twinkle in the eye of George Osbourne" (the UK chancellor who launched the new 'devolution revolution' in 2015). On the other hand, the Liverpool City Region Combined Authority was characterised as effectively 'starting from scratch' and the failure of the remaining parts of the North West to form a combined authority, notably authorities in Lancashire, highlighted the high degree of dysfunction. This had a consequence for building trust through co-creation. For example, one voluntary sector stakeholder explained that in Greater Manchester there was 'a real commitment to co-design and co-production' but in other parts of the North West it was less clear whether the rhetoric of co-production and co-creation would be delivered in reality. This finding is consistent with existing research on trust which suggests that building trust is a time-consuming and challenging task. Therefore, the adoption of co-creation or co-production to build trust with civil society actors or the wider general public is likely to be most challenging where this shared history or identity is largely absent.

The second overarching theme that shaped the character of trust relations across the three states and six sub-national territories was the extent to which the restructuring of governance arrangements within a territory impacted cooperation. In those territories where reorganisation was relatively recent it was more likely that trust would face specific challenges related to ongoing spatial tensions. These issues were most clearly illustrated in the case of Auvergne-Rhône-Alpes where the 2015 reforms led to a turf war between the newly created region and prominent cities, notably Lyon, in terms of policy areas such as economic planning. In addition, there were tensions around the relative influence and power of different parts of the region. For example, one interviewee explained that 'Lyon has an overpowering weight and squeezes out all other territories'. The impact of restructuring or reorganisation can also be found to a lesser extent in Saxony-Anhalt and both of the UK territories. The case of Saxony-Anhalt is somewhat different, processes of local government reorganisation have led to the creation of structures which are bigger in both size and scope but delivering services for a declining population. An interviewee noted that this had meant that trust in public service delivery has suffered as a result. Once again, the context in North West England and Wales varies considerably. On the one hand, the shifting governance arrangements in the North West has meant that tensions have bubbled to the surface; for example, in the negotiations around transport functions in the Liverpool City Region and the aborted attempts around the Lancashire Combined Authority. Similarly, in Wales the continued debates around the structure of local government introduced in 1996 and the relationship between the local and devolved levels means that tensions are never far from the surface. While these potential barriers are by no means insurmountable, they create an additional challenge for building the trust between key actors in delivering collaboration and co-creation.

The third theme highlighted by the project's fieldwork focused on the mechanisms that were introduced across our cases to support the building of trust and, in particular, the relative formality or informality of those arrangements. The six sub-national territories were distributed along a continuum from an emphasis being placed on fairly informal mechanisms based primarily on inter-personal relations to highly formalised legal agreements. The two ends of the spectrum are perhaps best exemplified by Wales in the UK context and the German cases, respectively. A consistent theme within the Welsh fieldwork was the importance played by tight-knit interpersonal relations which characterised policy communities. In particular, these linkages moved beyond professional shared history and encompassed the personal domain, such as having attended the same school or being related. In stark contrast, relations in the German Länder were more reliant on formal legal agreements. The other territories across our states are placed somewhere between these points, for example, in North West England, while interpersonal relations were important, there was much greater focus on the creation of formal agreements and compacts between organisations. On the one hand, these types of formal agreements were probably not as deep as the more personalised form of trust highlighted in Wales, but on the other, they were seen as more resilient in terms of changes of personnel. In the French cases, Bretagne was perhaps closer to the Welsh model than Auvergne-Rhône-Alpes. Importantly, the fieldwork does not identify a specific approach as being more or less effective at building trust, rather the mechanism has to respond to the specific territorial context. The highly interpersonal nature of trust in Wales, for example, was seen as having both positives and negatives. One interviewee explained that it meant 'you know which buttons to press and which levers to pull', but it was also seen as risking a degree of groupthink. Similarly, formal agreements, such as concordats and memoranda of understanding, were seen as useful mechanisms but building more informal forms of interpersonal trust remained important.

The final overarching theme identified by the project's fieldwork was illustrated most clearly in the French and German cases, and highlighted the potentially significant influence of political conflict on building trust at the sub-national level. In both of the French sub-national territories, the far-right National Rally (Rassemblement national) and the gilets jaunes (yellow vests) movement significantly impacted regional politics (Charmes 2019; Tran 2021). This is particularly noteworthy in Bretagne, where the Breton model was historically characterised as a driving force for cross-partisan, territorial cohesion. However, a recurring theme of the fieldwork in 2018 was that Bretagne was no longer isolated from the political disaggregation and social disaffection that fuelled both the Rassemblement national and gilets jaunes across France. Indeed, one interviewee observed that 'the Breton partisan model is an old Christian democratic tradition, which says nothing today to those who are under 50'. The rise of Alternative für Deutschland (AfD) in both Hesse and Saxony-Anhalt also highlighted the importance of the political context in shaping trust among political actors at the sub-national or regional level. In both German regions, the established parties combined to counter the threat of the AfD, but whereas in Hesse this coalition was characterised as having a coherent progressive agenda, the Saxony–Anhalt coalition was portrayed as simply a defensive coalition. In an interesting contrast, despite the perceived rise of populism in the UK in recent years, this political dimension was relatively absent from the sub-national cases (Ford and Goodwin 2017; Eatwell and Goodwin 2018). Despite the attention given to the populist agenda put forward by the United Kingdom Independence Party (UKIP) and then the Brexit Party, both failed to achieve a significant foothold in UK elections, particularly at the local and devolved levels. Although the Additional Member System used for devolved elections in Wales delivered seven seats for UKIP in 2016, during the fifth Senedd term these members were perhaps more a source of irritation, rather than a genuine challenge to the established political parties. Indeed, their time in the Senedd was marked more by political infighting and changes of party allegiance than disrupting the status quo. It was illustrative that at the 2021 Senedd election the various right-wing populist parties, Abolish the Welsh Assembly, UKIP and Reform UK (the new incarnation of the Brexit Party), failed to come close to winning a seat.

This short discussion of the key factors which shaped processes of building and maintaining trust between civil society actors at the sub-national level highlights the importance of understanding the wider context within which increasingly complex forms of multi-level governance are emerging. These themes highlight the importance of what Worthy and Grimmelikhuijsen (2012) characterise as external or macro influences, the wider political environment, and the significance that they can play in providing the backdrop for internal or micro influences, the individual level factors. Given that concepts such as trust are deeply embedded in the wider web of social, economic and political features of society, it is essential to recognise that in terms of building or rebuilding trust the context may differ as much within states as between them. Therefore, the potential role of co-creation in building trust, either among civil society actors or the wider general public, would need to recognise the wider social, economic and political landscape within which these efforts would take place.

Conclusion: building back better or *plus ça change*?

This chapter began by noting that the decline of political trust and perceived existential threat that it poses to democracy have become deeply engrained narratives within contemporary debates. The COVID-19 pandemic has had some interesting effects on the state of political trust and the potential agenda around restoring it. As noted earlier in the chapter, following an initial 'rally-round-the-flag' effect, the gains around political trust have steadily been eroded across many states (Jennings 2020; Edelman Trust Barometer 2021). However, there appears to be a territorial dimension to the impact that COVID-19 has had on political trust, and, particularly in the case of the UK, this has provided a platform for the devolved level which is usually absent. For example, a March 2021 YouGov poll reported that 60 per cent of respondents felt that the Welsh government had handled the COVID-19 crisis 'very well' or 'fairly well' in comparison to 39 per cent who gave the same answer for the UK government (Wales Online 2021). Indeed, public confidence in First Minister, Mark Drakeford, around the handling of COVID-19 and the raised profile provided by the crisis have been identified as key factors in explaining Labour's performance in the 2021 Welsh Parliament elections. Similarly, the crisis provided Metro Mayors, such as Andy Burnham in Greater Manchester and Steve Rotheram in the Liverpool City Region, with a platform to play a prominent role with public debate. However, what relevance, if any, does this have for the potential role of civil society and ideas such as co-creation and co-production in restoring trust?

The sub-national level, as highlighted in this chapter, potentially provides an ideal platform for the building or rebuilding of public trust, although it is important to note that the existing evidence is somewhat mixed and it is possible that the perceived performance of government remains the key variable in driving trust (Denters 2002). Furthermore, the analysis of the six territories across the three country cases highlighted that it is not simply the case that greater levels of devolution will equate to higher levels of trust between actors in civil society and government. The cases highlighted that the wider context played a key role in terms of creating obstacles that made the process of building or rebuilding trust harder, or alternatively providing factors which helped overcome these obstacles. For example, the presence of institutional continuity and a shared history of cooperation between different actors provided a reservoir of goodwill and the foundations for further partnership-working. However, a shared history of cooperation was neither a necessary nor a sufficient factor in building trust; indeed, if that shared history was negative then it could act as an obstacle (to restoring trust). Instead, a shared history can be seen as a useful foundation upon which to build trust, but other factors, such as the restructuring of governance arrangements or political conflict, could undermine this process. Furthermore, there was no 'one way' of building trust in terms of the tools and arrangements that were put in place across our territories. A range of informal and formal mechanisms were utilised, and there was no clear evidence that one approach was more effective than another. However, once again what was clear was that these arrangements were shaped by the wider political and social environments within which they had emerged. Therefore, the process of drawing lessons from one territory to another or, to put it another way, identifying 'what works' in terms of building or rebuilding trust, is likely to be highly challenging.

The research carried out as part of our project centred on trust within the context of civil society at the sub-national level, and although civil society organisations are frequently identified as playing a key role in processes of co-creation and co-production, the primary focus tends to be on citizens and service users themselves. Therefore, our analysis may only offer clues about building trust via co-production or co-creation among the general public. In the pre-COVID-19 setting of our research, a common theme was that the public was relatively unengaged with what we might characterise as the regional or sub-national level. For example, in the YouGov survey carried out in France, trust was highest at the municipality level, and the regional and national levels performed at a similar level. Furthermore, the regional or sub-national tiers were frequently characterised as being the result of top-down and elite-driven processes. This would appear to suggest that it is problematic to see them as the panacea for rebuilding political trust among the public via processes of co-creation and co-production. However, the COVID-19 context undoubtedly provides an opportunity to reboot political trust and democratic processes, and in many contexts, public awareness of the potential role that sub-national levels of governance can perform has never been higher. The narrative of 'building back better' has become almost omnipresent and there is clearly a potential role for co-creation and co-production at the sub-national level in this process. However, as Hamann (2021) notes 'different people will have different views of what "better" actually means and how to achieve it'. A key lesson for these processes from our analysis of building trust in the context of civil society would be the importance of tailoring arrangements to the specific territorial context. Therefore, adopting a one-size-fits-all approach to 'building back better' is unlikely to work and ignores valuable opportunities provided by the specific settings in each locality or territory. In some senses, this is part of the promise that genuine co-creation and co-production could provide, but there is a risk that these ideas become watered down and act simply as a rebranding exercise or 'faux production' for the status quo.

References

Alford, J. (2009) 'A public management road less travelled: Clients as co-producers of public services', *Australian Journal of Public Administration*, 57(4): 128–137.

Allen, N. and Birch, S. (2015) *Ethics and Integrity in British Politics: How citizens judge their politicians' conduct and why it matters*, Cambridge: Cambridge University Press.

Ansell, C. and Torfing, J. (2021) 'Co-creation: The new kid on the block in public governance', *Policy and Politics*, 49(2): 211–230.

Ayalon, L. (2021) 'Trust and compliance with Covid-19 preventive behaviors during the pandemic', *International Journal of Environmental Research and Public Health*, 18(5): 1–10. https://doi.org/10.3390/ijerph18052643

Bachmann, R. and Inkpen, A. C. (2011) 'Understanding institutional based trust building processes in inter-organizational relationships', *Organization Studies*, 32(2): 281–301.

Baker, D. W. (2020) 'Trust in health care in the time of COVID-19', *JAMA*, 324(23): 2373–2375. DOI:10.1001/jama.2020.23343

Bargain, O. and Aminjonov, U. (2020) 'Trust and compliance to public health policies in times of COVID-19', *Journal of Public Economics*, 192: 104316. https://doi.org/10.1016/j.jpubeco.2020.104316

BBC (2021) 'Report of The Dyson investigation by the Right Honourable Lord Dyson', BBC, 20 May 2021. Available at: http://downloads.bbc.co.uk/aboutthebbc/reports/reports/dyson-report-20-may-21.pdf

Bedock, C. (2019) 'Enquêter in situ par questionnaire sur une mobilisation', *Revue Française de Science Politique*, 69(5): 869–892.

Beel, D., Jones, M. and Jones, I. R. (2018) 'Regionalisation and civil society in a time of austerity: The cases of Manchester and Sheffield', in C. Berry and A. Giovannini (eds), *Developing England's North*, Cham, Switzerland: Palgrave Macmillan, pp 241–260.

Behnke, N. and Benz, A. (2008) 'The politics of constitutional change between reform and evolution', *Publius: The Journal of Federalism*, 39(2): 213–240.

Bennett, M. (2020) 'Should I do as I'm told? Trust, experts, and COVID-19', *Kennedy Institute of Ethics Journal*, 30(3–4), 243–263. DOI:10.1353/ken.2020.0014

Bol, D., Giani, M., Blais, A. and Loewen, P. J. (2020) 'The effect of COVID-19 lockdowns on political support: Some good news for democracy?', *European Journal of Political Research*, 60(2): 497–505.

Brandsen, T. and Honingh, M. (2016) 'Distinguishing different types of coproduction: A conceptual analysis based on the classical definition', *Public Administration Review* 76(3): 427–435.

Brandsen, T. and Honingh, M. (2018) 'Definitions of co-production and co-creation', in T. Brandsen, T. Steen and B. Verschuere (eds), *Co-Production and Co-Creation: Engaging citizens in public services*, London: Routledge, pp 9–17.

Brandsen, T., Pestoff, V. and Verschuere, B. (2011) 'Co-production as a maturing concept', in V. Pestoff, T. Brandsen and B. Verschuere (eds), *New Public Governance, the Third Sector and Co-production*, Abingdon: Routledge.

Bristow, G., Entwistle, T., Jines, F. and Martin, S. (2009) 'New spaces for inclusion? Lessons from the "Three-Thirds" partnerships in Wales', *International Journal of Urban and Regional Research*, 32(4): 903–921.

Cairney, P. and Wellstead, A. (2021) 'COVID-19: Effective policymaking depends on trust in experts, politicians, and the public', *Policy Design and Practice*, 4(1): 1–14. DOI: 10.1080/25741292.2020.1837466

CEVIPOF (2009) *La confiance dans tous ses états: les dimensions politique, économique, institutionnelle, sociétale et individuelle de la confiance*, Paris: CEVIPOF.

CEVIPOF (2014) '*Le baromètre de la confiance politique 5*', CEVIPOF [online]. Available at: http://www.cevipof.com/fr/le-barometre-de-la-confiance-politique-du-cevipof/resultats-1/vague5/

Charmes, E. (2019) *La revanche des villages: Essai sur la France périurbaine*, Paris: Seuil.

Cheurfa, M. and Chanvri, F. (2019) *2009–2019: la crise de la confiance politique*, Paris: CEVIPOF.

Cole, A. (2019) *Emmanuel Macron and the Two Years that Changed France*, Manchester: Manchester University Press.

Cole, A. and Pasquier, R. (2015) 'The Breton model between convergence and capacity', *Territory, Politics, Governance*, 3(1): 51–72.

Cook, K. S. (ed.) (2001) '*Trust in Society*', New York: Russell Sage Foundation.

Créhange, P. (2019) *Le mystérieux Club des trente, enquête sur le plus influent des lobbys Bretons*, Langrolay-sur-Rance: Du coin de la rue.

Denk, T. (2012) 'Size and political support on the local level in Sweden', *Local Government Studies*, 38(6): 777–793.

Denters, B. (2002) 'Size and political trust: Evidence from Denmark, the Netherlands, Norway, and the United Kingdom', *Environment and Planning C: Government and Policy*, 20(6): 793–812.

Depoux, A., Martin, S., Karafillakis, E., Preet, R., Wilder-Smith, A. and Larson, H. (2020) 'The pandemic of social media panic travels faster than the COVID-19 outbreak', *Journal of Travel Medicine*, 27(3): taaa031. https://doi.org/10.1093/jtm/taaa031

Devine, D., Gaskell, J., Jennings, W. and Stoker, G. (2021) 'Trust and the Coronavirus pandemic: What are the consequences of and for trust? An early review of the literature', *Political Studies Review*, 19(2): 274–285. Doi:10.1177/1478929920948684

Easton, D. (1965) *A Systems Analysis of Political Life*, New York: Wiley.

Eatwell, R. and Goodwin, M. (2018) *National Populism: The revolt against liberal democracy*, London: Penguin Books.

Edelenbos, J. and Eshuis, J. (2012) 'The interplay between trust and control in governance processes: A conceptual and empirical investigation', *Administration and Society*, 44(6): 647–674.

Edelenbos, J. and Klijn, E. (2007) 'Trust in complex decision-making networks: A theoretical and empirical exploration', *Administration and Society*, 39(1): 25–50.

Edelman, R. (2020) *Edelman Trust Barometer 2020*, New York: Edelman.

Edelman, R. (2021a) *Edelman Trust Barometer 2021*, New York: Edelman.

Entwistle, T. (2006) 'The distinctiveness of the Welsh partnership agenda', *International Journal of Public Sector Management*, 19(3): 228–237.

Falcone, R., Coli, E., Felletti, S., Sapienza, A., Castelfranchi, C. and Paglieri, F. (2020) 'All we need is trust: How the COVID-19 outbreak reconfigured trust in Italian public institutions', *Frontiers in Psychology*, 11: 561747.

Fledderus, J. (2015) 'Building trust through public service co-production', *International Journal of Public Sector Management*, 28(7): 550–565.

Fledderus, J. (2018) 'The effects of co-production on trust', in T. Brandsen, T. Steen and B. Verschuere (eds), *Co-Production and Co-Creation: Engaging citizens in public services*, London: Routledge, pp 258–265.

Fledderus, J., Brandsen, T. and Honingh, M. (2014) 'Restoring trust through the co-production of public services: A theoretical elaboration', *Public Management Review*, 16(3): 424–443.

Ford, R. and Goodwin, M. (2017) *Revolt on the Right: Explaining support for the radical right in Britain*, London: Routledge.

Fuglsang, L. and Jagd, S. (2015) 'Making sense of institutional trust in organizations: Bridging institutional context and trust', *Organization*, 22(1): 23–39.

Fukuyama, F. (1995) *Trust: Social virtues and the creation of prosperity*, New York: Free Press.

Fukuyama, F. (1999) 'Social Capital and Civil Society', International Monetary Fund, [online] 1 October. Available at: http://www.imf.org/external/pubs/ft/seminar/1999/reforms/fukuyama.htm#6

Giddens, A. (1984) *The Constitution of Society*, Berkeley, CA: University of California Press.

Goldfinch, S., Taplin, R. and Gauld, R. (2021) 'Trust in government increased during the Covid-19 pandemic in Australia and New Zealand', *Australian Journal of Public Administration*, 80(1): 1–11. https://doi.org/10.1111/1467-8500.12459

Grimmelikhuijsen, S. (2012) 'Linking transparency, knowledge and citizen trust in government: an experiment', *International Review of Administrative Sciences*, 78(1): 50–73.

Grimmelikhuijsen, S. G., Porumbescu, G., Hong, B. and Im, T. (2013) 'The effect of transparency on trust in government: A cross-national comparative experiment', *Public Administration Review*, 73(4): 575–586.

Gunlicks, A. and Lees, C. (2003) *The Lander and German Federalism*, Manchester: Manchester University Press.

Hall, T. (2020) 'Trust in the age of disruption'. Speech to the Global Business Summit on Saturday 7 March 2020, BBC website. Available at: https://www.bbc.co.uk/mediacentre/speeches/2020/trust-in-the-age-of-disruption

Hamann, R. (2021) ' "Building back better" may seem like a noble idea. But caution is needed', *The Conversation*, 4 February 2021. Available at: https://theconversation.com/building-back-better-may-seem-like-a-noble-idea-but-caution-is-needed-154587

Hansen, S. W. (2013) 'Polity size and local political trust: A quasi-experiment using municipal mergers in Denmark', *Scandinavian Political Studies*, 36(1): 43–66.

Hardin, R. (2006) *Trust*, Cambridge: Polity Press.

Harris, S. M. and Sandal, G. M. (2021) 'COVID-19 and psychological distress in Norway: the role of trust in the healthcare system', *Scandanavian Journal of Public Health*, 49: 96–103. https://doi.org/10.1177/1403494820971512

Hodgson, L. (2004a) 'Manufactured civil society: Counting the cost', *Critical Social Policy*, 24(2): 139–164.

Hodgson, L. (2004b) 'The National Assembly for Wales, civil society and consultation', *Politics*, 24(2): 88–95.

Hooghe, L. and Marks, G. (2003) 'Unraveling the central state, but how? Types of multi-level governance', *American Political Science Review*, 97(2): 222–243.

Hooghe, L., Marks, G. and Schakel, A. H. (2010) *The rise of Regional Authority: A comparative study of 42 democracies*, London: Routledge.

Hooghe, L., Marks, G., Schakel, A. H., Chapman Osterkatz, S., Niedzwiecki, S. and Shair-Rosenfield, S. (2016) *Measuring Regional Authority: A postfunctionalist theory of governance*, vol. 1, Oxford: Oxford University Press.

Hooghe, M. and Zmerli, S. (2011) 'Introduction: The context of political trust', in S. Zmerli and M. Hooghe (eds), *Political Trust: Why context matters*, Colchester: ECPR Press, pp 1–11.

Huxham, C. and Vangen, S. (2005) *Managing to Collaborate: The theory and practice of collaborative advantage*, London: Routledge.

Jeffery, C. (2014) 'Introduction: Regional public attitudes beyond methodological nationalism', in A. Henderson, C. Jeffery and D. Wincott (eds), *Citizenship after the Nation State: Regionalism, nationalism and public attitudes in Europe*, Basingstoke: Palgrave Macmillan, pp 1–30.

Jennings, W. (2020) 'COVID-19 and the "rally-around-the flag" effect', UK in a Changing Europe [online], 30 March. Available at: https://ukandeu.ac.uk/covid-19-and-the-rally-round-the-flag-effect/

Jennings, W. and Lodge, M. (2019) 'Brexit, the tides and Canute: The fracturing politics of the British state', *Journal of European Public Policy*, 26(5): 772–789.

Jennings, W., Stoker, G. and Twyman, J. (2016) 'The dimensions and impact of political discontent in Britain', *Parliamentary Affairs*, 69(4): 876–900.

Jennings, W., Clarke, N., Moss, J. T. and Stoker, G. (2017) 'The decline in diffuse support for national politics: The long view on political discontent in Britain', *Public Opinion Quarterly*, 81(3): 748–758.

Jennings, W., Valgarðsson, V., Stoker, G., Devine, D., Gaskell, J. and Evans, M. (2021) *Political Trust and the COVID-19 Crisis: Pushing populism to the backburner?* Canberra: Democracy 2025.

Jobert, B. and Muller, P. (1987) *L'Etat en Action*, Paris: Presses universitaires de France.

Khodyakov, D. (2007) 'Trust as a process: A three-dimensional approach', *Sociology*, 41(1): 115–132.

Klijn, E. H. and Koppenjan, J. (2016) *Governance Networks in the Public Sector*, London: Routledge.

Lane, C. (1998) 'Introduction: Theories and issues in the study of trust', in C. Lane and R. Bachmann (eds), *Trust Within and Between Organisations: Conceptual issues and empirical applications*, Oxford: Oxford University Press, pp 1–30.

Lane, C. and Bachmann, R. (eds) (1998) *Trust Within and Between Organisations: Conceptual issues and empirical applications*, Oxford: Oxford University Press.

Lenard, P. T. (2005) 'The decline of trust, the decline of democracy?', *Critical Review of International Social and Political Philosophy*, 8(3): 363–378.

Loeffler, E. (2021) *Co-Production of Public Services and Outcomes*, Cham, Switzerland: Palgrave Macmillan.

Lucas, C. (2011) *Le lobby Breton*, Paris: Nouveau monde éditions.

Luhmann, N. (1979) *Trust and Power*, Cambridge: Polity Press.

Mayer, N. and Perrineau, P. (1989) *Le Front National à découvert*, Paris: Presses de la Fondation Nationale des Sciences Politiques.

Mény, Y. (1986) 'La légitimation des groupes d'intérêt par l'administration française', *Revue Française de l'administration publique*, 39: 99–110.

Muller, P. (1984) *Le technocrate et le paysan*, Paris: Economie et humanisme.

Newton, K. (2007) 'Social and political trust', in R. J. Dalton and H. Klingemann (eds), *The Oxford Handbook of Political Behavior*, Oxford: Oxford University Press, pp 342–361.

Newton, K. (2020) 'Government communications, political trust and compliant social behaviour: The politics of Covid-19 in Britain', *The Political Quarterly*, 91: 502–513. https://doi.org/10.1111/1467-923X.12901

Nielsen, H. J. (1981) 'Size and evaluation of government: Danish attitudes towards politics at multiple levels of government', *European Journal of Political Research*, 9(1): 47–60.

Nooteboom, B. (1996) 'Trust, opportunism and governance: A process and control model', *Organization Studies*, 17(6): 985–1010.

Nutbeam, D. (2020) 'COVID-19: Lessons in risk communication and public trust', *Public Health Research and Practice*, 30(2): e3022006.

Offe, C. (1999) 'How can we trust our fellow citizens?', in M. E. Warren (ed.), *Democracy and Trust*, Cambridge: Cambridge University Press, pp 42–87.

Ostrom, E. (1996) 'Crossing the great divide: Coproduction, synergy and development', *World Development*, 24(6):1073–1087.

Page, E. (2012) *Policy without Politicians*, Oxford: Oxford University Press.

Parks, R. B., Baker, P. C., Kiser, L., Oakerson, R., Ostrom, E., Ostrom, V., Percy, S. L., Vandivort, M. B., Whitaker, G. P. and Wilson, R. (1981) 'Consumers as co-producers of public services: Some economic and institutional considerations', *Policy Studies Journal*, 9(7): 1001–1011.

Passey, A. and Tonkiss, F. (2000) 'Trust, voluntary association and civil society', in F. Tonkiss and A. Passey (eds), *Trust and Civil Society*, Basingstoke: Macmillan, pp 31–51.

Pattie, C. and Johnson, C. (2012) 'The electoral impact of the UK 2009 MPs' Expenses Scandal', *Political Studies*, 60(4): 730–750.

Piattoni, S. (2010) *The Theory of Multi-level Governance: Conceptual, empirical, and normative challenges*, Oxford: Oxford University Press.

Plohl, N. and Musil, B. (2020) *'Modeling compliance with COVID-19 prevention guidelines: The critical role of trust in science'*, PsyArXiv, 6 April. https://psyar xiv.com/6a2cx/

Porumbescu, G. (2015) 'Linking transparency to trust in government and voice', *American Review of Public Administration*, 47(5): 520–537.

Putnam, R. D. (2000) *Bowling Alone: The collapse and revival of American community*, New York: Simon and Schuster.

Reinl, A. and Schäfer, C. (2020) 'How the 2017 federal election in Germany affected satisfaction with democracy among AfD voters', *German Politics*, 30(4): 463–484. doi.org/10.1080/09644008.2020.1741550

Ring, P. S. and Van de Ven, A. H. (1994) 'Developmental processes of cooperative interorganizational relationships', *The Academy of Management Review*, 19(1): 90–118.

Rodríguez-Pose, A. and Gill, N. (2003) 'The global trend towards devolution and its implications', *Environment and Planning C: Government and Policy*, 21(3): 333–351.

Rothstein, B. and Uslaner, E. (2005). 'All for all: Equality, corruption, and social trust', *World Politics*, 58(1): 41–72. doi:10.1353/wp.2006.0022

Rumbul, R. (2016a) 'Critical friend or absent partner? Institutional and organisational barriers to the development of regional civil society', *European Urban and Regional Studies*, 23(4): 848–861.

Rumbul, R. (2016b) 'The trouble with civil society in Wales', *Agenda – Journal of the Institute of Welsh Affairs* [online] 3 March. Available at: https:// www.iwa.wales/agenda/2016/03/the-trouble-with-civil-society-in-wales/

Schmidt, V. A. (2006). 'Democracy in Europe: The EU and national polities', *Oxford: Oxford Scholarship Online*. Available at: https://oxford.universityp ressscholarship.com/view/10.1093/acprof:oso/9780199266975.001.0001/ acprof-9780199266975

Schraff, D. (2020) 'Political trust during the Covid-19 pandemic: Rally around the flag or lockdown effects?', *European Journal of Political Research*, 30(4): 1007–1017. https://ejpr.onlinelibrary.wiley.com/doi/10.1111/ 1475-6765.12425

Shair-Rosenfield, S., Schakel, A. H., Niedzwiecki, A., Marks, G., Hooghe, L. and Chapman-Osterkatz, S. (2021) 'Language difference and regional authority', *Regional and Federal Studies*, 31(1): 73–97.

Sturm, R. (2018) 'Unitary federalism: Germany ignores the original spirit of its constitution', *Revista d'estudis Autonòmics i Federals*, 28: 17–46.

Sullivan, H. and Skelcher, C. (2002) *Working Across Boundaries: Collaboration in public services*, Basingstoke: Palgrave.

Swenden, W. (2006) *Federalism and Regionalism in Western Europe: A comparative and thematic analysis*, Basingstoke: Palgrave Macmillan.

Sydow, J. (2006) 'How can systems trust systems? Structuration perspective on trust-building in inter-organisational relations', in R. Bachmann and A. Zaheer (eds), *Handbook of Trust Research*, Cheltenham: Edward Elgar, pp 377–392.

Torcal, M. and Montero, J. R. (2006) *Political Disaffection in Contemporary Democracies: Social capital, institutions and politics* (1st edn), London: Routledge. https://doi.org/10.4324/9780203086186

Trades Union Congress (2013) *Making Co-Production Work: Lessons from local government*. London: Trade Union Congress.

Tran, E. (2021) 'The Yellow Vests Movement: Causes, consequences and significance', in H. Drake, A. Cole, S. Meunier and V. Tiberi (eds), *Developments in French Politics 6*, Basingstoke: Palgrave, pp 179–198.

Transparency International (2020) *Corruption Perceptions Index 2020*, Berlin: Transparency International.

Uslaner, E. M. (2002) *The Moral Foundations of Trust*, Cambridge: Cambridge University Press.

van der Meer, T. W. G. (2017) 'Political trust and the "crisis of democracy"', *Oxford Research Encyclopedias*, Oxford: Oxford University Press.

van Deth, J. W., Montero, J. R. and Westholm, A. (2007) *Citizenship and involvement in European Democracies: A comparative analysis*, London: Routledge.

Voorberg, W. H., Bekkers, V. J. J. M. and Tummers, L. G. (2015) 'A systematic review of co-creation and co-production: Embarking on the social innovation journey', *Public Management Review*, 17(9): 1333–1357.

Wales Online (2021) 'Why do people trust Mark Drakeford to handle coronavirus well but don't want him to be First Minister?' *Wales Online website*. Available at: https://www.walesonline.co.uk/news/politics/drakef ord-yougov-poll-senedd-election-19922279

Weinberg, J. (2020) 'Can political trust help to explain elite policy support and public behaviour in times of crisis? Evidence from the United Kingdom at the height of the 2020 Coronavirus pandemic', *Political Studies* (online first), https://journals.sagepub.com/doi/full/10.1177/0032321720980900

Weisskircher, M. (2020) 'The strength of far-right AfD in Eastern Germany: The East-West divide and the multiple causes behind "populism"', *The Political Quarterly*, 91(3): 614–622.

Welling Hansen, S. (2013) 'Polity Size and Local Political Trust: A Quasi-experiment Using Municipal Mergers in Denmark', *Scandinavian Political Studies*, 36(1): 43–66.

Whiteley, P., Clarke, H. D., Sanders, D. and Stewart, M. (2016) 'Why do voters lose trust in governments? Public perceptions of government honesty and trustworthiness in Britain 2000–2013', *The British Journal of Politics and International Relations*, 18(1): 234–254.

Worthy, B. and Grimmelikhuijsen, S. (2012) Transparency and trust in the UK and Netherlands, January 2012, Conference: The Transatlantic Conference on Transparency Research. https://www.researchgate.net/publication/291835752_Transparency_and_trust_in_the_UK_and_Neth erlands

Xiao, X., Borah, P. and Su, Y. (2021) 'The dangers of blind trust: Examining the interplay among social media news use, misinformation identification, and news trust on conspiracy beliefs', *Public Understanding of Science*, 30(8): 977–992. doi: 10.1177/0963662521998025

Zaheer, A., McEvily, B. and Perrone, V. (1998) 'Does trust matter? Exploring the effects of interorganizational and interpersonal trust on performance', *Organization Science*, 9(2): 141–159.

Zand, D. E. (1972) 'Trust and problem solving', *Administrative Science Quarterly*, 17(2): 229–239.

Zucker, L. G. (1986) 'Production of trust: Institutional sources of economic structure, 1840–1920', *Research in Organizational Behavior*, 8: 53–111.

8

Xenophobia, hostility and austerity: European migrants and civil society in Wales

Stephen Drinkwater, Taulant Guma and Rhys Dafydd Jones

The last few years have often been characterised by turbulence and uncertainty. The election of populist leaders in the USA, India, Italy, the Philippines, Indonesia, Brazil and Hungary, the notable electoral performance of far-right and populist parties in France, Germany, Sweden and elsewhere, and the UK's decision to withdraw from the European Union have seen a disruption to the established expectations of liberal–democratic states following neo-liberal practice. However, these did not emerge in 2016. Austerity politics, population displacement following conflict, and climate emergencies over the previous decade and beyond – and the perceived failure of states to deal with these justly – have contributed to this condition. What is clear, however, is that the world is a less certain place on issues of migration and beyond through the unsettling of previously established norms and conventions. Furthermore, specific questions about the UK's future relationship with the European Union pose uncertainty regarding several fields, including future movement of people.

The UK's 2016 EU membership referendum marked the culmination of restrictive immigration legislation and policy over the last two decades. The Asylum and Immigration Act, 1999, for example, introduced a number of restrictions, including replacing monetary support for refugees and asylum seekers with vouchers, and the forcible dispersal of asylum seekers across the UK (Kofman 2002; Hubbard 2005; Darling 2011). In the following decade, Prime Minister Gordon Brown made his plea for 'British jobs for British workers' at his first Labour Party conference as prime minister, restrictions and surveillance were placed on marriages between UK and non-UK citizens in the UK (Mulvey 2010; Wray 2011; Yuval-Davis et al 2017), and on non-EU citizens accessing benefits and the NHS (Guentner et al 2016; Hiam et al 2018). The policing of state boundaries further encroached into everyday life with the requirement of landlords and employers to verify tenants' and employees' migration statuses under the Immigration Acts of 2014 and 2016 (Hall 2015; Yuval-Davis et al 2017). These developments, which constituted a policy of maintaining a 'hostile environment' against immigrants in the UK during Theresa May's tenure as Home Secretary, and which placed extensive restrictions on immigrants to the UK, criticised as overly complex by the Court of Appeal of England and Wales (Yeo 2017), continued after her elevation to the premiership (Burrell and Schweyher 2019). As has been noted extensively, the 2016 Brexit referendum, with its inflammatory discourse surrounding immigration, saw a sharp increase in reported hate crimes, with many EU citizens targeted in xenoracist incidents (Rzepnikowska 2019; Guma and Dafydd Jones 2019).

A focus on migration, and its target to reduce immigration to 'tens of thousands', can be characterised as one of three major features of the Cameron governments (2010–2016), while another concerned civic participation. However, many have commented on the intertwining of this approach with a context of austerity, the third characteristic of that government, which saw a substantial reduction in public spending and cuts to public services. As others have noted (Wolch 1989; Beaumont 2008), volunteering and civic participation is framed as a shadow state: providing the services associated with the state at an arm's length. However, not all areas are placed to contribute to and benefit from voluntary activity, revealing spatial inequalities of participation (Lowndes and Pratchett 2012; Williams et al 2014).

While much attention has been paid to many aspects of participation and civil society, including youth movements and young people (Mills and Waite 2017, 2018), older people (Heley and Jones 2013; Jones and Heley 2014), and around specific issues such as solidarity and place-making (Guma et al 2019) and at different scales (Heley et al 2019), there has been little engagement with migrants' roles and their experiences of civil society, especially in the context of ongoing hostile and austere environments that we described above. Examining this issue is important for several reasons. First, many accounts of migrants' participation in the UK present them as passive and requiring support (Light and Young 2009; Spigelman 2013), rather than as being resourceful agents and civil society makers, participating and providing support in their own right. These constructions are largely underpinned by integrationist discourses (Meissner and Heil 2020), which tend to problematise migrants' engagement and roles, while taking the integration of the host society for granted. Second, participation allows for understanding how attachments to places, people and communities are created through activity. By examining participation as an anchoring practice (Grzymala-Kazlowska 2018), insight is gained in understanding relationships with localities which go beyond accounts associated with identity and belonging. Third, there is scope for understanding how participation and civil society are impacted by and help reduce hostility. We know from existing research, for example, that marginalised groups (such as people of colour) are often expected to police their own behaviour in encounters with dominant groups to give a 'good encounter' and avoid being cast in stereotypical and racialised terms, thus limiting their agency to confront injustice (Jones and Norwood 2017). At the same time, as our findings in this chapter demonstrate, hostility also prompted some migrant individuals to act more proactively, setting up and running new civil society initiatives in order to tackle dominant negative discourses of migrants in the UK.

This chapter presents data on European migrants' involvement in civil society in Wales, collected as part of WISERD's Civil Society research programme. It highlights the ways many people became involved in civil society, broadly conceived, as a way of 'giving something back' or 'doing something worthwhile'. However, despite such actions, migrants' participation in civil society is challenged by austerity, abuse and mobility. We begin with a brief discussion of current work conceptualising uncertainty in the context of migration. We then offer methodological and ethical reflections. The fourth section examines the motivations of migrants engaging with civil society in a hostile environment in Wales, while the fifth examines the challenges in the context of austerity and precarity. Succinct conclusions are offered in the sixth section.

Turbulence, precarity and liquid migration

Bauman (2000) argued that late capitalism is characterised by its liquidity: constant shape-shifting and free-flowing forms that are difficult to grasp. Similarly, Engberson and Snel (2013) have argued that contemporary migration can be characterised by this liquid ontology. European Union citizenship – gained by virtue of national citizenship of member states – for example, allows free movement of people (albeit with several caveats), while communication technologies, the proliferation of the smartphone and low-cost air travel have facilitated hyper-mobile lifestyles (Lulle et al 2018). Rather than migrating to start a new life in a new world, as migration in the nineteenth and early twentieth century was characterised, contemporary migration is more fluid, circular and non-linear. People may move to gain experience or financial, social and cultural capital; they move speculatively to see if things work out, in the knowledge that moving onwards or returning 'home' is often easy. Along with this liquidity, plans can be more contingent, and respond to situations as they unfold (Drinkwater and Garapich 2015).

Many accounts of liquid migration often emphasise the experiences of those who have significant social, financial or cultural capital to move onwards, or do not have commitments, responsibilities or attachments that inhibit further mobility (Guma and Dafydd Jones 2019). In liquid modernity, there is often a lack of predictability that may affect migrants' everyday lives. Policies may change, restricting or placing conditions on access to welfare;

automation may mean that their work can be done cheaper robotically; austere politics may mean that their job or support is cut. Furthermore, migrants often work under exploitative conditions, where safety concerns may not be fully considered (Song 2004) and where third-party agents or 'gangmasters' have influence on living conditions (Spigelman 2013). Migrants, including (central and eastern) European migrants, are often highly qualified, they frequently work in jobs for which they are deemed overqualified (Gill and Bialsky 2011).

Against this backdrop, there are several studies which examine migrants' anchoring practices. Indeed, the metaphor is appropriate in thinking of giving some notion of stability and reference against the roll of the waves and the draw of the current. Studies have emphasised the ways in which meeting a partner, raising children, making friends, joining a place of worship and developing a career in a happy workplace can contribute to anchoring practices (Grzymala-Kazlowska 2018). We contend in this chapter that volunteering and participation also functions as an anchoring practice, helping individuals bond with their communities, both in terms of people and places.

Brexit presents a further challenge to EU migrants in the UK. The referendum result made many feel that they no longer belonged or were wanted (Guma and Dafydd Jones 2019). While some planned to leave the UK – or to relocate to parts which voted to remain and were perceived as more tolerant – others felt that they could not do so due to familial or legal connections with particular localities or the country in general. Uncertainty about future legal rights or obligations once the UK leaves the EU, and the advantages of European citizenship recede, are also noted (Lulle et al 2018; Lulle et al 2019; Miller 2019; Ranta and Nancheva 2019). Furthermore, the context of hate crime directed at migrants and minority groups also means people question their belonging to a place beyond the broader socio-legal implications that come with Brexit.

Methodology

Data were collected in two distinct strands. The first involved analysis of quantitative data on civic participation using large-scale survey data as well as on hate crimes using administrative data. This is intended to complement and provide a background context for the qualitative analysis that also appears in this chapter, thereby essentially relating to a mixed-methods approach. The analysis of civic participation focuses on differences by country of birth using the *UK Household Longitudinal Study*, also known as *Understanding Society.* Further details about the survey, especially from the perspective of ethnic minorities and migrants, can be found in McFall et al (2014). Although questions on civic participation have been asked in two waves of the survey (the third and sixth), the analysis appearing in this chapter only relates to the third wave, which took place in 2011–12. The reason for this is because the sample size is larger in this wave than in the sixth wave. However, the broad patterns that can be identified in the data for different groups of migrants are fairly similar in the two waves. In terms of measuring civic participation, we generally follow the approach used by Heath and Li (2015), who define an overall civic participation rate in their study of religious groups in the UK as well as other measures including the number of civic memberships and activities reported by the respondents. These memberships and activities relate to 16 different organisations, including religious groups or church associations, sports and social clubs, political parties, trades unions and professional associations and other community groups.

The quantitative analysis of hate crimes relates to police recorded crimes, as opposed to the Crime Survey for England and Wales, which also contains information from respondents on hate crime incidents. Hate crimes recorded by the police relate to 'any criminal offence which is perceived, by the victim or any other person, to be motivated by hostility or prejudice towards someone based on a personal characteristic' (Home Office 2018: 8). This definition contains five types of hate crime: race or ethnicity, religion or beliefs, sexual orientation, disability and transgender identity. The Home Office (2018) highlights the steep rise in reported hate crimes in recent years, especially since 2014/15, which they attribute to improvements in crime recording by the police, a growing awareness of hate crimes as well as certain events such as the 2016 EU referendum vote and the 2017 terrorist attacks.

The second strand focused on qualitative analysis of European migrants' participation in civil society in Wales. Forty-two individuals, representing 25 organisations were interviewed in a range of localities, including Wrexham, Cardiff, Swansea, Bridgend, Merthyr Tydfil, Newport and Llanelli. The majority of these respondents were involved with organisations that explicitly engaged with migrants' issues and cohesion, and varied from welfare-focused and advocacy groups, to those which focused on particular national cultural reproduction and representation (such as Czech-language classes for children). Some groups existed formally and legally, while others were less formal; we also included the creators/moderators of a number of online groups which we had found, stretching the conceptualisation of participation to one that exists beyond the actual/material world. The majority of respondents were migrants, and their time in the UK and Wales ranged from over 45 years to six months. Most respondents came from Poland, Czechia, Slovakia, Hungary or Latvia; states which acceded to the EU in 2004. Due to similarities in the labour profile, and interactions in communities which included sharing resources observed during preliminary fieldwork, we also included Portuguese respondents. Some of these respondents had been born in former Portuguese colonies in Africa, while others from central

Europe were Roma; consequently, we had a range of diverse experiences among a cohort which is often represented as homogeneously white and from 'mainland' Europe's 'metropolitan' powers (McDowell 2009; Guma and Dafydd Jones 2019).

The interviews were conducted mainly in English; however, respondents were invited to express themselves in their own native language if they were unable to communicate certain words or expressions in English. With one of the researchers being proficient in Slovak, some Slovak respondents spoke both in English and Slovak during the interview. In addition, the fact that one of the researchers was a 'fellow migrant' and a non-native English speaker may have also helped the interviewees to understand themselves as equal partners in the communication. The interviews were open ended, allowing participants to talk freely and openly about the organisations/groups/initiatives that they were involved in. Participants were asked questions which included the aim and purpose of these groups, their programme, activities and membership, their use of social media, as well as questions around personal motivation and experiences of participating in these organisations. Interviews were recorded with participants' consent, transcribed verbatim and analysed with the aid of NVivo software. Ethical clearance was obtained from Aberystwyth University, and their guidelines and identified best practice in the field were followed.

Migrants' participation in civil society

Table 8.1 contains information on the civic participation of people who were born outside the UK compared to those who were born in the UK, both for Wales and the rest of the UK. It shows that the civic participation rate (CPR) for non-UK-born residents in Wales is higher (62.9 per cent) than for UK-born residents in Wales (58.6 per cent). This differs from the rest of the UK, where the CPR for UK-born residents (60.3 per cent) is higher than for non-UK-born residents (53.1 per cent). While the difference between UK-born residents in Wales and the rest of the UK is small, but slightly lower in Wales, there is a bigger difference between non-UK-born residents in Wales and elsewhere in the UK, with the former being higher in this instance. There are also differences between migrant groups, with Polish migrants reporting lower CPRs both within Wales and the rest of the UK compared to other migrant groups from the EU or the Commonwealth of Nations. The number of observations in Wales, especially for people born overseas, is relatively small, which limits more detailed analysis for specific groups of migrants. The table indicates that the difference was around 10 percentage points and significantly different from the rest of the UK at the 5 per cent level. However, this is partly due to variations in the composition of migrants in terms of their countries of origin, as shown in

Table 8.1: The migrant/non-migrant participation gap: civic participation in Wales and rest of UK, 2011–12

	Wales			Rest of the UK		
	CPR	Average civ. acts or membs	N	CPR	Average civ. acts or membs	N
UK born	58.6*	1.07***	3,328	60.3	1.16	35,258
Foreign born	62.9**	1.15	132	53.1	0.99	5,823
Country of origin	%			%		
Ireland	8.3			5.1		
France/Germany/Italy/Spain	7.6			5.7		
Poland	2.3			3.6		
Australia/NZ/Canada/US	7.6			4.2		
India	9.9			12.3		
Pakistan/Bangladesh	10.6			18.1		
Other	53.8			51.1		

Source: Understanding Society (authors' calculations).

Notes: N is the number of observations. The stars indicate whether there are statistically significant differences between Wales and the rest of the UK. * indicates significance at the 10% level, ** at the 5% level and *** at the 1% level.

the table. In particular, there was a far higher percentage of respondents who were born in Pakistan and Bangladesh, who have the lowest levels of civic engagement, living in the rest of the UK (Demireva and Heath 2014; Heath and Li 2015).

Only a small percentage of respondents in the survey were born in Poland both in terms of Wales and the rest of the UK. This makes it difficult to provide a clear indication of the relative levels of civic participation among recent Polish migrants and those from other EU accession countries. Nevertheless, using the larger sample provided for the whole of the UK in the Understanding Society dataset, Drinkwater et al (2019) report that CPRs for migrants from Poland were comparatively low in wave 3 and were quite well behind the rates seen for migrants from most other countries, including from other parts of Europe such as Germany, France, Italy and Spain. However, the CPR had risen by around 10 percentage points, which may indicate the importance of the duration of stay in the host community (Aleksynska 2011). The number of civic activities and memberships display a similar pattern to the CPRs, with a slightly higher average seen in the rest of the UK compared to Wales for the native-born but this was again reversed for people born outside the UK.

Anxiety, xenophobia and hate crime motivation

The rise in hate crimes that have been recorded by police in England and Wales in recent years is presented in Table 8.2. The percentage increase in total hate crimes over the period 2011/12 to 2017/18 was slightly higher in England than in Wales, with a particularly noticeable change observed in both countries since 2015/16, which is consistent with a post-referendum shift in relation to hate crimes (Rzepnikowska 2019). The table also reveals that the relatively large growth in total hate crimes has been fairly evenly spread across the different categories in percentage terms, including for race- and religion-motivated offences.

Figure 8.1 provides information on hate crimes by Welsh police force area over this period. It reveals a generally upward trend for each area, especially since 2015/16. This is particularly noticeable in North Wales and Gwent. In contrast, a reduction in total, and racially/religiously motivated, hate crimes was recorded in South Wales in 2017/18 compared to 2016/17. Moreover, South Wales was only one of four police force areas in Wales and England to report a fall in hate crimes between these two years (the others being the City of London, Metropolitan London and Merseyside). Interestingly with regards to the latter, the recent decline in hate crimes has been attributed to the positive effect that Liverpool's star football player, Mo Salah, has had on attitudes and behaviours in this area (Alrababa'h et al 2021). The possible contributory factor of the longstanding boycott of the tabloid, *The Sun*, on Merseyside may also be relevant.

Table 8.2: Hate crimes in Wales and England, 2011/12, 2014/15 and 2017/18 (number of reported crimes)

	Wales			England		
	2011–12	2015–16	2017–18	2011–12	2014–15	2017–18
Race	1,368	1,747	2,298	36,016	47,672	68,953
Religion	54	119	198	1,622	4,281	8,138
Sexual orientation	244	372	670	4,362	6,822	10,968
Disability	122	244	308	1,757	3,385	6,918
Transgender	21	35	64	309	823	1,587
Total	1,809	2,517	3,538	44,066	62,983	96,564
Change	–	708	1,021	–	18,917	33,581
% change	–	39.1	40.6	–	42.9	53.3

Source: Home Office.

Note: Hate crimes reported to British Transport Police have been excluded.

Figure 8.1: Total hate crimes by police force areas in Wales, 2011/12–2017/18

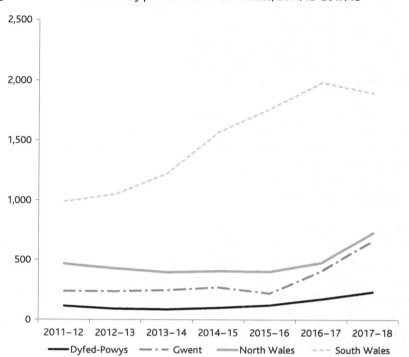

Many migrants that we interviewed spoke about the hostility and abuse they had received in Wales. While there was a reported increase in abuse during the 2016 EU membership referendum campaign and its aftermath, much abuse had taken place over a number of years. As Branca, a Portuguese national, notes, her café became a visible target of difference:

'The Portuguese café they were easy targets in the following days, especially where we're just being [inaudible]. All sorts of racism going on. People bossing, shouting. "Now you have to go home". "Go, go, go" and things like that. It's just ridiculous but you have that constantly. I was sitting down outside for an hour me and [colleague] just an hour there was four incidents happening ... we have to understand 59 per cent voted to leave because of the immigration. Yeah, and they were clear. They could vote to leave for anything. They hate the EU. They want to make their own rules, da, da, da, da, da. Fine, we understand. We have to deal with it because we live here, and whatever we need to ... we can help you to achieve your goals. That's why we're here for, but now tell me want to leave because you don't want me here. That's a different way of looking at things.' (Branca, Portuguese, 42 years old)

As Rzenipovska (2019) has noted, everyday markers of difference, such as accent, cars (through number plates or steering wheels on the left), and dress distinguish European nationals from UK citizens. However, some participants spoke of being particularly marginalised due to their Roma ethnicity, which sometimes intersected with migration status. As Milan, a Roma participant from Slovakia notes, racist prejudice took a number of forms:

> 'Since Brexit there were a few incidents where parents reported, they had some racial abuse on the street, but we tried to educate them how to deal with it. You know, record it. Report it. You can't just let it go because some people are so … used to racism or they've not even recognised there's racism because they don't see it as being racist, perhaps.' (Milan, Slovak, 22)

In Milan's experience, these incidents were not always understood as racist. The perpetrators may not have understood that their actions were racist, or have reflected on what impact their words and deeds had on people, and those subjected to it were often so used to microaggressive racism that they did not consider it worth reporting. As other studies of racism in rural areas (de Lima 2004; Malcolm 2004; Robinson and Gardener 2004) demonstrate, some aspects of abuse, such as microaggression, staring and avoidance, while hurtful, may not be understood or recorded as hate incidents, while there is often an underreporting of hate incidents; some are reluctant to report it or to engage with the police, while such events may not be recorded as hate incidents. For Johanna, a Polish woman who had set up an initiative to help newly arrived migrants living in southern Wales, such incidents demonstrated a need to address the structural issues of hate:

> 'We believe that [the] root cause is language and cultural difference but also public opinion created by media and political campaign. We support children and their parents who find it difficult to live and work in UK and as a result isolate themselves. We need to change people's attitudes to the migration, to educate people about difficulties and political attacks we experience.' (Johanna, Polish, 32)

Thus, our interview data revealed that political campaigns and the media created a permissive environment for xenophobia and xenoracism. In turn, this underlined that broader, structural efforts are needed to challenge the difficulties.

Many respondents spoke about the hostility they had encountered, either directly as migrants, or as members of civil society groups focused on migration issues. The increasingly hostile environment and construction of immigrants as people who 'took jobs and benefits', required additional support and contributed 'nothing' was something that affected many respondents, who felt motivated to challenge this widespread discourse. This underpinned Piotr's reason to create an informal group in Cardiff aimed at the Polish community living in the city. He spoke about how he felt 'fed up' with the negative image of Polish people in the British media, adding that such images also affected Poles themselves; for example, some would feel ashamed to speak Polish in public. His initiative aimed to tackle this by promoting the Polish language, culture, food, music and theatre in Wales and the UK and educating the Welsh/British public about these cultural values; as well as teaching children of Polish parents born in Wales/UK about them, since, as he put it, they often "don't know about Polish identity".

For others, becoming involved in civil society was motivated by personal experience of migration. As Agata and Jana note, helping others have an easier time in moving to Wales than they did was an important factor:

'I faced the same challenges as Polish people who arrived in Swansea who could not speak English well. My motivation was to help them.' (Agata, Polish, 41)

'We should help the others. That was the initiative to help the others so they don't have these hard beginnings like I had, but not everybody shared it at the beginning but now they understand and they're more willing to help others.' (Jana, Czech, 38)

As Johanna notes, having migrants involved in civil society supported integration through having some common language and national background, as well as experience of having migrated themselves:

'We have a committee of seven and 14 supporters. Currently all the volunteers and supporters come from Poland but we are building a group for people from all over the world who are new arrivals to Bridgend. The reason why we were brought together was that we felt the need to help newly arrived migrants who find it difficult to integrate into British society because of language and culture differences.' (Johanna, Polish, 32)

For others, participating with civil society organisations was something that allowed more involvement with a community. For Tomasz, volunteering brought an opportunity to meet people:

'I wanted to meet different people from different communities. I wanted to volunteer and do something worthwhile. So all these things together, you know, there happened to be that opportunity to become this so called "community champion" … these volunteers would be involved in different ways in the aims of Mosaic project which was to increase the participation of minority ethnic communities in the upkeep of national parks. So my friend was actually the Mosaic Project Officer for Pembrokeshire Coast National Park and I became one of the champions, so called.' (Tomasz, Polish, 36)

Participation can be considered an anchoring practice in this context. Contributing to an organisation allows interaction with longer-term residents and other newcomers. Having a migrant visible and audible in a role such as community champion can also contribute to the positive image of a migrant that Piotr mentioned, although others, such as Ahmed (2011) have noted that such roles, which involved promoting equality, diversity and cohesion, are often targeted towards people of colour, and women of colour in particular, as a physical manifestation of institutions' diversity.

While interaction with a broad range of people in the community was a priority for Tomasz, anchoring is not restricted to intercultural exchanges. For others, anchoring can take the place of supporting other migrants and fostering a nationally focused network in a community, through the medium of particular national languages. As Branca notes, supporting fellow Portuguese nationals and Portuguese-speaking residents was important to allow services to develop:

'If it's the Portuguese requesting [translation] I'm not going to charge anything, but with that what happened because we'd been serving so many people every time I need my car fixed that [they?] will do it for free, that Portuguese if I need it. That gentleman yesterday, "Oh, I've got some cheese. Can you try it or took a picture". Everybody wanted to buy this morning in the café because it was good. It's kind of creating, building a community in what my aim. I know I'm a bit, maybe ahead of what's going on. If we don't support each other along we're not going to go anywhere. So that's why I keep saying, okay we don't need money for many things because all of us have a quality.' (Branca)

For Branca, the importance of maintaining a sense of community among local Portuguese speakers was more important than having payment for her translation services. In fostering social capital among fellow Portuguese nationals and speakers, she felt that she also supported their financial capital through allowing networking.

While a number of factors motivated European migrants to participate in civil society, other factors inhibited participation. As Jana, a coordinator with an EU migrant project run by a local charity in Newport, notes, single male economic migrants were less likely to participate:

'So we have a lot of single males living in Newport. Single European males which they come to work. Nothing to do. Stay home. No clubs for them or they want to play chess or something, nothing like that. Lots of young males and they feel the youth provision is not for me. It's for Asians because there's lots of Asians. That's what they're thinking, it's not for me. So they don't join in basically. They do not integrate whatsoever. The Roma community is a completely different story. They do not want to integrate with any other one. [They do] Everything [on] their own because they don't trust them.' (Jana)

As others have noted (Batnitzky et al 2009; Dyer et al 2008; Thompson et al 2010), single male economic migrants are often in vulnerable positions. Many prioritise work and earning money, which may be sent home to origin countries as remittances. There are also suggestions that having partners or families at hand encourages anchoring practices (Grzymala-Kazlowska 2018). However, studies have also suggested that younger males are more likely to feel isolated and less integrated (Gill 2010; Gill and Bialsky 2011), and there is scope to suggest that this is a cohort that could see an increase in their well-being through greater participation in civil society. However, one respondent countered this view, reporting that from his experiences of working in a major Polish organisation in southern Wales it was older migrant men who felt more isolation, rather than younger people:

'Most of the young Polish people who come here basically they are integrated already because they wanted to be part of this society. They're learning English in their homeland. So they come here knowing English or if they don't know they want to learn as quickly as possible, because they know the more English they will have the better job they will get, but I think most of the Polish people I know they wanted to have British friends. ... What they do, we've got angling associations and people want to join the angling because they like this. They want to join the angling association. Then we talk about the British friends. They are really interested.' (Andrzej, Polish, 39)

Furthermore, many European citizens in Wales work and live in precarious situations. Writing on the context of Polish migration, Thompson et al (2010) note that accommodation is sometimes provided through agencies or gangmasters, and workers are often bussed in and out from different locations, limiting opportunities for participation and interaction with local civil society (Sporton 2013). These precarious situations, along with some exploitative practices, mean that some people have less time and opportunity to participate; for others, the need to maximise time spent working and earning may lead to participation being viewed as less of a priority.

While there is much discussion in many of the cases we have presented thus far, and in the literature more broadly, of reproducing national culture and languages among migrants' organisations (Gill 2010), we also note that another factor limiting participation among the groups we studied was disassociation, as Jana explains:

> 'For the community they do not integrate with settled Welsh community. Very rarely and between themselves as well. So when we organised the first Christmas party it was, "Oh I'm not coming because the person works in the office is coming and she's not very nice", but then eventually they realise why not, we can keep our traditions. We can meet up. There's nothing wrong with that. Somehow they felt, we don't want to do anything else with the Slovak community. We just came to the UK to live the UK life, but in their eyes it's not possible. We have about ten to 15 people are very proactive on the Facebook and they organise the things themselves as well, and they're helping others.' (Jana, Czech, 38)

For some migrants, whose emigration to the UK represented a clear distinction from their life in Slovakia or elsewhere, there was a desire to limit association with fellow migrants, which may be seen as inhibiting integration in a zero-sum conceptualisation. For Jana, and her fellow organisers, maintaining connections with co-nationals does not restrict integration; indeed, through providing support she argues that integration is facilitated. However, not all efforts led to integration. As Irena notes below, some initiatives were met with indifference:

> 'Nobody was interested. So I had to distribute them here in the Polish Centre here. So we had a trip, sort of, half people from Llanelli and half from Llanybydder. You can't do anything with them. You try to organise events. You know, take part in some barbecues or things like that. It just doesn't go. So they keep to themselves, both communities. They've even made a [TV] programme about it.' (Irena, Polish, 65)

As the accounts here demonstrate, many European migrants are motivated to participate in civil society to provide a good example of an immigrant or of a particular nationality, challenging the perceptions circulated around migration throughout the 2000s and 2010s. Many were also motivated to help people who were in a similar situation to them when they had migrated, and to give others the benefits of their experiences and skills. As these accounts also demonstrate, participation in civil society is also an anchoring experience. People can build connections with communities and feel attached to a locality. To this end, it allows some stability in what can be new or unfamiliar settings. However, many factors challenge this stability, providing a turbulent experience of civil society. We turn now to explore these factors.

Austerity, precarity and participation

Following the financial crisis of 2008, many states embarked on a programme of austerity. As Collett (2011) has noted, these policies had particular impact on public spending on groups working with immigrants, as services, such as language support for migrants, were targeted in the spending cuts. Such measures resonated with anti-immigrant sentiments, and migrant services were often perceived as 'softer' targets for cuts while having potential to make some political capital at the same time. One impact of these cuts is the loss of expertise when local authorities, for example, have been faced with the need to make savings. In order to retain a range of services (some of which may be a statutory requirement), fewer people are doing the same amount of work:

> 'The cutbacks in local authority [spending] have been such that there are less people doing more work within the local authority. So people can't have time to go to meetings or to do things they normally would do. Also I think there's a real issue with people taking on responsibility for things that they're not really qualified in.' (Jennifer, British, 58)

As Jennifer notes, expertise is lost following the reduction of the staff base, with people taking responsibility for fields in which they have no experience or qualification. Consequently, there is both less work due to the individuals trying to cover too many bases, and in having less knowledge and experience to deal adequately with the issues that arise.

In light of these cuts to local authorities, increasing pressure is put on civil society organisations to plug the gap. Many organisations and groups provide support in an informal way. That is, migrant assistance is not the purpose of the group, but they wish to adapt their activities to offer support. Much of this work is related to supporting engagements with state bureaucracies or potential employers, such as signposting services, helping with paperwork, and so forth:

> 'That's the way. There's only the one support. The Facebook page is very good at helping me in that way, but advocacy work is still here and the people need basic help with their paperwork. With their [social security/welfare] benefits. With their CVs. With the letters to employers. If it wasn't here lots of people wouldn't get the benefits they're having. They wouldn't be able to survive. Lots of people would

end up at social services. It's vital that something like this is here, but I'm here fifth year and I'm coming to the end of my passion because I see it every day and I see the frustration that nothing else is happening. We're coming to all these meetings and trying for all this funding, my bosses, and I feel like it's not going anywhere and it's getting only worse, the situation, but I somehow feel old. The problem is getting solved these problems. So I feel like, okay I should stop. So maybe a new life. You see what I mean?'

I: You're a bit overworked, yes, because of this situation?
R: It is. This is draining because you see all these people and you know you can't do any more and there should be more for them. (Jana, Czech, 38)

As Jana notes, she feels frustrated with the lack of progress and direction. She notes the embodied effect that this has on her, feeling old and drained. She worries about the situation, and feels that maybe she should stop for her own well-being. While initiatives such as GwirVol in Wales, and the Big Society in England, which has received far more attention in public discourse, are presented as opportunities, the impact of volunteers' emotional labour is rarely seen in media and policy discussions. Increasing reliance on civil society to make up the shortfall in public services has an effect where people may stop volunteering. This may be heightened when working on cases with upsetting or unjust aspects, which are plentiful under the government's hostile environment policies, which have seen families separated and people removed from the communities in which they have built their lives.

Alongside the emotional toll of participating in migrant-facing movements in civil society, there are also reductions to the core funding of organisations. In many cases, these organisations face uncertainty due to not knowing whether funding will continue:

R: Yeah, this is the second year now I think funding us and it's up to 1st of December, but we don't know it will be next year, if we will be here or not.
I: Are you gonna ... are you worried about?
R: Well, er ...
I: I heard your colleagues talking about this ...
R: We lose our job if we won't have the funding you know but, I don't know after that. (Maja, Polish, 34)

The uncertainty is not limited to whether the organisation can carry on, but also whether those paid for their labour will continue to have employment.

The often short turnaround before people knew if funding would continue often created a 'cliff-edge', which made planning difficult. In the case of one organisation, which worked extensively with Polish nationals in southern Wales, the uncertainty over future funding meant that they decided to wind-down the organisation:

I: We will close it because I've had enough of hassle. Once they miss it maybe something will happen, but I said to [Wales' then-First Minister] Carwyn Jones I'm not going to jump through any hoops for you because he was offering new grant, new money and whatever. I said, I want a service contract and nothing else, because that's the only way that you can guarantee some stability. I talked to the guy who put so much work in this town with the multicultural network. … No funding and that's it. So he works in a completely different sector now and everything fell apart. So we've been doing so much good work in line of cohesion and integration and stuff like that. He was really, really good for a few years.

I: It's not possible to extend, to ask the Department of Work and Pensions to extend this?

R: No, no. We've moved heaven and earth. Every politician. Every MP. We've had a meeting with the minister responsible for it, and all we got, no money. No money. No money. Everybody else is in the same position. You know, austerity, cuts and whatever. We're not going to beg any more. (Irena)

The continuous 'jumping through hoops' to secure funding and continue to operate, as well as the broader austerity context meant that Irena felt that she did not want to continue. While there has been an assumption that voluntary organisations will support the roll-back of the state, fatigue from dealing with state bureaucracy and other pressures may mean that volunteers and civil society practitioners reduce or stop their contribution (Jones and Heley 2014). For Irena, who had been active in her community for several years, the decision to step back means that her experience, skills and knowledge are lost. Without funding, or the energy, enthusiasm and experience demonstrated here, a further gap develops in the coverage of the shadow state.

The experience of coordinating an organisation in civil society in the context of a hostile environment also means that people may consider futures elsewhere; not just out of the movement, but also out of the country, as Branca notes:

'It was bad really. Even now I still feel sad but I'm like, I don't care. This is where I live. This is where I'm working with you. I've done nothing wrong with you. So please don't tell me that I'm coming here to do this or do that, because this is not true, but it took me a while. I was telling my daughter we're going. I don't want to stay here anymore. I don't want you to grow up in a country where you're not welcome. I don't want you to grow up where you're feeling oppressed. We're going, and she was like, oh mum what about Portugal, and I said Portugal, your first language is not Portuguese fluent because it's the first time ever we're going to have Portuguese classes. We've been requesting but it'll never happen, and I was saying, I think we should go to Scotland. I like them there. I was like, we're just not moving to Iceland because it's too cold. I'm always very cold, but Scotland is also cold. She said, I like the idea of Scotland. They're very open minded. Okay, we'll go to Scotland then, but then I remember I'm the Portuguese councillor. I can't just leave my boat like that. I have to be here until the end.' (Branca)

For Branca, the experience of Brexit means that she considered moving to Scotland, which she saw as more welcoming than Wales, which is itself constructed, somewhat selectively, and often in comparison to England, as a 'tolerant' nation (Williams et al 2003; Jackson and Dafydd Jones 2014). However, considering her roles in the community, and among the area's Portuguese speakers and Portuguese nationals, Branca feels that she cannot leave. Such a decision is not taken lightly, and demonstrates the commitment many participants in civil society have to their roles and organisations. Such participation, while seen as benevolent and altruistic, can often come to the detriment of individuals' well-being, if they feel under pressure and unable to move away from their commitments.

As this section has noted, there are a number of challenges to European migrants' continued participation in civil society in Wales. Austerity, fatigue, hostility and possible onward or return migration in light of Brexit all make people question their continued involvement with civil society. When there is a lack of funds, or key people do not feel that they can carry on, the ability of organisations to continue is threatened.

Conclusions

In this chapter we have outlined the role of European migrants in civil society in Wales. We have demonstrated that rather than the discourse of immigrants as passive and requiring care, many are active and provide support for others. These accounts demonstrate that migrants are involved in a range of organisations, formal and informal, online and offline, based around various localities around Wales. For the migrants we spoke with, involvement with civil society provided them with an opportunity to develop and use their skills, knowledge and experience, and to foster connections with people and places where they built their lives. To this end, civil society functions as an anchoring practice, allowing attachments to be developed, facilitating integration.

However, our findings also show that a number of challenges destabilise civil society organisations and European migrants' involvements with them. A key example is austerity, meaning more competition for reducing pots of money, and anxiety and stress in attempting to do more with less. This threatens the viability of many organisations and the role they play in the 'shadow state', leading to them being wound-up or for participants to reduce their roles. The loss of participants is also brought about by Brexit, and the increased prevalence of hate, hostility and abuse that has surfaced during the referendum campaign and its aftermath. The withdrawal of the UK from the EU may lead many European migrants to reconsider their futures in Wales. The hostile environment and the climate of permissive vilification of immigrants may ease that decision for some: in January 2020 Wales reported lower rates of application for settled status than other constituent countries of the UK (BBC 2020). This means that active people prepared to spend their time and energy in benevolent activities may be lost. These conditions contribute to the ongoing uncertain conditions: challenges which make it difficult to plot the future course of migrant-oriented civil society organisations.

This broader climate of uncertainty should alert governments to the precarious situation of civil society, and to the people in precarious situations they often support. If organisations wind up due to uncertainty around future budgets, or people stop their involvement due to moving away or not feeling that their contributions are valued, their ability to function as part of a shadow state is curtailed, limiting its reach. Given the way in which precarity and uncertainty contribute to the turbulence of the age, our findings raise serious concerns about the support and wider policy environment that sustains civil society.

References

Ahmed, A. (2011) 'Belonging out of context: The intersection of place, networks and ethnic identity among retired British migrants living in the Costa Blanca', *Journal of Identity and Migration Studies*, 5(2), 33–45.

Alrababa'h, A., Marble, W., Mousa, S. and Siegel, A. (2021) 'Can exposure to celebrities reduce prejudice? The effect of Mohammed Salah on Islamophobic behaviors and attitues', *American Political Science Review* (online first). Available at: https://www.cambridge.org/core/journals/american-political-science-review/article/can-exposure-to-celebrities-reduce-prejudice-the-effect-of-mohamed-salah-on-islamophobic-behaviors-and-attitudes/A1DA34F9F5BCE905850AC8FBAC78BE58

Aleksynska, M. (2011) 'Civic participation of immigrants in Europe: Assimilation, origin and destination country effects', *European Journal of Political Economy*, 27(3): 566–585.

Batnitzky, A., McDowell, L. and Dyer, S. (2009) Flexible and strategic masculinities: The working lives and gendered identities of male migrants in London. *Journal of Ethnic and Migration Studies*, 35(8): 1275–1293.

Bauman, Z. (2000) *Liquid Modernity*, Cambridge: Polity Press.

BBC (2020) 'Brexit: Wales' EU citizens behind in applications to stay', 29 January 2020. Available at: https://www.bbc.co.uk/news/uk-wales-51285843]

Beaumont, J. (2008) 'Introduction: Faith-based organisations and urban social justice', *Urban Studies*, 45(10): 2011–2017.

Burrell, K. and Schweyher, M. (2019) 'Conditional citizens and hostile environments', *Geoforum*, 106: 193–201.

Collet, B. (2011). 'The sociocultural reality of French-Foreign mixed marriages: An analysis of statistical data from a survey of new immigrants', *Revue européenne des migrations internationales*, 27, 7–34. https://doi.org/10.4000/remi.5516

Darling, J. (2011) 'Domopolitics, governmentality and the regulation of asylum accommodation', *Political Geography*, 30(5): 263–271.

de Lima, P. J. F. (2004) 'John O'Groats to Land's End: Racial equality in Britain?' in N. Chakraborti and J. Garland (eds), *Rural Racism*, Oxford: Willan, pp 36–60.

Demireva, N. and Heath, A. (2014) 'Diversity and the civic spirit in British neighbourhoods: An investigation with MCDS and EMBES 2010 data', *Sociology*, 48(4): 643–662.

Drinkwater, S. and Garapich, M. (2015) 'Migration strategies of recent Polish migrants to England and Wales: Do they have any at all'? *Journal of Ethnic and Migration Studies*, 41(12): 1909–1931.

Drinkwater, S., Jones, R. D. and Guma, T. (2019) *Civic participation among migrants to the UK*, mimeo, WISERD.

Dyer, S., McDowell, L. and Batnitzky, A. (2008) 'Emotional labour/body work: The caring labours of migrants in the UK's National Health Service', *Geoforum*, 39(6): 2030–2038.

Engbersen, G. and Snel, E. (2013) 'Liquid migration: Dynamic and fluid patterns of post-accession migration', in B. Glorius, I. Grabowska-Lusinska and A. Rindoks (eds), *Mobility in Transition: Migration patterns after EU enlargement*, Amsterdam: Amsterdam University Press, pp 21–40.

Gill, N. (2010) 'Pathologies of migrant place-making: polish migration to the UK', *Environment and Planning A*, 5(42): 1157–1173.

Gill, N. and Bialsky, P. (2011) 'New friends in new places: Network formation during the migration process among Poles in the UK', *Geoforum*, 42(2): 241–249.

Grzymala-Kazlowska, A. (2018) 'From connecting to social anchoring: Adaptation and "settlement" of Polish migrants in the UK', *Journal of Ethnic and Migration Studies*, 44(2): 252–269.

Guentner, S., Lukes, S., Stanton, R., Vollmer, B.A. and Wilding, J. (2016) 'Bordering practices in the UK welfare system', *Critical Social Policy*, 36(3): 391–411.

Guma, T. and Dafydd Jones, Rh. (2019) "Where are we going to go now?" European Union migrants' experiences of hostility, anxiety, and (non-) belonging during Brexit, Volume 25, Issue 1, Special Issue: Negotiating Brexit: Migrant spatialities and identities in a changing Europe, e2198. https://doi.org/10.1002/psp.2198

Guma, T., Woods, M., Yarker, S. and Anderson, T. (2019) 'It's that kind of place here: Solidarity, place-making and civil society response to the 2015 refugee crisis in Wales', *Social Issues*, 7(2) 96–105.

Hall, S. M. (2015) 'Migrant urbanisms: Ordinary cities and everyday resistance', *Sociology*, 49(5): 853–869.

Heath, A. and Li, Y. (2015) 'Review of the relationship between religion and poverty: An analysis for the Joseph Rowntree Foundation', *Centre for Social Investigation Working Paper: 2015–01*, Oxford: Nuffield College, University of Oxford.

Heley, J. and Jones, L. (2013) 'Growing older and social sustainability: Considering the "serious leisure" practices of the over 60s in rural communities', *Social and Cultural Geography*, 14(3): 276–299.

Heley, J., Yarker, S. and Jones, L. (2019) 'Volunteering in the bath? Microvolunteering and the implications for policy', *Journal of Policy Studies* (online first). Available at: https://www.tandfonline.com/doi/full/10.1080/01442872.2019.1645324

Hiam, L., Steele, S. and McKee, M. (2018) 'Creating a "hostile environment for migrants": The British government's use of health service data to restrict immigration is a very bad idea', *Health Economics, Policy and Law*, 13: 107–117.

Home Office (2018) *Hate Crime, England and Wales, 2017/18*. Home Office Statistical Bulletin 20/18, London: Home Office.

Hubbard, P. (2005). 'Accommodating otherness: Anti-asylum centre protest and the maintenance of white privilege', *Transactions of the Institute of British Geographers*, 30(1), 52–65. http://www.jstor.org/stable/3804529

Jackson, L. and Jones, R. D. (2014) "'We'll keep a welcome"? Proximity, distance, and hospitality towards migrants in Wales', *Contemporary Wales*, 27(1): 82–104.

Jones, L. and Heley, J. (2014) 'Practices of participation and voluntarism among older people in rural Wales: Choice, obligation, and constraints to active ageing', *Socioligia Ruralis*, 56(2): 176–196.

Jones, T. and Norwood, K. J. (2017) 'Aggressive encounters and white fragility: Deconstructing the trope of the Angry Black Woman', *Iowa Law Review*, 102: 2017–2069.

Kofman, E. (2002) 'Contemporary European migrations, civic stratification and citizenship', *Political Geography*, 21(8): 1035–1054.

Light, D. and Young, C. (2009) 'European Union enlargement, post-accession migration and imaginative geographies of the "New Europe": Media discourses in Romania and the United Kingdom', *Journal of Cultural Geography*, 16(3): 281–303.

Lowndes, V. and Pratchett, L. (2012) 'Local governance under the coalition government: Austerity, localism, and the "Big Society"', *Local Government Studies*, 38(1): 21–40.

Lulle, A., Moroşanu, L. and King, R. (2018) 'And then came Brexit: Experiences and future plans of young EU migrants in the London region', *Population, Space & Place*, 24(1): e2122.

Lulle, A., King, R., Dvorakova, V. and Szkudlarek, A. (2019) 'Between disruptions and connections: "New" European Union migrants in the United Kingdom before and after Brexit', *Population, Space & Place*, 25(1): e2200.

Malcolm, D. (2004) 'Outsiders within: The reality of rural racism', in N. Chakraborti and J. Garland (eds), *Rural Racism*, Oxford: Willan, pp 63–84.

McDowell, L. (2009) 'Old and new European economic migrants: Whiteness and managed migration policies', *Journal of Ethnic and Migration Studies*, 35(1): 19–36. DOI: 10.1080/13691830802488988

McFall, S., Nandi, A. and Platt, L. (2014) *Understanding Society: UK Household Longitudinal Study: User guide to ethnicity research*, Institute of Social and Economic Research, University of Essex.

Meissner, F. and Heil, T. (2020) 'Deromanticising integration: On the importance of convivial disintegration', *Migration Studies*, 9(3): 740–758. https://doi.org/10.1093/migration/mnz056

Miller, R. G. (2019) '(Un)settling home during the Brexit process', *Population, Space & Place*, 25(1): e2203. https://doi.org/10.1002/psp.2203

Mills, S. and Waite, C. (2017) 'Brands of youth citizenship and the politics of scale: National Citizen Service in the United Kingdom', *Political Geography*, 56(1): 66–76.

Mills, S. and Waite, C. (2018) 'From big society to shared society? Geographies of social cohesion and encounter in the UK's National Citizen Service', *Geografiskker Annaler: Series B Human Geography*, 100(2): 131–148.

Mulvey, G. (2010) 'When policy creates bad politics: The problematizing of immigration and the consequences for refugee integration in the UK', *Journal of Refugee Studies*, 25(4): 437–462.

Ranta, R. and Nancheva, N. (2019) 'Unsettled: Brexit and European Union nationals' sense of belonging', *Population, Space & Place*, 25(1): e2199. https://doi.org/10.1002/psp.2199

Robinson, V. and Gardner, H. (2004) 'Unravelling a stereotype: The lived experience of black and minority ethnic people in rural Wales', in N. Chakraborti and J. Garland (eds), *Rural Racism*, Oxford: Willan, pp 85–107.

Rzepnikowska, R. (2019) 'Racism and xenophobia experienced by Polish migrants in the UK before and after Brexit vote', *Journal of Ethnic and Migration Studies*, 45(1): 61–77.

Song, M. (2004) 'When the "global chain" does not lead to satisfaction all round: A comment on the Morecambe Bay tragedy', *Feminist Review*, 77(1): 137–140.

Spigelman, A. (2013) 'The depiction of Polish migrants in the United Kingdom by the British press after Poland's accession to the European Union', *International Journal of Sociology and Social Policy*, 33(1/2): 98–113.

Sporton, D. (2013) '"They control my life": The role of recruitment agencies in east European migration to the UK', *Population, Space & Place*, 19(3): 443–458.

Thompson, A., Lever, J. and Knight, J. (2010) 'The Labour Market Mobility of Polish Migrants: A comparative study of three regions in South Wales, UK', *Central and East European Migration Review*, 3(2): 61–78.

Williams, A., Goodwin, M. and Cloke, P. (2014) 'Neoliberalism, big society, and progressive localism', *Environment and Planning A*, 46(12): 2798–2815.

Williams, C., Evans, N. and O'Leary, P. (2003) *A Tolerant Nation? Exploring race and ethnic diversity in Wales*, Cardiff: University of Wales Press.

Wolch, J. (1989) 'The shadow state: Transformations in the voluntary sector', in J. Wolch and M. Dear (eds), *The Power of Geography: How territory shapes social life*, London: Routledge, pp 197–221.

Wray, H. (2011) *Regulating Marriage Migration into the UK*, London: Routledge.

Yeo, C. (2017) How complex is UK immigration law and is this a problem? Freemovement, 24 January. Available at: https://www.freemovement.org.uk/how-complex-are-the-uk-immigration-rules-and-is-this-a-problem/

Yuval-Davis, N., Wemyss, G. and Cassidy, K. (2017) 'Everyday bordering, belonging and the reorientation of the British immigration legislation', *Sociology*, 52(2): 228–244.

9

Meeting the challenge? Prospects and perils for civil society in the twenty-first century

Paul Chaney and Ian Rees Jones

The chapters in this edited collection have examined how the uncertainties of the age present diverse challenges to civil society at the beginning of the twenty-first century. We have drawn on a wide range of studies from WISERD's Civil Society research programme. The first part of this concluding chapter summarises the different existential challenges with reference to the principal findings of each study and how they link to civic stratification. The second part outlines the common themes emerging from this volume and the associated prospects and perils for civil society organisations.

Principal findings, existential challenges and civic stratification

Drawing upon David Lockwood's (1996) conceptualisation, the present volume underlines how the existential challenges and the uncertainties facing civil society impact on civic stratification in the form of civic deficit and exclusion as well as civic expansion and gain. Lockwood posits that 'the institutional unity of citizenship, market and bureaucratic relations is central to social cohesion' (1996: 531). However, in a specific and qualified sense, the studies presented here point to the demise of institutional unity of citizenship. This is because of the global trend of state decentralisation and the rise of meso – or 'regional' – governance. Lockwood cannot be blamed for not foreseeing the full impact of this. He did, however, view demands for constitutional reform as a mode of civic expansion (p 535). His seminal work was formed in an era largely characterised by what Wimmer and Glick Schiller (2002: 301) term 'methodological nationalism', or the assumption that the state-wide practices are the natural social and political form of the modern world. As this volume's findings illustrate, devolution in the UK is leading to the territorialisation of welfare citizenship, trust, identity and rights (see Chaney 2013, 2015, 2021c). For so-called 'sub-state' nations such as Wales and Scotland, the present may be a stepping-off point, a transitional stage on the way to independent statehood. What we do know from the studies in this volume is that the rise of territorial electoral politics and meso-government is significant because prevailing policy approaches in each UK nation are grounded in the different ideological orientations of the dominant parties. As Morris (2016: 697) explains, 'civic stratification constitutes a system of inequality by virtue of the granting or denial of rights by the state'. The present findings show how Left-of-Centre socialist and civic nationalist governments in Wales and Scotland have eschewed the neo-liberal policy prescriptions of successive Westminster governments and, supporting Lockwood's prescient observation about constitutional reform, have (with varying degrees of effectiveness) pursued programmes to advance rights, recognition and redistribution and promote civic expansion (Fraser 1997; Fraser and Honneth 2003).[1]

As Lockwood (1996: 534; emphasis added) asserts 'at the most abstract level, the unity and coherence of market, bureaucratic, and citizenship relations is to be found in *the manner in which they combine to create a social universe*'. This resonates with contingency theory (compare Chapter 1) and emphasises temporality (changing governance contexts and challenges facing civil society organisations over time) and spatiality.

Such themes are to the fore in Chapter 3 'Civil society and the governance of city region economic development'. David Beel, Martin Jones and Ian Rees Jones analysed how new spatial political units of governance for economic development are (re-)positioning civil society. This is important because, hitherto, much of the academic work on the city region agenda has been primarily focused upon economic development, often overlooking the implications for civil society autonomy and criticality.

In the UK, regional disparities have perpetuated over time and are continuing. City regions are reinforcing this by developing at contrasting rates and adopting different forms. They are spatial fixes for several economic deficiencies in the UK's growth model and align with academic and policy literatures that vaunt economic growth through agglomeration. Agglomeration at the city region scale features in ideological discourse that is dominant within the neo-liberal growth model of urban development thinking. This celebrates the development of the urban while ignoring the structural inequality it creates. The political project of city regionalism is, therefore, to rescale the central city into a much larger territory and to bring surrounding territories under its control. Due to this, everything else becomes a secondary concern.

Viewed through the lens of civic stratification, the rise of city regions poses 'questions of how inequalities of class and status affect the institutionalization of citizenship and thereby its integrative function' (Lockwood 1996: 531). To unpack this, the analysis in Chapter 3 shows the challenges posed to civil society by agglomerative, city regional models. These have been primarily focused upon economic development, often to the detriment more social concerns. In turn, this suggests new modes of civic deficit and civic exclusion in relation to civil society's participation and influence in the new decision-making institutions of city regions. In a spatial sense, it also points to the rise of differential economic (and political) citizenship rights depending on whether, with their higher levels of state investment, citizens are located within or outside the geographical boundaries of city regions. As the analysis notes, those outside are in danger of civic exclusion and civic deficit. The overall potential effect is increased class inequalities and stratification, as well as a pronounced urban–rural divide in cases such as the Swansea City Region.

The analysis also highlights gaps in the political justification for city regions' agglomerative 'trickle-down' approach. If proponents are correct and it leads to what the current Tory Westminster government alludes to as 'levelling-up', city regions are institutionalising mechanisms for class restructuring. Yet the same is true if, more likely, the result is less of a case of levelling-up than a respatialising of inequalities (Etherington and Jones 2018). It is also the case that city regions are reshaping welfare rights within the respective national policy frameworks of Wales and England. This is more pronounced in the case of England. For example, with distinctive, territorialised approaches to employment, skills and welfare policies in the Sheffield City Region (Etherington and Jones 2016, 2018; Beatty et al 2019; Hoole and Hincks 2020). The authors conclude with a bleak prognosis, noting that in relation to city regions and the latest Westminster 'levelling up' and post-pandemic recovery agendas, civil society actors are struggling to get to the debating table. In consequence, the limited extent of social mobilisation and civil society engagement identified in this chapter looks set to continue.

Chapter 4, 'Civil society, pandemic, and the crisis of welfare: exploring mixed economy models of welfare in domiciliary adult social care in a devolved UK' by Paul Chaney and Christala Sophocleous, explored mixed economy of welfare models in domiciliary adult social care (ASC) in a devolved UK. Over recent decades there have been significant cuts to welfare services and extensive outsourcing to the private sector. The resultant crisis in state welfare provision is an issue that has international salience with a burgeoning literature covering Europe (Smith 2004; Yerkes and van der Veen 2011; Brewis et al 2021), the Americas (Skocpol 2011) and beyond (Lee and Chan 2007; Kwon 2009). It has led to the rise of welfare pluralism, whereby state welfare delivery is complemented by civil society and private sector organisations. Comparative analysis of stakeholders' views in the four nations of the UK is instructive because devolution in the UK has created a natural experiment in welfare mixes. Chapter 4 examined whether mixed economy approaches are the answer to meeting modern welfare needs with reference to the pre-COVID policy frameworks and the subsequent pandemic responses. The analysis revealed key contrasts and commonalities across polities. The Welsh model of ASC delivery was revealed to be distinctive for its interventionist underpinnings, notably, with a legal duty placed on local government to promote third sector organisations in the delivery of domiciliary ASC. However, a key finding was the importance of effective policy implementation, for while legislation may be innovative, the results may be counterproductive. The new legislation, far from promoting collectivism, has led to marketisation. The comparative analysis further revealed that a marketised approach to ASC was a key failing across polities. In each country there was widespread use of spot contracts and brokerage systems, as well as insufficient funding for contracts to deliver ASC. These factors were found to prevent third sector and private organisations from paying staff sufficiently and promoted commissioning-led income insecurity. In turn, this has a negative impact on interactions with service users.

Moreover, this analysis of the crisis of welfare and community–domiciliary ASC revealed mixed patterns and processes of civic deficit and exclusion. Stakeholders underlined how ethnic minorities and poorer communities were subject to heightened inequalities during the pandemic, often struggling to access care during the COVID-19 crisis. In addition, access to affordable social care was shaped by contrasting policy frameworks in the different nations of the UK. Marketised approaches to ASC provision were evident in each nation, but their impact played out in strikingly different ways. Notwithstanding a plethora of caveats and conditions, ASC is 'free' at the point of use in Northern Ireland and Scotland. In contrast, it is means-tested in Wales and England. However, in Wales the threshold of permissible retained property and savings before payment is due to the local authority is double that of England. Moreover, the pursuit of neo-liberal policies in England has resulted in the near extinction of the state sector in ASC provision and resulted in the highest level of self-funders of all UK countries. The findings tell us that for those families in England that cannot afford to pay for care the situation is precarious. Often responsibility for delivering care falls entirely on family members' shoulders, regardless of their health, well-being and ability to provide such assistance. In consequence, stakeholders referred to the increasingly common practice of families forced to make informal arrangements with charities and/or other providers in a 'grey economy' of ASC that largely falls outside statutory processes. The prevailing crisis of care in England provides a troubling illustration of what Lockwood (1996: 535) refers to as 'the endemic contradiction between citizenship and capital'. As Chapter 4 reveals, devolution and the territorialisation of welfare citizenship presents a dynamic picture of civic stratification across UK nations. This is driven by multilevel electoral politics (Chaney 2021a) and, when compared to England, grounded in the markedly different political and ideological orientations of governments in Wales, Scotland and Northern Ireland. Thus, a key finding is the often-overlooked political provenance of social policy and how the policy frameworks on ASC outside of England seek to deliver civic expansion by conveying broader, more universalistic welfare rights.

The experience of the pandemic confirmed the need for systemic reform of ASC delivery in each nation. In the view of stakeholders this will require both leadership and political ownership across the whole system of care and support. Without the adoption of new approaches to mixed-economy ASC delivery, the longer-term impact of the pandemic is likely to see the continuation of short-term funding of not-for-profit organisations by government. This transfers risk and responsibility without securing civil society organisations' longer-term survival. Future success will depend upon the state–market–family–community configurations in social welfare provision and the power relationship between the state and the third sector. A further crucial factor guiding the success of the reforms is whether politicians and policy-makers listen to the situated knowledge of civil society providers – as well as the views of service users. Past evidence does not bode well.

In Chapter 5 'The contemporary threat to minority languages and cultures: civil society, young people and Celtic language use in Scotland and Wales', Rhys Jones, Elin Royles, Fiona O'Hanlon and Lindsay Paterson explored civil society's past and present roles in addressing the existential threat facing two 'minority' languages, Welsh and Scottish Gaelic. This is an internationally salient issue with many minority languages under threat (Mooko 2006; Sherris and Penfield 2011). In part driven by globalisation, a predicted half of the estimated 6,800 languages spoken today will have disappeared by the end of the twenty-first century. Language death is preceded by language shift, involving the reduction in overall numbers of speakers, the breaking down of intergenerational transmission and a downturn in the use of minority languages both in everyday settings and in different areas of life. In consequence, the speakers of minority languages choose, instead, to speak 'majority' languages. The existential challenges facing both Welsh and Scottish Gaelic are revealed to be stark. Both are in a precarious demographic and sociolinguistic position. From an estimated 95 per cent of the population able to speak Welsh in 1801, the current figure is approximately 19 per cent. In Scotland, the 1891 census showed 6.8 per cent of the Scottish population (254,415 people) to be Gaelic speaking. Today this figure is 1.1 per cent. The new analysis in Chapter 5 highlights the key past role played by civil society organisations in staving off language death and reversing language decline in the two countries. This involved mobilisation, protest and civil disobedience and has resulted in new legal rights and a significant expansion of minority language education.

The analysis also presented a series of new findings on the contemporary role of national festivals in seeking to promote minority language use in social contexts. This matters because while both languages have seen an increase in the number of speakers, much of the gain has been associated with formal state education. The wider literature warns us that a language which is confined to the educational sector is not a living language. Therefore, much depends on civil society organisations' co-working with state agencies to promote language use in social settings. The case studies were the *Eisteddfod Cenedlaethol* (National Eisteddfod) in Wales and *Am Mòd Nàiseanta Rìoghail* (Mòd) in Scotland, the latter being an eight-day annual Gaelic language and culture festival which aims to support and develop all aspects of the Gaelic language, culture, history and heritage.

Viewed through the civic stratification lens, this analysis of the contemporary threat to minority languages provides mixed evidence. The historical overview in the first part of the chapter reminds us of how civil society mobilisation and protest, largely from the 1960s onwards, led to civic expansion through new legal language rights (for example, the Welsh Language Act 1967; the Welsh Language Act 1993; the Welsh Language (Wales) Measure 2011; and the Gaelic Language (Scotland Act 2005)) accompanied by a significant programme of state support for both minority languages, notably in compulsory phase education. These are the actions of 'those seeking to establish new rights of citizenship as "civic activists"' (Lockwood 1996: 542). Yet the chapter also tells us that Welsh and Scottish Gaelic speakers are still subject to civic deficit and often they are not able to live all aspects of their lives through Welsh or Scottish Gaelic. In turn, this underlines the contingent nature of this aspect of civic deficit and its temporal and spatial grounding in past, historical rounds of exclusion. Against the backdrop of a shift to more favourable social attitudes towards the two languages, the analysis in Chapter 5 underlines the importance of cultural festivals in helping to reverse language decline by providing opportunities for young people to expand their minority language use to informal, social settings. It also provides rich insights into how young people experience opportunities or contexts very differently depending on their identities, attitudes and motivations, leading to different patterns of participation in minority language events. The findings also suggest that potentially negative associations of minority language promotion within different settings is changing. While minority languages may well have contributed in the past to the formation of divisions within civil society, today there is growing awareness and recognition of their inclusive potential to act as facilitators of social interaction, civic expansion and positive identity formation. Recent policy statements in relation to race equality and minority languages and contemporary academic research on such themes emphasise this positive potential (for example, Jones and Royles, 2020b). Thus, over coming years, civil society will have a key role in determining the nature of further civic expansion. This includes holding political elites to account for policies such as the Welsh government's 'Cymraeg 2050: A million Welsh speakers' (Welsh Government 2017) that aims to achieve one million Welsh speakers by 2050.

In Chapter 6, 'Digital threat or opportunity? Local civil society in an age of global inter-connectivity', Michael Woods, Taulant Guma and Sophie Yarker examined the challenges and opportunities for local civil society posed by digital technologies, especially social media. Drawing upon case studies of local civil society groups in three localities in Wales – Aberystwyth, Cardiff and Swansea – they explored the dynamics of reconfiguration of local civil society and how the new digital technologies have created a new universal space of social awareness, identity, belonging and collective action. This is underpinned by a growth in global consciousness and values, mediated by transnational institutions and NGOs. A key issue is whether this presents an existential threat to local civil society, with the global and the local pitted against each other in a zero-sum game, or whether more sophisticated processes are at work.

The emerging evidence points to the latter. Digital technologies have had both positive and negative impacts. Interviewees spoke of the perceived weakening of established social networks and sites of engagement within communities. In contrast, others saw digital technologies as affording opportunities to rebuild local community identities through hyper-local platforms, providing new ways of connecting neighbours and new vehicles for civil society action. Grounding global issues in local concerns and actions was shown to enable individuals to identify manageable responses in their locality. The flexibility of digital technologies offers local civil society groups tools and resources for new ways of organising that are less constrained by the formalised structures of older groups and more open to collaboration and interactive participation. Thus, Woods et al's analysis provides mixed evidence on the impact of new digital technologies on social stratification. On the one hand, it found that digital technologies have enabled civic expansion as local civil society groups forge connections beyond their locale. These external contacts can form a resource that may be mobilised to support local civil society objectives. Social media also allow local civil society activists to connect with other individuals involved with similar groups and campaigns in other places, providing mutual support. In contrast, the analysis also points to the potential for civic deficit and exclusion. For example, over-reliance on social media can exclude members of local communities that are not online, especially older residents, thus creating a new digital 'participation gap'. In addition, there was evidence of social exclusion and how social media can expose local civil society groups in ways not encountered historically, with incidences of online trolling and refugee support groups targeted with racist and xenophobic abuse.

Overall, the analysis underlines that digital technologies have raised consciousness of global issues and many individuals respond to the enormity of such problems through grounded actions in their own localities, reconnecting with local civil society organisations or forming new groups oriented around issues such as environmental change, food and refugees. The greatest asset of local civil society is that it is embedded in real places and that, as such, digital technologies are most effective and empowering when they are used to reinforce and not replace the physical coming together of community members.

In Chapter 7, 'Democratic decline? Civil society and trust in government', Alistair Cole, Ian Stafford and Dominic Heinz examined the contemporary decline of political trust and the potential existential threat that it poses to democracy. Drawing on comparative analysis from the UK, France and Germany it analysed governance–trust configurations and their likely propensity to foster co-production and co-creation between state and civil society. A key finding was the extent to which the development of trust within civil society varies as much within as between states. The analysis also highlighted how the COVID-19 pandemic has generally accelerated the erosion of trust. Specifically, it has created 'trust bubbles' characterised by an initial increase, then a decline in trust in government. As the study findings show, this bubble already appears to have burst in the UK, shrunk to a smaller degree in Germany, and grown between May 2020 and January 2021 in France. The study argues that potential solutions for restoring political trust and reversing the perceived decline of democracy have civil society at their heart and include the adoption of more diverse and effective forms of citizen engagement. Yet the discussion in Chapter 7 also warns that this is fraught with difficulties. Notably, the authors argue that the adoption of co-creation or co-production to build trust with civil society actors is likely to be most challenging in new governance regions where a shared history or identity is largely absent. A further key finding is that the character of trust relations across the three states and six sub-national territories is shaped by the extent to which the restructuring of governance arrangements within a territory impacted cooperation between the state and civil spheres. In those territories where governance reorganisation was a relatively recent event it was more likely that rebuilding trust would face specific challenges related to ongoing spatial tensions. Importantly, while the fieldwork did not identify a single, specific approach as being effective at building trust, it emphasised that the mechanism must respond to the territorial context.

When positing his framework for examining social stratification, Lockwood makes no direct mention of trust. Rather it is implicit in the category he refers to as 'moral resources' – or 'the advantages conferred by social standing and social networks, command of information, and general know-how, including the ability to attain one's ends through the activation of shared moral sentiments, whether or not the actor's orientation to such standards is sincere or disingenuous' (Lockwood 1996: 536). Cole et al's analysis underlines how decline in trust is complex and the importance of tailoring restorative arrangements to the territorial context. Using Lockwood's framework (1996: 537), lack of trust in government can be viewed as a specific type of civic deficit, namely a power deficit. This is because, as the literature on democratic legitimacy (for example, Suchman 1995; Seligman 1997) explains, the power of governments is derived from the legitimacy conveyed by the people (namely, the electorate). A decline in trust can undermine the perceived legitimacy of government and its right to rule. In extreme cases – such as the Heath and Callaghan Westminster governments (1974 and 1979, respectively), the decline may reach a tipping point when loss of trust leads to widespread civil protest and unrest, and ultimately a parliamentary vote of no confidence in the government, fresh elections and regime change.

In contrast to state-wide government, examination of trust between civil society actors at the 'sub-national' level highlighted the importance of understanding the wider context within which increasingly complex forms of multi-level governance are emerging. In addition, there appears to be a territorial dimension to the impact of COVID-19 on political trust, particularly in the case of the UK. It has provided a political and mass media platform for the devolved level which is usually absent. Thus, the Welsh government is subject to far higher trust levels for its handling of the COVID-19 emergency, compared to the UK government. This finding suggests that the sub-national level potentially provides an ideal platform for the building or rebuilding of public trust, although it is important to note that the existing evidence is somewhat mixed, and it is possible that the perceived performance of government remains the key variable in driving trust.

The findings from Chapter 8, 'Xenophobia, hostility and austerity: European migrants and civil society in Wales' by Stephen Drinkwater, Taulant Guma and Rhys Dafydd Jones, highlight turbulence and uncertainty in relation to contemporary patterns and processes of migration. This has been driven by a variety of causes, including the international rise of populism and Brexit. The latter has seen inflammatory discourse surrounding immigration, and an accompanying sharp increase in reported hate crimes. Many EU citizens have been targeted in xenoracist incidents. Further drivers of uncertainty include substantial cuts to public services, including those for immigrants, refugees and asylum seekers, as well as Brexit's implications for migration. Drinkwater et al's study provides further mixed evidence in relation to civic stratification. Viewed from today's perspective and contemporary international protest under the banner of Black Lives Matter, writing a quarter a century ago

Lockwood (1996: 554) offered another prescient assessment when, referring to racial inequality he noted:

> This fault line in civic integration is likely to widen under conditions of high unemployment, the voluntary or involuntary ghettoization of ethnic minorities, and uncertainty about, and therefore obsession with, national identity. Perhaps the question then is, not why minorities protest against such discrimination, but why protest does not take on a more widespread political form.

This chapter's exploration of migrants' roles and their experiences of civil society revealed civic exclusion stemming from the ongoing hostile environment created by Brexit that made many feel that they no longer belonged or were wanted in the UK. The analysis also reveals a civic participation gap between migrants and non-migrants. Weighed against these negative factors, it also provided evidence of civic expansion and gain. In contrast to dominant integrationist views of migrants' participation that presents them as passive and requiring support (for example, Home Office 2020), Chapter 8 provided rich evidence of immigrants being resourceful agents and civil society makers, setting up and running new civil society initiatives to tackle dominant negative discourses about migrants. Following the UK's move to quasi-federalism, policy on refugees and asylum seekers is increasingly territorialised, with civic expansion of social welfare rights (including in relation to health, housing, social services, education and training) in the devolved countries (Chaney 2021b).

The discussion also highlighted the likely under-recording of hate incidents because study participants said they did not report some aspects of abuse, such as microaggression, staring and avoidance. In addition, the interview data revealed that political campaigns and the media created a permissive environment for xenophobia and xenoracism. In turn, this underlined that broader, structural efforts are needed to challenge racism and xenophobia. The migrants interviewed also spoke of how participation in civil society was an anchoring practice. Contributing to an organisation allows interaction with longer-term residents and other newcomers. Having a migrant visible and audible in a role such as community champion was also seen as contributing to the creation of positive images of migrants. Furthermore, the analysis showed several challenges to European migrants' continued participation in civil society in Wales, including austerity, fatigue and hostility. For immigrants the experience of coordinating an organisation in civil society in the context of a hostile environment often led them to consider futures elsewhere. Given the way in which precarity and uncertainty contribute to the turbulence of the age, the findings raise serious concerns about the wider policy environment that sustains civil society.

Emerging themes: prospects and perils facing civil society organisations

We conclude by highlighting a number of common, non-discrete themes that emerge from the empirical analysis in this volume. These capture the prospects and perils associated with the existential challenges facing civil society in an age of uncertainty.

Precarity, neo-liberalism and marketisation

There are a number of dimensions to the current precarious situation of civil society. One of the principal aspects of precarity emerging from the analysis in this volume is the need for civil society organisations to maintain their financial and operational sustainability. This is an enduring issue, *inter alia*, stemming from tensions between capitalism – notably the rise of neo-liberalism, voluntarism and welfare. Over recent decades there have been significant cuts to welfare services and extensive outsourcing to the private sector. The latter has been based on cost-based tendering and marketisation. The resultant crisis in third sector funding is an issue that has international salience (Suárez and Gugerty 2016; Civicus 2019). Brexit is a further factor to note here because European structural funding was an important income source for many civil society organisations in the UK (Mahoney and Beckstrand 2016).

Addressing precarity and safeguarding civil society's strengths is overtly political in nature. Its roots go back to foundational writings on civil society's role as a potential watchdog of democracy (compare De Tocqueville 1835/ 2000; Cohen and Arato 1992; Kumar 1993), as well as classic liberal theorists' work on participatory democracy (compare Hobbes, Locke and Rousseau). A key role for contemporary civil society is questioning the rise of neo-liberalism, marketisation and attendant outsourcing to the private sector. As noted, this has been associated with significant cuts to state welfare services. At its heart this is a debate about policy based on the neo-liberal imperative of capital accumulation through profit-seeking and personal/corporate gain, versus civil society values of civility, collectivism, voluntarism and acting for the greater good. Inherent in this dyad is the role of civil society in holding governments to account for their policy programmes. As the discussion of city regions and the neo-liberal growth model of urban development in Chapter 3 illustrates, there is a particular need for civil society to question the evidence-base of ideologically grounded programmes and call out governments that justify their policy agendas on partial and selective evidence. As the analysis of city regions also underlines, a further key challenge for civil society is to make its voice heard. Often it is government that decides the 'rules of the game' and, as the city regions analysis tells us, this can result in civil society voices being silenced or marginalised in institutional processes designed by those in power.

New governance structures, spatial processes and institutional change

As Barberis (2001: 115) notes, among the characteristics of modernity are 'disorganization, decomposition, disaggregation, flexibility, variegation and even incongruence – whether of structures, systems, processes or values. ... Structures have become more fragmented, organisations more difficult to classify, procedures more convoluted'. Accordingly, governance complexity is a further, internationally resonant challenge for civil society to negotiate. As this volume attests (Chapters 4 and 7), it may undermine transparency, and in turn cause a decline in trust, accountability and social cohesion (Chandler 2014; Jessop 2016). At the same time, rescaling national governance and the impact of devolution can also be singularly beneficial, allowing policy to better reflect Welsh, Scottish and Northern Irish needs and priorities. This can take the form of new legal rights and welfare entitlements, as well as new policy priorities and modes of government engagement with civil society. At the local level, as the analysis in Chapter 4 highlights, there can be associated challenges. For example, failure to coordinate the development of new regulatory, participatory and decision-making institutions can result in overlapping remits, a lack of transparency and declining trust (Chaney and Sophocleous 2021). Moreover, the imposition of UK government initiatives (for example, city regions) in the devolved nations can be seen as conflicting with local structures, political values and priorities. As Chapter 6 underlines, new threats and opportunities for civil society also stem from spatial processes associated with digital technologies. These may enable local civil society groups to forge connections beyond their locale. Again, civil society groups may also face associated challenges, such as the potential for civic deficit and exclusion arising from limited access to such technologies. Brexit is a further example of new governance structures, spatial processes and institutional change that presents manifold challenges to civil society (Chapter 8). The latter include changes in the justiciability of human rights law and, as noted, the loss of structural funding and the rise of racism and xenophobia.

Inclusion and exclusion, cultures and identities in uncertain times

Safeguarding local cultures, identities and languages in the face of globalisation is a key issue that civil society organisations also need to address (Alonso 2000; Clark 2014). As the foregoing analysis of Welsh and Scottish Gaelic shows (Chapter 5), civil society can play a pivotal role in mobilising for new legal rights and shaping social practices, such as the intergenerational transmission of minority languages (see also Maurais and Morris 2003). A further key dimension of the threat of globalisation is how civil society responds to new digital technologies. While these may pose a threat to a local sense of belonging and community, in the face of emerging artificial intelligence technologies, this may be the tip of the iceberg, with major implications for patterns and processes of mobilisation, as well as the potential for state infiltration and surveillance of civil society (OECD 2020; Deibert 2021). Future resilience against this threat will require effective coordination and co-working between civil society organisations. As noted, the rise of neo-liberalism is a further key challenge. In particular, there is a need to safeguard local cultures and practices in the face of a relentless globalised economy and the homogenising effects of international corporations.

A further test facing civil society is the promotion of citizens' rights in the wake of Brexit and its associated populist politics. As Ryder (2019: 115) notes when weighing up the post-Brexit prospects, 'civil society can constitute a discursive arena where the marginalized can invent and promote counter discourses and formulate oppositional interpretations of their identities, interests, and needs, furthering the politics and policies of redistribution, recognition, and representation'. Allied to this, as the foregoing discussion of civic stratification notes, a further threat to civil society comes from increased social and economic inequalities. The danger is that groups subject to marginalisation and exclusion retreat to separatist identities and cultures, not all of which are benign or promote wider well-being. This is evident in contemporary attitudes and behaviour towards immigrants (Chapter 8) and, as noted, the rise of xenophobia and racism. Moreover, it is intimately linked to declining trust in government (Chapter 7), with negative implications for governmentality and social cohesion.

Resilience

In the face of these manifold threats, the need to maintain civil society resilience is a key overarching challenge (Hall and Lamont 2013). As graphically illustrated by the accounts of the pandemic (Chapter 4), many civil society organisations entered the COVID-19 emergency in a weak and vulnerable state. This was due to years of under-funding, austerity, poor pay, staff-cuts and the negative impacts of marketised tendering processes and unpredictable, short-term contracts. As the literature on social capital reveals, rebuilding associative life with its norms of trust and reciprocity can be challenging because key aspects are embedded in localities and cultures (Portes 1998). Extant work on social-ecological resilience (Ebbesson and Hey 2013: 28) provides a potential framework for civic repair. *Inter alia*, it calls for: flexibility in social systems and institutions to deal with change;

openness of institutions to provide for extensive citizen participation; effective multi-level governance; and social structures that promote learning and adaptability without limiting options for future development. This volume's empirical analysis has also underlined the need for more effective government interventions to increase the resilience of third sector service providers; notably by greater official awareness of civil society organisations' need for longer-term funding cycles, less bureaucracy and financial reserves to withstand emergencies, such as the COVID-19 pandemic.

Overall, whether civil society is equal to these perils and uncertainties is linked to another key challenge: retaining its autonomy and criticality and resisting repression and co-option by the state. A survey of the international literature is salutary. For example, Naidoo (2003: 237) notes 'the ways that democracy, freedom and nation-building by free citizens ... appear to be under threat by the actions of some of our oldest democracies'. Around the globe, governments are introducing restrictive legislation, such as 'Foreign Agent' laws,[2] that limit civil society activism, breach human rights obligations on freedom of expression and association, and restrict civil society organisations' ability to hold government to account (Kreienkamp 2017; Chaney 2018a, 2018b, 2019, 2021d, 2022a, 2022b; Chaney and Sahoo 2020). Against this backdrop, this volume has sought to provide new insights into a range of contemporary challenges facing civil society organisations in the early twenty-first century. The analysis reveals how each may arrest or subvert the beneficial effects of associative life and negatively impact upon governance, culture and welfare. This underlines the importance of civil society to individual and collective well-being, as well as the health of democracy. On the one hand, there is evidence of the resilience of civil society and its adaptability to meet uncertainties, yet on the other, the present study suggests that civil society's ability to prevail in the face of existential challenges is far from assured. Rather, it is contingent in nature and requires ongoing vigilance, social self-organisation and criticality. While the contemporary 'project' to reconfigure the state might be normatively sound, its execution can be subverted by dogma, as well as civil society organisations' mistrust and lack of capacity to engage.

Accordingly, whether the challenges of the present age of uncertainty are addressed in an effective manner will depend upon the extent to which politicians and policy-makers listen to the situated knowledge of civil society actors. In a manner consistent with existential humanist studies of social welfare, this is an invaluable information source. It tells us about the direct experiences of individuals who, as part of their quest for meaning, take part in associative life to promote the well-being of others. In this regard, past government unresponsiveness does not bode well for the future. In coming years, effective civil society agency, advocacy and mobilisation will be more important than ever.

Notes

[1] The situation under Northern Ireland's consociationalist arrangements is much harder to interpret owing to periods of direct rule from Westminster and current constitutional uncertainties.

[2] These require non-profit organisations that receive foreign donations and engage in 'political' activities (often broadly and/or vaguely defined to include most regular types of NGO advocacy and criticality) to register and declare themselves to government as 'foreign agents'. Such enactments allow governments to ban NGOs from operating in their territories. They also introduce a wide range of sanctions and enable state surveillance.

References

Alonso, J. A. (2000) 'Globalisation, civil society, and the multilateral system', *Development in Practice*, 10(3–4): 38–49.

Barberis, P. (2001) 'Civil society, virtue, trust: Implications for the public service ethos in the age of modernity', *Public Policy and Administration*, 16(3): 111–126.

Beatty, C., Crisp, R., Ferrari, E., Gore, T. and Parkes, S. (2019) *Embedding Inclusive Growth in the Sheffield City Region*, Sheffield: Sheffield Hallam University Centre for Regional Economic and Social Growth. Available at: https://sheffieldcityregion.org.uk/wp-content/uploads/2019/09/SCR-Inclusive-growth-report-FINAL.pdf

Brewis, G., Ellis Paine, A., Hardill I., Lindsey, R. and Macmillan, R. (2021) *A World Turned Upside Down: What next for voluntary action?* Bristol: Policy Press.

Chandler, D. (2014) *Resilience: The governance of complexity*, London, New York: Routledge.

Chaney, P. (2013) 'Older people, equality and territorial justice: Devolution and social policy in the UK', *Critical Social Policy*, 33(1): 114–139.

Chaney, P. (2015) '"Post-feminist" era of social investment and territorial welfare? Exploring the issue-salience and policy framing of childcare in UK elections 1983–2011', *SAGE Open*, 5(1): 1–14.

Chaney, P. (2018a) 'Civil society, human rights and religious freedom in the People's Republic of China', *International Journal of Human Rights*, 22(4): 503–524.

Chaney, P. (2018b) 'Civil society, "traditional values" and LGBT resistance to heteronormative rights hegemony: Analysis of the UN Universal Periodic Review in the Russian Federation', *Europe-Asia Studies*, 70(4): 638–665.

Chaney, P. (2019) 'India at the crossroads? Civil society, human rights and religious freedom: Critical analysis of CSOs' Third Cycle Universal Periodic Review Discourse 2012–2017', *International Journal of Human Rights*, 25(5): 531–562.

Chaney, P. (2021a) 'Exploring the politicisation and territorialisation of adult social care in the UK: Electoral discourse analysis of state-wide and meso elections 1998–2019', *Global Social Policy*, SAGE Publishing (online first). Available at: https://journals.sagepub.com/eprint/AXFIYEECR KWXTYSSNBAA/full

Chaney, P. (2021b) 'Examining political parties' record on refugees and asylum seekers in UK party manifestos 1964–2019: The rise of territorial approaches to welfare?' *Journal of Immigrant & Refugee Studies* (online first). Available at: https://www.tandfonline.com/eprint/J6W5JTQV4FGNZ W7GMJZQ/full?target=10.1080/15562948.2020.1839620

Chaney, P. (2021c) 'Human rights and social welfare pathologies: Civil society perspectives on contemporary practice across UK jurisdictions', *International Journal of Human Rights*, 25(4): 639–674.

Chaney, P. (2021d) 'Civil society perspectives on children's rights in the occupied Palestinian territories', *International Journal of Children's Rights* (online first). Available at: https://brill.com/view/journals/chil/chil-overv iew.xml

Chaney, P. (2022a forthcoming) 'Exploring civil society perspectives on the human rights situation of LGBT+ people in the Caribbean community', *Journal of Civil Society*.

Chaney, P. (2022b forthcoming) 'Shrinking civil space? Exploring state and civil society perspectives on the contemporary situation of human rights defenders in South Asia', *Journal of South Asian Development*.

Chaney, P. and Sahoo, S. (2020) 'Civil society and the contemporary threat to religious freedom in Bangladesh', *Journal of Civil Society*, 16(3): 191–215.

Chaney, P. and Sophocleous, C. (2021) 'Trust, transparency and welfare: Third sector adult social care delivery and the COVID-19 pandemic in the UK', *Journal of Risk and Financial Management*, 14(12): 572–583.

Civicus (2019) *Understanding the Resourcing Landscape for Small and Informal Civil Society Groups in the Global South*, Johannesburg: Civicus. Available at: https://www.civicus.org/documents/understanding-the-resources-lan dscape_july2019.pdf

Clark, J. (ed.) (2014) *Worlds Apart: Civil society and the battle for ethical globalization*, London: Routledge.

Cohen, J. and Arato, A. (1992) *Civil Society and Political Theory*, Cambridge, MA: MIT Press.

Deibert, R. J. (2021) *Reset: Reclaiming the internet for civil society*, Tewkesbury: September Publishing.

De Tocqueville, A. (1835/2000) *De la démocratie en Amérique (1835/1840) – Democracy in America*, trans. and eds, Harvey C. Mansfield and Delba Winthrop, Chicago, IL: University of Chicago Press.

Ebbesson, J. and Hey, E. (2013) 'Introduction: Where in law is social-ecological resilience?' *Ecology and Society*, 18(3): 25.

Etherington, D. and Jones, M. (2016) *Devolution and Disadvantage in the Sheffield City Region: An assessment of employment, skills, and welfare policies*, Sheffield, Sheffield University. Available at: https://www.sheffield.ac.uk/polopoly_fs/1.645005!/file/SSDevolutionPolicy.pdf

Etherington, D. and Jones, M. (2018) 'Re-stating the post-political: Depoliticization, social inequalities, and city-region growth', *Environment and Planning A: Economy and Space*, 50(1): 51–72.

Foucault, M. (2008) *The Birth of Biopolitics: Lectures at the Collège de France 1978–1979*, New York: Palgrave MacMillan.

Fraser, N. (1997) *Justice Interruptus: Critical reflections on the 'postsocialist' condition*, New York: Routledge.

Fraser, N. and Honneth, A. (2003) *Redistribution or Recognition? A political-philosophical exchange*, London, New York: Verso.

Hall, P. and Lamont, M. (eds) (2013) *Social Resilience in the Neoliberal Era*, Cambridge: Cambridge University Press.

Home Office (2020) *Home Office Indicators of Integration Framework 2019* (3rd edn), ISBN 978-1-78655-833-6, Home Office Research Report 109, London: Home Office.

Hoole, C. and Hincks, S. (2020) 'Performing the city-region: Imagineering, devolution and the search for legitimacy', *Environment and Planning A: Economy and Space*, 52(8): 1583–1601.

Jessop, B. (2016) 'Territory, politics, governance and multispatial metagovernance', *Territory, Politics, Governance*, 4(1): 8–32.

Kreienkamp, J. (2017) *Responding to the Global Crack-Down on Civil Society*, Policy Briefing, London: University College London: Global Governance Institute. Available at: https://www.ucl.ac.uk/global-governance/sites/global-governance/files/policy-brief-civil-society.pdf

Kumar, K. (1993) 'Civil society: An inquiry into the usefulness of an historical term', *British Journal of Sociology*, 44(3): 375–395.

Kwon, H. (2009) 'The reform of the developmental welfare state in East Asia', *International Journal of Social Welfare*, 18(s1): S12–S21.

Lee, J. and Chan, K. (2007) *The Crisis of Welfare in East Asia*, Lanham, MD: Lexington Books.

Lockwood, D. (1996) 'Civic integration and class formation', *The British Journal of Sociology*, 47(3): 531–550.

Mahoney, C. and Beckstrand, M. J. (2016) 'Following the money: European Union funding of civil society organizations', *Journal of Common Market Studies*, 49(6): 1339–1361.

Maurais, J. and Morris, M. (eds) (2003) *Languages in a Globalising World*, London: Routledge.

Mooko, T. (2006) 'Counteracting the threat of language death: The case of minority languages in Botswana', *Journal of Multilingual and Multicultural Development*, 27(2): 109–125.

Morris, L. (2016) 'Squaring the circle: Domestic welfare, migrants rights, and human rights', *Citizenship Studies*, 20(6–7): 693–709.

Naidoo, K. (2003) 'Civil society at a time of global uncertainty, Organisation for Economic Cooperation and Development', *The OECD Observer*, May 2003, p 237.

OECD (2020) *Digital Transformation and the Futures of Civic Space to 2030, Development Policy Paper*, Paris: OECD Publishing. Available at: https://www.oecd.org/dac/Digital-Transformation-and-the-Futures-of-Civic-Space-to-2030.pdf

Portes, A. (1998) 'Social capital: Its origin and applications in modern sociology', *Annual Review of Sociology*, 24: 1–2.

Ryder, A. (2019) 'Transforming Brexit Britain', *Corvinus Journal of Sociology and Social Policy*, 10(2): 103–123.

Seligman, A. B. (1997) *The Problem of Trust*, Princeton, NJ: Princeton University Press.

Sherris, A. and Penfield, S. (2011) *Rejecting the Marginalized Status of Minority Languages: Educational projects pushing back against language endangerment*, Bristol: Channel View Publications.

Skocpol, T. (2011) *Social Policy in the United States: Future possibilities in historical perspective*, Princeton, NJ: Princeton University Press.

Smith, T. (2004) *France in Crisis: Welfare, inequality, and globalization since 1980*, Cambridge: Cambridge University Press.

Suárez, D. and Gugerty, M. K. (2016) 'Funding civil society? Bilateral government support for development NGOs', *Voluntas: International Journal of Voluntary and Nonprofit Organizations*, 27: 2617–2640.

Suchman, M. (1995) 'Managing legitimacy: Strategic and institutional approaches', *The Academy of Management Review*, 20(3): 571–610.

Welsh Government (2017) *Cymraeg 2050: A million Welsh speakers*, Cardiff: Welsh Government.

Wimmer, A. and Glick Schiller, N. (2002) 'Methodological nationalism and beyond: Nation–state building, migration and the social sciences', *Global Networks*, 2(4): 301–334.

Yerkes, M. and van der Veen, R. (2011) 'Crisis and welfare state change in the Netherlands', *Social Policy & Administration*, 45(4): 430–444.

Index

References to figures appear in *italic* type;
those in **bold** type refer to tables.